My Max Score

SAT U.S. HISTORY SUBJECT TEST

Maximize Your Score in Less Time

Cara Cantarella

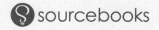 sourcebooks

This publication is designed to provide accurate and authoritative information in regard
to the subject matter covered. It is sold with the understanding that the publisher is
not engaged in rendering legal, accounting, or other professional service. If legal advice
or other expert assistance is required, the services of a competent professional person
should be sought.—*From a Declaration of Principles Jointly Adopted by a Committee of the
American Bar Association and a Committee of Publishers and Associations*

Published by Sourcebooks, Inc.
P.O. Box 4410, Naperville, Illinois 60567-4410
(630) 961-3900
Fax: (630) 961-2168
www.sourcebooks.com

CIP data is on file with the publisher.

Printed and bound in the United States of America.
VP 10 9 8 7 6 5 4 3 2 1

Contents

Introduction

Many high school students who plan to go to college take SAT subject tests, but they prepare for these tests in different ways. Some take a given exam once and spend only a few days cramming beforehand. Others take the test multiple times, hoping that practice will improve their score and make them more competitive for college admission. Some even add to what they learn in school by pursuing outside resources on their own.

Regardless of how you approach the exam, this guidebook can boost your performance on test-taking day. The book's content is presented in three sections:

- A last-minute study guide designed for use over a short period of time
- A more comprehensive study guide for students who have more than a few days to prepare
- A long-term study plan to guide those who want to begin preparing far ahead of time

If your schedule allows, it's a good idea to check out all three sections of the book. You're likely to find useful information in each part. It's also a good strategy to take more than one practice test. Before you begin studying, however, there are some things you'll want to know about the test itself.

About the Test

The SAT U.S. History Subject Test consists of 90 to 95 multiple-choice questions, and you will have one hour to answer them. For each question, you'll select one answer from five possible choices, and you'll mark your selection on a separate answer sheet. Before starting the test, you'll be asked to fill out a background questionnaire; your answers to these questions will not affect your test score.

Test questions deal with a wide range of topics and cover U.S. history from before Columbus discovered the New World through the present day. The percentage of questions allocated to each aspect of U.S. history varies slightly from year to year, but the following list shows the range of percentages devoted to each subject area, regardless of the time frame. This list is arranged from highest percentage to lowest.

- 32–36 percent: political history
- 18–22 percent: social history
- 18–20 percent: economic history
- 13–17 percent: foreign policy
- 10–12 percent: intellectual and cultural history

Knowing which subject areas count most when your test is scored can help you establish priorities as you prepare.

It's also useful to know the percentage of questions devoted to various periods of U.S. history. The following percentages are arranged according to three chronological time periods:

- 20 percent: Pre-Columbian history to 1789
- 40 percent: 1790 to 1898
- 40 percent: 1899 to the present

How Your Test Will Be Scored

Your performance on the test will be assessed by three scores: a raw score, a percentile score, and a scaled score.

Your Raw Score

Although you won't be able to find out your raw score, knowing how it's calculated can help you make wise choices as you take the test. Your raw score will be determined by how many questions you answer correctly, how many you answer incorrectly, and how many you don't answer at all.

- You'll receive 1 point for every answer that's correct.
- You'll forfeit a quarter of a point for every answer that's incorrect.
- You won't receive any points for a question you don't answer.

Here's the method that will be used to calculate your raw score:

- The number of correct answers will be tallied.
- The number of incorrect answers will be tallied.
- A fourth of the incorrect answers will be subtracted from the number of correct answers.

For example, if you get 67 questions right and 28 questions wrong—and you don't leave any answers blank—your raw score will be 60 (67 minus one fourth of 28).

Your Percentile Score

Your percentile score indicates how your performance compares with that of all the other students who took the same test you took. This score reflects the percentage of that group of students who scored lower than you did. For example, if your score puts you in the 60th percentile, this means your raw score was higher than the raw scores of 60 percent of the other students who took the test and lower than the raw scores of 40 percent of the other students.

Your Scaled Score

Your scaled score indicates how your performance compares with that of everyone who has ever taken the SAT U.S. History Subject Test. This score is calculated by means of a formula that converts your raw score to a scaled score ranging between 200 and 800. Scaled scores are intended to account for variations in student performance and fluctuations in the test's degree of difficulty from year to year.

You might be surprised to know that it's possible to receive a scaled score of 800 without answering every question correctly. If the test you take consists of 95 questions, you could earn a scaled score of 800 with a raw score no higher than 82 (if, for example, you answer 84 questions correctly, 8 incorrectly, and leave 3 answers blank). It's possible to get a scaled score of 700 with a raw score as low as 64 and a scaled score of 600 with a raw score as low as 48.

There are two take-away messages here:

- You don't have to know the answer to every question to do well on the test.
- You can maximize your score by responding to all the questions you can answer with confidence within the allotted time, and then making educated guesses for answers you're not so sure about.

Visit mymaxscore.com for an additional practice test for the SAT U.S. History Subject Test, as well as practice tests for other subjects.

THE ESSENTIALS: A LAST-MINUTE STUDY GUIDE

If you have only a few days before taking the test and you're not feeling as ready as you'd like, don't freak out. Take a deep breath, set aside some quiet time to focus on getting better prepared, and begin gathering the materials you'll need to take with you to the test.

Check Out Our Test-Taking Tips

The best way to start preparing is to look over the "Test-Taking Strategies" outlined in the next section of this book. If time permits, you can also check out the more detailed strategies provided in the following section.

Review the Basics

If you've registered for this test, you've probably taken a year-long class in U.S. history as part of your high school curriculum. A good way to recall the information stored in your brain is to study the section of this book titled "The Big Ideas of U.S. History." This section is designed to remind you of the most significant people, events, and policies you've already learned about so that the test questions will trigger your memory and enable you to choose the correct answers.

Take a Practice Test

The most effective way to identify which aspects of U.S. history you know well and which ones you need to brush up on is to take a practice test. A trial run is also the best way to assess the usefulness of your test-taking strategies. Try to simulate as closely as possible the conditions you'll encounter during the actual test, timing yourself and making sure you won't be interrupted.

Memorize the test instructions. These directions are the same from test to test, so if you're familiar with them ahead of time, you won't need to waste valuable time pondering them when you take the actual test. Also, study the sample questions so you'll be familiar with how they're formatted.

Unlike the real test, a practice test gives you the opportunity to calculate your score and to make a list of all the questions you got wrong and all the answers you left blank. Think about why you missed these questions and what you could have done to answer them correctly. This exercise will reveal your strengths and weaknesses and indicate which topics you need to concentrate on as you study for the actual test. Focus your review on the subject areas you found most troublesome. If time allows, you can study this material in greater detail in the comprehensive review provided in a later section of this book.

What to Do the Night before the Test

You don't want to be racing around the house the morning of the test searching for the things you'll need to take along with you. You'll be much more relaxed if you collect all these items beforehand. The night before the test, put all the items in a backpack or large purse that you can grab on your way out the door the next morning.

Here's a checklist of the essentials:

- Directions to the test center
- Your admission ticket obtained from the company administering the test
- A photo ID (driver's license, school- or state-issued ID card, or valid passport)
- Several number 2 pencils with clean erasers
- A watch or clock (in the test room, you can't have any electronic devices that would allow communication with the outside world, so you won't be able to use a cell phone to check the time)
- A bottle of water
- Optional item: a light snack that's not messy to eat (perhaps an apple or an energy bar)

Check the time your admission ticket says you should arrive at the test site, and decide what time you'll need to leave home in order to get there a little early. You won't be allowed to take the test if you're late. Build in plenty of time to get ready—including time for breakfast—and set your alarm accordingly. Then go to bed early enough to get a good night's sleep. Whatever you do, don't pull an all-nighter. Scientists have proved that our brains work better when we're rested.

What to Do on Test Day

The sound of your alarm is your signal to implement the plan you made the night before. Because you've had enough sleep, you'll be able to get in gear quickly and easily. Here are some additional guidelines to help you feel your best as you take the test:

- Dress for comfort rather than looks.
- Wear layers so you'll be comfortable regardless of the temperature in the test room.
- Eat a light breakfast consisting mainly of protein (for example, eggs, cheese, or nuts). Avoid foods that are fatty or heavy.

- Drink coffee only if that's how you normally start your day, and drink the same amount as usual. Too much caffeine can make you feel jumpy, especially if you're not accustomed to it.

- Read something like a magazine or newspaper. This will stimulate your brain, like priming a pump.

- Leave home no later than the time you've designated in order to reach the test site early.

- Remind yourself that you've prepared for the test and that you don't have to answer every question correctly to score well.

- Just before you start the test, get into a positive mind-set. Say to yourself something like, "I'm taking this test with skill and confidence." (Repeat as necessary.)

Test-Taking Strategies

Of course your performance on the SAT U.S. History Subject Test will hinge primarily on your knowledge of the subject matter and your ability to analyze information. Still, even if you can't figure out the answer to every question, you can improve your chances of scoring well by following the proven test-taking strategies outlined in this section.

How to Approach the Test

One of the most important approaches to taking a standardized test is to use your time wisely. The following lists of strategies are designed to help you accomplish this. If you've taken a practice test, you already have several of the strategies under your belt.

Housekeeping Tips

- **Mark your answer sheet carefully.** Because standardized tests are graded by machines, it's crucial that you mark your answers in the right place. The safest approach is to talk yourself through the process each time. In your head, say the question number and the letter corresponding to your answer as you search out the exact spot on the answer sheet (Number 31, A; Number 32, C; Number 33, E;

and so on). Fill in the oval shapes completely and make sure they're dark.

- **Periodically check your answer sheet.** Verify the accuracy of your answer sheet by checking it after every 10 questions. This is especially important if you skip questions with the intention of returning to them later. If you have to make corrections, erase completely.

- **Keep your answer sheet clean.** Because the machine processing your answer sheet can misinterpret extraneous marks or incomplete erasures as incorrect answers, don't sully the sheet with any marks outside the ovals intended for your answers.

- **Use your test booklet to make notes**. Unlike your answer sheet, your test booklet is fair game for scribbling. Write reminders to yourself, put check marks beside the answers you select, and circle the questions you want to return to so you can find them easily.

Test-Taking Tips

- **Be familiar with the format.** The test's format is always the same—90 to 95 multiple-choice questions, each with five possible answers. You'll select one choice for each question.

- **Know the instructions.** The instructions are also the same from test to test. Memorize these directions ahead of time so you won't have to waste time reading them on test-taking day.

- **Read carefully.** Make sure you understand exactly what the question is asking before you look at the answers.

- **Budget your time.** Because you'll have only an hour to take the test, it's important to pace yourself. Agonizing about a question you find particularly challenging can prevent you from getting through the entire test. Work at a steady rate and keep moving through the test. Check your watch periodically to monitor your progress.

- **Formulate your answer before reading the choices offered.** If you know the answer to a question, you can select the right choice quickly without having to ponder all the options. Thinking about possible answers before considering the actual choices can also keep you from getting sidetracked by answers that are incorrect or misleading.

- **Answer the easiest questions first.** If you address every question on the test, you'll need to spend an average of less than a minute per question. (Bet that got your attention!) Therefore, it makes sense to devote the largest percentage of your time to addressing questions you're likely to answer correctly. Fortunately, the questions are generally presented in order of difficulty.

- **Eliminate incorrect choices.** If you don't know the answer to a question, read all the choices and identify any you know are incorrect. Mark through all the wrong choices in your test booklet, and reread only the options that remain. The more choices you can get rid of, the better chance you have of selecting the correct answer. If after eliminating the choices that are wrong, you're left with two reasonable options, select the one that answers the question most completely or most precisely. (You'll find more detailed guidelines on how to go about eliminating incorrect choices later in this chapter, with sample questions and explanations of how to arrive at the correct answers.)

- **Make an educated guess or skip the question.** If you're able to eliminate one or two wrong answer choices, making an *educated* guess is a good idea (you lose only a quarter of a point for a wrong guess, and you get a whole point for a right one). On the other hand, making a *random* guess—selecting an answer without having a clue as to which choice might be right—is a bad idea (your chance of guessing correctly is only one in five). If you find yourself spending too much time puzzling over a single question, circle it in your test booklet and come back to it at the end of the test if you have time. More guidance on how to make educated guesses is available in the section containing sample questions.

- **Leave an answer blank if you must.** If you're completely stumped and can't eliminate any of the answer choices, it's better to leave the answer blank than to make a random guess.

- **Underline key words or phrases.** This will help you focus on the main point of a question. Key words often provide clues that can point you toward a correct answer or help you eliminate an incorrect one.

- **Rewrite questions you find to be confusing.** If you're having a hard time figuring out what's being asked by a particular question, you may find it helpful to rewrite the question and the possible answers in your own words.

- **Go back to the questions you're not sure about.** After answering all the easy questions, look back at the questions you skipped the first time through. Maybe an answer will suddenly be more apparent, or perhaps another question will have jogged your memory and you'll remember an answer you knew all along.

How to Identify and Answer Different Types of Questions

The multiple-choice questions that comprise the SAT U.S. History Subject Test can be divided into seven types or categories. If you grasp the distinctions among these seven types, you'll be better equipped to zero in on the main point of each question and to focus on the kind of answer that's appropriate. This section uses examples to illustrate how each type of question works. The seven categories are:

- Factual/Content Questions
- Cause/Effect and Significance Questions
- EXCEPT and LEAST Questions
- Graph/Chart Questions
- Excerpt/Quotation Questions
- Political Cartoon, Illustration, or Photograph Questions
- Map Interpretation Questions

Factual/Content Questions

Factual/content questions are the least complicated questions on the test because they simply require you to recall a basic fact, term, or concept. The following is an example of a basic factual/content question.

Which of the following men was an important transcendentalist writer?

A. Ernest Hemingway
B. F. Scott Fitzgerald
C. William Faulkner
D. John Steinbeck
E. Ralph Waldo Emerson

To select the correct answer to this question (E), you only need to recall one fact—Ralph Waldo Emerson was a central figure in the American Transcendentalist movement. However, considering this sample question can also help you to learn how to go about eliminating incorrect answer choices. If you also remember that Transcendentalism was at its height during the 1830s, you can eliminate the other four choices because the rest of these men were twentieth-century writers.

Cause/Effect and Significance Questions

Cause/effect questions are more complex because they ask you to analyze information and draw conclusions. They also call for more comprehensive knowledge of historical periods because they require you to remember when certain events occurred and how they relate to one another. The following question is an example of a cause/effect and significance question.

One result of the National Origin Act of 1924 was that

A. immigration from China was banned
B. the United States adopted a literacy test for new immigrants
C. immigrants from northern and western Europe were directly discriminated against

D.   paupers were denied admission to the United States
E.   quotas were established that specifically limited the number of immigrants from eastern and southern Europe to the United States

To select the correct answer to this question (E), you need to do more than simply recall the events cited in the five answer choices. In addition to remembering that the National Origin Act spelled out the quota system restricting the number of eastern and southern Europeans allowed to enter the United States, you also need to remember the time period in which each event cited occurred.

Remember our suggestion that you underline key words or phrases in the questions? In this question, the key term is the date 1924. You can figure out the correct answer if you know that Chinese immigrants were denied admission to the United States in 1882, the literacy test for immigrants was adopted in 1917, the United States did not discriminate against immigrants from northern and western European countries in the 1920s, and paupers were not allowed into the United States during the late 1880s.

Except and *Least* Questions

The best strategy for addressing this type of question is to underline or circle the key word EXCEPT the moment you spot it. Other key words that are used in EXCEPT questions include LEAST, NOT, and INCONSISTENT. (Even though these words always appear in capital letters, these questions can be confusing because they ask you to choose an answer that would be incorrect if the word EXCEPT or one of its counterparts weren't there.) Next, mark through the answer choices that would be correct if the word EXCEPT was left out. Then select the one answer that remains. The following is an example of an EXCEPT question.

All of the following countries were represented at the Versailles Conference in January 1919 EXCEPT

A. Russia
B. France
C. Italy
D. United States
E. Great Britain

To answer this sample question, you need to recall that the 1919 Treaty of Versailles officially ended the state of war between Germany and the Allied forces at the conclusion of World War I, that the Bolshevik Revolution establishing Communist rule in Russia occurred in 1917, and that a separate treaty, signed by Germany and the Russian Communist leaders in 1918, ended Russian involvement in the war. Recalling this information will remind you that of all the countries listed in the answer choices, Russia was the only one not represented at Versailles. Thus A is your only option for answering this EXCEPT question. Representatives from the other four countries offered as choices were present at the Versailles Conference.

Graph/Chart Questions

A graph/chart question requires you to use the data presented in a graph or chart to help you come up with the correct answer. The chart in the sample graph/chart question presented here provides all the data you need in order to answer the question. However, some graph/chart questions on the actual test may require you to combine information from a chart or graph with your own knowledge in order to arrive at the correct answer. Use the chart provided to help you answer the following example of a graph/chart question.

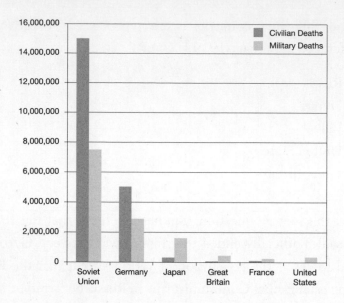

Which of the following statements is best supported by the graph shown?

A. All countries experienced both civilian and military deaths during World War II.
B. The British lost the least number of civilians during World War II.
C. The United States suffered the least number of military casualties in World War II.
D. The Japanese civilian deaths were the second largest after Soviet losses.
E. The Soviets suffered the largest number of civilian and military deaths during World War II.

The best approach to addressing a graph/chart question is to read the question and all the answer choices before you examine the graph or chart. First, identify the most important words in the question. Then look carefully at the title of the chart or graph, as well as any keys that will help you analyze the data. The key words in this sample question are "best supported." The key words in the answer choices are "civilian" and "military." The key in the upper right corner of the chart enables you to interpret the shaded bars (darker bars represent civilian deaths;

lighter bars represent military deaths), and the labels beneath the chart's horizontal axis indicate the country represented by each set of bars. Now you're ready to start eliminating the inaccurate answer choices.

You can mark through A and B because the chart indicates that no U.S. civilians died during World War II; thus, the United States, not Britain, lost the fewest civilians in the war. You can eliminate C because the chart clearly shows that France suffered the smallest number of military deaths. D is incorrect because the chart shows that the Germans, not the Japanese, experienced the most civilian deaths after the Soviets. The correct answer is E, because the Soviet Union suffered the largest number of civilian deaths (15 million, according to the chart) as well as the largest number of military deaths (7.5 million).

Excerpt/Quotation Questions

To answer an excerpt/quotation question, you'll be asked to identify either the author or the chief idea of the passage quoted. Underline or circle the words that convey the passage's main idea and try to recall the person most closely associated with this point of view (if applicable). The following is an example of an excerpt/quotation question.

"This, then is held to be the duty of the man of wealth;…to set an example of modest…living,…to consider all surplus revenues which come to him simply as trust funds, which he is called upon to administer… in the manner which, in his judgment, is best calculated to produce the most beneficial results for the community…the man of wealth thus becoming a trustee…for his poorer brethren."

The ideas in the passage are most closely associated with

A. Andrew Carnegie
B. John D. Rockefeller
C. James Hill
D. James Fiske
E. Cornelius Vanderbilt

The key words in this passage are "duty" and "trustee," and the chief idea expressed is the responsibility of the wealthy class to the rest of society. If you're not familiar with the passage itself, you can eliminate answer B, C, and E because Rockefeller, Hill, and Vanderbilt are typically considered robber barons who amassed their fortunes without regard to ethical concerns or consideration for others. You can also eliminate D, James Fiske, who was a Wall Street stockbroker associated with the financial panic of 1869. That leaves you with A, Andrew Carnegie, the correct answer. In 1889, Carnegie wrote an essay titled "The Gospel of Wealth" in which he espoused the opinion that wealthy individuals should manage their money in ways that would improve the lives of people who were less fortunate.

Political Cartoon, Illustration, or Photograph Questions

Questions in this category require you to discern the message or viewpoint conveyed by a piece of artwork such as a political cartoon, illustration, or photo. In contrast to our recommendation for addressing a graph/chart question, we suggest you approach this type of question by looking at the artwork first. Examine the image itself, read any title or caption accompanying it, and pay special attention to any symbolism depicted in the image. Scrutinizing the artwork before reading the question should help you eliminate answer choices that are inconsistent with the message communicated by the image. The following sample question is based on a political cartoon.

Which viewpoint is expressed in the above cartoon?

A. Congress and Jackson worked closely together to enact legislation.
B. Jackson sought a return to British traditions.
C. Jackson was a weak president.
D. Jackson had monarchical ambitions.
E. The wealthy class in the United States supported Jackson.

This cartoon portrays Andrew Jackson as a king—he's wearing a crown, holding a royal scepter, and decked out in royal robes. The details of the image are difficult to determine in this tiny reproduction, but if you look closely, you'll see that King Andrew's left hand holds a piece of paper bearing the word *veto*. You'll also notice a copy of the U.S. Constitution and a bank charter under his feet. The fact that he's standing on these documents implies that he has no respect for them. The image implies that Jackson abused his executive power and showed contempt for the Constitution when he vetoed legislation that would have rechartered the country's national bank.

In selecting an answer to this question, you would first eliminate choices A, C, and E because the cartoon does not suggest that Jackson worked with Congress, was a weak leader, or was allied with members of the wealthy class. You can also eliminate B because although the monarchy is a central part of British tradition, the Constitution and the bank charter indicate that the cartoon has more to do with the United States than with Britain. D is the correct answer because the cartoon suggests that Jackson's veto of the bank charter signaled a desire to rule the United States like a monarch rather than a willingness to work cooperatively with the other two branches of government.

Map Interpretation Questions

In addition to illustrating geographic boundaries, maps can be used to depict information about social, economic, and political issues. When faced with a question requiring you to interpret a map, examine the map thoroughly, read any title or legend that indicates what the map is intended to show, and check out any keys that can help you make sense of the graphic information. Use the map below to help you arrive at the correct answer to the following map interpretation question.

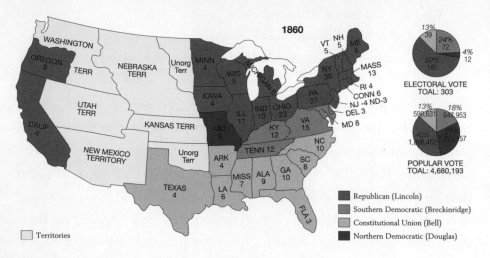

The Electoral Map of 1860 shows that

    A.   Lincoln was a national candidate who won electoral votes in all sections of the country.

    B.   Breckinridge's popular vote exceeded that of Douglas.

    C.   The Northern working class supported Lincoln.

    D.   Lincoln won a minority of the popular vote but a majority of the electoral vote.

    E.   Bell received the lowest number of electoral votes.

This map doesn't include a title to tell you what it's about, but the date above the map and the two pie charts to the right indicate that the map shows a breakdown of the popular and electoral votes cast in the 1860 presidential election. Although there's no key to verify this assumption, the numbers on the map itself appear to be the number of electoral votes each state had in 1860.

Answering this question can be tricky because it requires you to differentiate between electoral votes and popular votes. You can eliminate A because the map clearly shows that Lincoln didn't win any Southern state's electoral votes. B is incorrect because the lower pie chart shows that Douglas received more popular votes than Breckinridge. C has to be eliminated because the map offers no information about how the working class voted in the election. E must also be eliminated because the pie chart on the top shows that Douglas received the fewest electoral votes. The correct answer has to be D.

The Big Ideas of U.S. History

The purpose of this chapter is to help you review the most important ideas and terms for the U.S. History Subject Test. In the pages that follow, you'll review nine major themes likely to appear on the exam. Each theme is accompanied by a summary of key terms and references for more extensive review later in the book.

Leadership

The theme of leadership is predominant throughout U.S. history. Two elements of American leadership are particularly important: U.S. presidents and the United States as a world leader.

U.S. Presidents

An understanding of the order of the presidencies will help you place each leader in historical context. It is not necessary to memorize the exact order or dates in office, but it is helpful to have a general understanding of which presidents served during what periods in U.S. history. The major contributions of each president are discussed in the Comprehensive Strategies and Review portion of the book.

The table below lists the presidents in order and shows their terms in office. Presidents who died while in office are marked in bold, and assassinated presidents are shown in italics.

TERM	PRESIDENT	ORDER
1789–1797	George Washington	1
1797–1801	John Adams	2
1801–1809	Thomas Jefferson	3
1809–1817	James Madison	4
1817–1825	James Monroe	5
1825–1829	John Quincy Adams	6
1829–1837	Andrew Jackson	7
1837–1841	Martin Van Buren	8
1841	**William Henry Harrison**	9
1841–1845	John Tyler	10
1845–1849	James Polk	11
1849–1850	**Zachary Taylor**	12
1850–1853	Millard Fillmore	13
1853–1857	Franklin Pierce	14
1857–1861	James Buchanan	15
1861–1865	*Abraham Lincoln*	16
1865–1869	Andrew Johnson	17
1869–1877	Ulysses S. Grant	18
1877–1881	Rutherford B. Hayes	19
1881	*James A. Garfield*	20
1881–1885	Chester A. Arthur	21
1885–1889	Grover Cleveland	22
1889–1893	Benjamin Harrison	23
1893–1897	Grover Cleveland	24
1897–1901	*William McKinley*	25
1901–1909	Theodore Roosevelt	26
1909–1913	William Taft	27
1913–1921	Woodrow Wilson	28
1921–1923	**Warren G. Harding**	29

TERM	PRESIDENT	ORDER
1923–1929	Calvin Coolidge	30
1929–1933	Herbert Hoover	31
1933–1945	**Franklin D. Roosevelt**	32
1945–1953	Harry Truman	33
1953–1961	Dwight D. Eisenhower	34
1961–1963	*John F. Kennedy*	35
1963–1969	Lyndon B. Johnson	36
1969–1974	Richard Nixon	37
1974–1977	Gerald Ford	38
1977–1981	Jimmy Carter	39
1981–1989	Ronald Reagan	40
1989–1993	George Bush	41
1993–2001	Bill Clinton	42
2001–2009	George W. Bush	43
2009–present	Barack Obama	44

One president, Grover Cleveland, was elected for two nonconsecutive terms. Two presidents have been impeached (Andrew Johnson and Bill Clinton), but both were acquitted. Richard Nixon resigned from office before he could be impeached.

The United States as a World Leader

As the United States has grown, so has its presence on the world stage. In its early stages, as the country was forming (mid-1700s), it remained isolated and then later expanded on the North American continent (early 1800s). It was protective of Latin America, though it stayed out of Europe's affairs.

The United States gained strength as a great power through imperial expansion between the Civil War and World War I (mid-1800s to early 1900s). It then became the strongest economic power in the world after World War II (1945). By the end of World War II, the United States was in a position to help rebuild Europe. By doing so, it dominated the world economy. It also began an intense rivalry with the Soviet Union during the Cold War (late 1900s).

The United States emerged as the strongest world leader overall when the Soviet Union collapsed, ending the Cold War (1989) and remains so to the present day. Its most significant foreign policy efforts currently involve the combat of terrorism.

KEY TERMS

Presidential term	Open Door Policy
Impeachment	Imperialism
Assassination	Neutrality
Isolationism	Marshall Plan
Manifest Destiny	Cold War
Monroe Doctrine	Superpower

To Learn More

To learn more about the theme of leadership in U.S. history, see the sections in the U.S. History Review listed below.

SUBJECT	U.S. HISTORY REVIEW SECTION
U.S. Presidents	Presidents and their contributions are presented chronologically, based on their terms in office.
The United States as a World Leader	Part 4 Part 5

Government

American government is a fundamental aspect of U.S. history, particularly its establishment and structure. The test may also contain questions about the democratic principles on which the U.S. government is based. Many of these principles have been codified through legal cases over time.

Establishment

The first European contact with the Americas came in 1492 by Christopher Columbus, whose voyage was sponsored by Spain. By the 1600s, British settlers had established colonies along the east coast of North America and were governed by British rule. American colonists became disgruntled with British colonial governance, particularly taxation policies. This discontent led the colonists to declare their independence from Britain in 1776. Independence was secured through the Revolutionary War, which ended with an American victory in 1783.

The U.S. Constitution was signed in 1787 and adopted in 1788, establishing the government of the country. The Constitution was developed in several stages:

- The **Declaration of Independence** (1776) declared the colonies independent and established certain principles on which the U.S. government would eventually be based.

- The **Founding Fathers** guided the process of establishing government by providing the vision for the new country and serving as its leaders.

- After the United States won its independence, an initial constitution called the **Articles of Confederation** was passed. Some of the principles of the Articles would later be incorporated into the Constitution.

- The **Federalist Papers** were written by Founding Fathers Alexander Hamilton, James Madison, and John Jay. These documents advocated ratification of the Constitution.

- Once the Constitution was ratified, it was expanded over time to include twenty-seven **Amendments**. The first ten of these are known as the **Bill of Rights**.

Structure

The U.S. government is based on a **federalist** system in which power is shared among a central governing body (the federal government) and the individual states. The government is divided into three branches: executive, legislative, and judicial. The **executive branch** of government executes the laws, the **legislative branch** makes the laws, and the **judicial branch** interprets the laws.

The government was set up in this fashion to ensure a **separation of powers** between the different branches. A system of **checks and balances** is built in to prevent any one branch from wielding too much power. The U.S. government also upholds the **separation of church and state**, keeping religion separate from political governance.

Principles

American political philosophy is based on certain democratic ideals. Among the most important are:

- Democratic **self-governance**, or rule by the people
- **Individual rights**, particularly the right to freedom regardless of an individual's social group
- **Civil rights**, including protection from discrimination
- **Political rights**, including the right to a fair trial and the right to vote
- **Human rights** that apply to all people regardless of citizenship and include humane treatment and freedom from oppression

Legal Cases

The principles of the U.S. government have been codified and refined over time through interpretation by the judicial branch in landmark court cases. Some Supreme Court decisions set precedents that have greatly affected the conduct of government and the treatment of individuals.

CASE	DATE	SIGNIFICANCE
Marbury v. Madison	1803	Establishes the Supreme Court's power of judicial review
McCulloch v. Maryland	1813	Establishes the supremacy of the federal government over states' rights

CASE	DATE	SIGNIFICANCE
Dred Scott v. Sandford	1857	Classifies slaves as property
Plessy v. Ferguson	1896	Establishes "separate but equal" facilities for blacks
Brown v. Board of Education	1954	Declares "separate but equal" facilities unconstitutional
Miranda v. Arizona	1966	Upholds the rights of those accused of crimes

KEY TERMS

Declaration of Independence

Founding Fathers

Federalist Papers

Articles of Confederation

Constitution

Amendments

Bill of Rights

Federalism

Separation of powers

Checks and balances

Separation of church and state

Self-governance

Individual rights

Civil rights

Political rights

Human rights

To Learn More

To learn more about the theme of government in U.S. history, see the sections in the U.S. History Review listed below.

SUBJECT	U.S. HISTORY REVIEW SECTION
Establishment	Part 2
Structure	Part 2
Principles	Part 2
Legal Cases	Legal cases are presented chronologically in the U.S. History Review section by the date of each case. The *Miranda* case is explained in the glossary.

Culture

Certain aspects of culture have been highlights in American history. These cultural elements, which reflect American values, stand out in particular for their impact on the country's development.

Asceticism

The **Puritans** were a Protestant group that comprised a significant population in colonial America. Their religious philosophy was tied in with their personal values, including a concept known as asceticism. **Asceticism** decried greed, laziness, and other distractions from a righteous life. Idleness was thought to be particularly threatening because it was believed that time should be continually spent doing work for God.

Under the ascetic view, individuals were considered blessed if they gained wealth through serving God by hard work. This belief laid the foundation for later American economic values of **capitalism** and **consumerism**.

Plantation Cultures

In the pre–Civil War United States, Northern economies were based on **industry**, while the economies of the Southern states were based on **agriculture**. The agricultural economies of the South centered around large plantations on which crops such as **tobacco** and **cotton** were grown. Plantations were operated using **slave labor** and were entirely dependent on the slave trade for their survival.

Because the Southern agricultural elite relied exclusively on slave labor to produce their crops, this group of influential citizens strongly resisted attempts by the Northern states to **abolish slavery**. The reliance of the South on its plantation-based economy ultimately led to the Civil War.

The Roaring Twenties

The **Roaring Twenties** was a period in U.S. history that occurred after the end of **World War I**. Although U.S. involvement in World War I had been more limited than that of other nations, the country was still recuperating from the tremendous losses incurred during the war. The casualties were not only in human lives but emotional as well. World War I represented a level of military devastation that the world had never seen. The United States and its allies had achieved their strategic objectives, but the wounds in the American psyche ran deep.

The Roaring Twenties era was a time in which Americans could find enjoyment again after the experience of war. Music, art, and cultural events saw a resurgence, particularly jazz and dancing. Jazz music was so popular that the period was nicknamed the **Jazz Age**. New developments in technology continued to propel industry forward.

- Young women in particular began to rebel and become more outspoken in this period. Women known as **flappers** symbolized the age with fringed dresses, short haircuts, and long cigarette holders.
- **Prohibition** was implemented via the Eighteenth Amendment to the Constitution, which banned alcohol. Establishments known as **speakeasies** arose and sold alcohol illegally.

Melting Pot

Another important element of U.S. culture is that of the **melting pot** theme. This refers to the view that Americans as a whole do not reflect a particular identity or ethnic heritage, but they are instead an amalgam or conglomeration of many cultures. The country is viewed as a melting pot in which individuals from all walks of life are embraced.

> "Give me your tired, your poor, / Your huddled masses yearning to breathe free"
>
> *This excerpt from a poem by Emma Lazarus is inscribed on a bronze plaque inside the Statue of Liberty. It reflects the degree to which the United States was seen as a haven of hope for many who immigrated in search of a new life.*

Immigration was particularly pronounced for the United States between 1850 and 1930. The **Statue of Liberty** was erected as a symbol of democracy and **freedom**.

KEY TERMS

Puritans	Roaring Twenties	Immigration
Asceticism	Jazz Age	Statue of Liberty
Northern industry	Flappers	Melting pot
Southern agriculture	Prohibition	
Tobacco	Eighteenth Amendment	
Cotton	Speakeasy	
Slave labor		

To Learn More

To learn more about the theme of culture in U.S. history, see the sections in the U.S. History Review listed below.

SUBJECT	U.S. HISTORY REVIEW SECTION
Asceticism	Part 1
Plantation Culture	Part 2
	Part 3
The Roaring Twenties	Part 3
Melting Pot	Part 3

Slavery

Of all the themes in U.S. history, perhaps none is more significant than that of **slavery**. Slavery represented a conflict with American democratic ideals. It helped establish the country's economy but was a glaring contradiction to what the nation stood for. Its abolition was an integral step toward aligning American identity with its values.

History and Plantation Culture

The **slave trade** brought slaves to the United States from Africa on **slave ships** under deplorable conditions. Slaves were sold as property on auction blocks and used to support the **plantation culture** of the South. Many key Southern agricultural products, such as **cotton** and **tobacco**, were directly produced through slave labor. Some of the Founding

Fathers were slave owners themselves, including George Washington and Thomas Jefferson.

Abolition

The **abolitionist movement** developed in the United States in the early 1800s and caused a great political divide. The movement was opposed by Southern plantation owners who relied on slave labor for their livelihood. Political pressure over the issue escalated as calls to action intensified on both sides.

In 1852, the antislavery novel *Uncle Tom's Cabin* was published by abolitionist **Harriet Beecher Stowe** and became a bestseller. The novel denounced the horrors of slavery and secured widespread popular support for abolition. Former slaves such as **Frederick Douglass** and **Harriet Jacobs** also spoke out in autobiographical slave narratives. The nation was at a turning point.

Civil War, Emancipation, and Reconstruction

In 1860, Abraham Lincoln was elected president on an **abolitionist platform**. Just prior to his taking office, proslavery Southern states **seceded from the Union**. The **Civil War** was fought from 1861 to 1865 to restore the Union. The North emerged victorious, though victory came with a cruel price and many lives were sacrificed.

Slavery was abolished by the **Thirteenth Amendment** in 1865, and the arduous process of **Reconstruction** was begun.

KEY TERMS

Slave trade	Abolition	Secession
Slave ships	Frederick Douglass	Confederacy
Plantation culture	Harriet Jacobs	Union
Cotton	Uncle Tom's Cabin	Emancipation
Tobacco	Harriet Beecher Stowe	Thirteenth Amendment
	Abraham Lincoln	Reconstruction

To Learn More

To learn more about the theme of slavery in U.S. history, see the sections in the U.S. History Review listed below.

SUBJECT	U.S. HISTORY REVIEW SECTION
History and Plantation Culture	Part 3
Abolition	Part 3
Civil War	Part 3
Emancipation	Part 3
Reconstruction	Part 3

Economics

The United States' economic progress is connected to four interrelated themes that are likely to appear on the test: individualism, capitalism, big business, and international economic cycles.

Individualism

One of the United States' prime economic values is **individualism**, which emphasizes self-reliance and personal responsibility for one's lot in life. American individualism had its start in the **Puritan work ethic** of seventeenth-century colonial America. As discussed in the culture section above, the Puritan philosophy emphasized hard work and a strict focus on service. Each person was expected to contribute his or her part; laziness was viewed as sinful.

This work ethic inculcated a driving belief in the importance of individual action. Nowhere was this seen more prominently than in the country's growth period between the two world wars. President Herbert Hoover

> "Individualism is a disturbing and disintegrating force. There lies its immense value. For what it seeks is to disturb monotony of type, slavery of custom, tyranny of habit, and the reduction of man to the level of a machine."
>
> —*Oscar Wilde*

> "The American system...is founded upon the conception that only through ordered liberty, freedom and equal opportunity to the individual will his initiative and enterprise spur on the march of progress."
>
> —*Herbert Hoover*

coined the term "**rugged individualism**" to emphasize the American values of independence and self-reliance.

Capitalism

Individualism as a personal value is highly connected with the American economic structure of **capitalism**, which is an economic philosophy based on individual enterprise and free markets. Companies compete to provide offerings to consumers. Free market forces encourage "survival of the fittest"—only the most effective businesses thrive.

In a capitalist system, businesses are owned by private individuals and groups, not by the government.

Big Business

Big business is another hallmark of the American economy. By the 1890s, advances in technology enabled businesses to grow and reap huge profits. Critics viewed some large businesses as advancing through greed and corporate corruption. The term **robber barons** was used to describe these businessmen, who were seen as gaining wealth unscrupulously the United States' **Gilded Age** of the late 1800s.

International Economic Cycles

As the United States grew more integrated with the world economy, international economic events had a greater financial impact. Here is a list of important periods and trends:

- Stock market crash (1929)
- The Great Depression (1930s)
- Postwar prosperity, restoration of Europe after World War II, and American economic supremacy (1945–1970)
- Inflation, the Oil Crisis, and recession (1970s)

- Deregulation under President Ronald Reagan (1980–1990)
- Dot-com and housing booms (1990s–2007)
- Global financial crisis and aftermath (2008–present)

KEY TERMS

Rugged individualism	Stock market crash (1929)
Self-reliance	Great Depression (1930s)
Puritan work ethic	Oil Crisis (1974)
Capitalism	Deregulation (1980–1990)
Big business	Reaganomics
Robber barons	Dot-com boom (1990s)
Gilded Age	Recession (2008–present)

To Learn More

To learn more about the theme of economics in U.S. history, see the sections in the U.S. History Review listed below.

SUBJECT	U.S. HISTORY REVIEW SECTION
Individualism	Part 1
Puritan work ethic	Part 1
Rugged individualism and self-reliance	Part 4
Capitalism	Part 3
Big Business	Part 3
International Economic Cycles	International economic cycles are presented chronologically, based on the dates of events.

Growth and Expansion

Closely related to economics is the theme of growth and expansion. The time period between the Civil War and World War I was ripe for U.S. expansion. During these years the country grew in size, expanding its territory westward. It grew economically in terms of its resources and production capacity. And it grew militarily, increasing its territory through imperialism.

Westward Expansion

In the mid-1800s, the United States expanded westward to the Pacific Coast. **Westward expansion** was fueled by:

- pioneers with a **frontier spirit**
- the **1848 Gold Rush** and rumors of wealth and opportunity
- inventions that promoted expansion, particularly the **steam engine** and the **transcontinental railroad**

The Gilded Age

As discussed in the Economics section, the United States grew economically during the **Gilded Age**. Big business increased with the help of industrial technology. Key names included businesses such as **U.S. Steel** and businessmen such as **Andrew Carnegie** and **John D. Rockefeller**. Monopolies were counteracted with antitrust legislation, such as the **Sherman Antitrust Act** of 1890.

Imperialism

The United States expanded its territory overseas through imperialism in the late 1800s. A schematic of imperialism shows its causes and effects.

U.S. IMPERIALISM, 1890s

Late 1800s	Late 1800s	1898	1898	1898	1898
Industrialization Big business	Markets needed for goods	U.S. wins Spanish-American War	Gains an empire: Philippines Guam Puerto Rico	Maintains control over Cuba	Annexes Hawaii

KEY TERMS

Westward expansion	Gilded Age	Monopolies
Frontier spirit	Big business	Sherman Antitrust Act
Gold Rush	U.S. Steel	Imperialism
Transcontinental railroad	Andrew Carnegie	Spanish-American War
Steam engine	John D. Rockefeller	U.S. territories

To Learn More

To learn more about the theme of growth and expansion in U.S. history, see the sections in the U.S. History Review listed below.

SUBJECT	U.S. HISTORY REVIEW SECTION
Westward Expansion	Part 2
	Part 3
The Gilded Age	Part 3
Imperialism	Part 3

Wars

The United States became a military superpower through its extensive experience in armed conflict over time. Some of the wars have been fought on U.S. soil, but most have been fought overseas either to defend American interests, to assist allies, or both.

KEY TERMS

When preparing for the test, the most important things to know about the wars are their names, when they began, when they ended, the main issues of the conflict, and the United States' role in the conflict. A summary of these aspects is presented below.

SUMMARY OF MAJOR WARS

DATES	WAR	CONFLICT/U.S. ROLE
1754–1760	French and Indian War	France enlisted Native Americans to fight against Great Britain and the American colonies over territory. The American colonists fought to retain possession of their land.
1775–1783	American Revolution	The American colonists fought against British soldiers to obtain political independence. The war established the United States as a separate country.

DATES	WAR	CONFLICT/U.S. ROLE
1812–1815	War of 1812	The United States fought against Great Britain over trade, territory, and British violations of U.S. neutrality.
1846–1848	Mexican War	The United States fought against Mexico over territory, particularly Texas. The United States won and purchased significant territory from Mexico.
1861–1865	Civil War	The Northern states fought against the Southern states over slavery. The North won, abolished slavery, and reunited the country.
1776–1918	Indian Wars	This series of wars was fought by the U.S. government against Native American populations. The United States fought to gain control of the territory from Native American tribes.
1898	Spanish-American War	The United States fought against Spain over territory. The United States won and gained the Philippines, Guam, and Puerto Rico.
1914–1918	World War I	The war was fought over territory, particularly the Balkans. The main powers were France, Britain, and the United States against Germany, Russia, Austria-Hungary, and the Ottoman Empire. The United States and its allies won and imposed a harsh peace on Germany.
1939–1945	World War II	Britain, France, the Soviet Union, and the United States fought against Germany, Italy, and Japan. Germany, Italy, and Japan were defeated.
1947–1991	Cold War	The United States and the Soviet Union struggled for influence and ideological domination (democracy versus Communism). The war was fought without the United States and the Soviet Union directly attacking each other's territories. The United States won when the Soviet Union dissolved in 1989.

DATES	WAR	CONFLICT/U.S. ROLE
1950–1953	Korean War	The United States supported South Korea when this country was invaded by North Korea, which was supported by China and the Soviet Union. The war ended in stalemate.
1955–1975	Vietnam War	The United States supported South Vietnam in its conflict against North Vietnam, which was supported by the Soviet Union. The war was drawn out, with many American casualties, and faced significant opposition beginning in the mid-1960s. The United States withdrew from the war in 1973, and North Vietnam won control of the country, ending the sovereignty of South Vietnam.
1990–1991	Gulf War	The United States fought against Iraq after Iraq invaded Kuwait, which controlled significant oil resources. The United States won and forced Iraq to withdraw from Kuwait.
2001–present	Afghanistan War	The United States launched the war with the expressed goal of preventing terrorists from using Afghanistan as a base of operations.
2003–present	Iraq War	The United States invaded Iraq with the expressed goal of preventing the country from using weapons of mass destruction (which were never found). The U.S. presence in Iraq was opposed by groups within the United States. U.S. combat troops left Iraq in 2010, but U.S. troops still remain in an advisory capacity.

To Learn More

To learn more about the theme of wars in U.S. history, see the sections in the U.S. History Review listed below.

SUBJECT	U.S. HISTORY REVIEW SECTION
French and Indian War	Part 1
American Revolution	Part 1
War of 1812	Part 2
Mexican War	Part 2
Civil War	Part 3
Indian Wars	Part 1
	Part 2
	Part 3
Spanish-American War	Part 3
World War I	Part 4
World War II	Part 4
Cold War	Part 5
Korean War	Part 5
Vietnam War	Part 5
Gulf War	Part 5
Afghanistan War	Part 5
Iraq War	Part 5

Social Groups

Among the social groups most prominent in American history are Native Americans, African Americans, and women. African American and women's concerns have historically revolved mainly around civil rights and equal rights.

Native Americans

Native Americans are the indigenous peoples who inhabited the Americas when the continents were discovered by Europeans. As far back as the 1400s, explorers had conflicts with Native Americans in their quest to claim territory. Conflicts intensified in colonial America when the territorial claims of the settlers increased.

During the period of **western expansion**, the U.S. government waged a series of battles with Native American tribes known as the **Indian Wars**. Through these wars, Indians were forced to concede their land and to give up their way of life. Permanent homes were established for various tribes on Native American **reservations**.

African Americans

As a social group, African Americans began their history in the United States under **slavery**. This marked the beginning of a long struggle to obtain civil rights, in keeping with American ideals.

- The **civil rights** movement has worked to secure equal citizenship rights for all social groups in the United States, regardless of race, gender, or ethnicity.

- After Reconstruction, in the 1880s, the Southern states continued to discriminate against former slaves through the passage of **Jim Crow laws** that kept blacks and whites separated. This legalized separation was known as **segregation** and persisted until 1954.

- In 1954, the landmark case *Brown v. Board of Education* declared "**separate but equal**" facilities unconstitutional. Resistance to ensuing **integration** efforts was substantial and sparked civil rights protests by leaders including **Dr. Martin Luther King Jr.** and **Malcolm X**.

- Martin Luther King Jr. was a pivotal leader whose speeches, personal example, and leadership vision did more for the civil rights movement—and indeed, American culture—than can ever be quantified. He was assassinated in Memphis, Tennessee, in April 1968.

Women

Unlike African Americans, women as a social group did not start their experience in the United States as personal property. But women have struggled to gain equal rights, such as the right to vote and equal pay for equal work.

- Women's right to vote was obtained through the efforts of the **suffrage movement**. Well-known suffragettes included **Susan B. Anthony** and **Elizabeth Cady Stanton**.

- Some suffragettes supported the abolitionist movement. However, there were conflicts for some suffrage activists over which political agenda to prioritize.

- Black men were granted the right to vote by the **Fifteenth Amendment** to the Constitution, which was passed in 1870 after the Civil War. Women were not granted this right until fifty years later, with the passage of the **Nineteenth Amendment** in 1920.

The **women's movement** gained prominence in the 1970s, when women demanded **equal pay for equal work**. Women benefited from the gains made by civil rights activists in the 1960s.

KEY TERMS

Native Americans	Slavery	Suffrage
Western expansion	Civil rights	Susan B. Anthony
Indian Wars	Segregation	Elizabeth Cady Stanton
Reservations	Separate but equal	Fifteenth Amendment (1870)
	Rosa Parks	Nineteenth Amendment (1920)
	Integration	Women's movement
	School busing	Equal pay for equal work
	Passive resistance	
	Civil disobedience	
	Martin Luther King Jr.	
	Black Power movement	
	Malcolm X	

To Learn More

To learn more about the theme of social groups in U.S. history, see the sections in the U.S. History Review listed below.

SUBJECT	U.S. HISTORY REVIEW SECTION
Native Americans	Part 1
	Part 2
	Part 3
Jim Crow Laws	Part 3
Segregation	Part 3
	Part 5
Civil Rights Activism	Part 5
Women's Suffrage	Part 2
Equal Rights Movement	Part 5
Legal Cases	Legal cases are presented chronologically, based on the date of the case.

Counterculture

Along with the theme of culture discussed above, the United States has also experienced the development of a **counterculture**. This counterculture was particularly pronounced during the time of the Vietnam War. It has continued since then in the form of resistance to authority.

> "When the power of love overcomes the love of power, the world will know peace."
>
> —*Jimi Hendrix*

- The **Vietnam War** was fought as part of the Cold War against the Soviet Union. It took place on Vietnamese soil and lasted twenty years. During the 1960s, U.S. **popular opposition** to the war became widespread. Young Americans in particular did not see the rationale for continuing American participation, which had a high cost in military casualties.

- A counterculture arose in the United States centering around themes of peace, love, sexual freedom, and drug experimentation. **Hippie** protesters known as **Flower Children** demonstrated against the war in the late 1960s and early 1970s.
- **Rock 'n' Roll** icons stemming from as far back as the 1950s were part of the emergence of American counterculture. **Elvis Presley**, **the Beatles**, **Jimi Hendrix**, and **the Grateful Dead** were particularly influential.

KEY TERMS

Counterculture	Rock 'n' Roll
Vietnam War	Elvis Presley
Popular opposition	The Beatles
Hippies	Jimi Hendrix
Flower children	The Grateful Dead

To Learn More

To learn more about the theme of counterculture in U.S. history, see the sections in the U.S. History Review listed below.

SUBJECT	U.S. HISTORY REVIEW SECTION
Counterculture	Part 5

THE MAIN COURSE: COMPREHENSIVE STRATEGIES AND REVIEW

If you have several weeks before you're scheduled to take the SAT U.S. History Subject Test, the following section of this book is for you!

More detailed than the brief section called "The Big Ideas of U.S. History," this Comprehensive Review section presents additional, more in-depth information about the highlights of U.S. history. A good way to maximize the value of this section is to use the following checklist as a guide.

- **Read the strategies for answering multiple-choice questions** discussed in the next few chapters to become familiar with the test.

- **Take a Practice Test** to evaluate the usefulness of these strategies and assess your knowledge of U.S. history. Compare your answers with the answers and explanations provided along with the practice test, and make a list of any areas of weakness you identify. Examine your incorrect answers and figure out why you got them wrong so you can avoid making the same types of mistakes on future tests. Did you make an error because you didn't read carefully enough or because you were confused and marked an answer in the wrong place on your answer sheet? Or was your knowledge of the material covered by a question simply incomplete?

- **Study the U.S. History Review chapters** in this section of the book. Although you'll want to go over all the material, you should concentrate intently on the areas you found challenging when you took the practice test.

- **Read the definitions in the glossary**. If you have trouble understanding or remembering particular events, terms, or concepts, you can put these definitions on flash cards and use them for review.

- **Take at least one more practice test** before taking the actual test.

- **Take another look at "A Last-Minute Study Guide"** section of this book. Review the "Housekeeping Tips" and the "Test-Taking Tips," as well as "The Big Ideas of U.S. History." Revisiting these tips several nights before test day is more effective than doing it the night before.

- **Do everything on your checklists** for the night before the test and for test day. Also, remember your positive mind-set!

Diagnostic Test

Directions: Choose the answer choice that best answers the question or incomplete statement below.

1. A drawing of the *Santa Maria*, *Pinta*, and *Niña* ships would most likely illustrate

   A. Robert de La Salle's voyage down the Mississippi River in 1680
   B. Ferdinand Magellan's circumnavigation of the globe in 1519
   C. Juan Ponce de León's voyage to Florida in 1513
   D. Christopher Columbus's voyage to the Bahama Islands in 1492
   E. Hernando de Soto's discovery of the Mississippi River in 1539

2. *McCulloch v. Maryland* was significant because it

   A. upheld the right of the individual to be protected against self-incrimination
   B. determined that school segregation was unconstitutional
   C. established the concept of judicial review
   D. established the supremacy of federal power over states' rights
   E. upheld students' rights to freedom of expression

3. In 1955, Rosa Parks was arrested in Montgomery, Alabama, for which of the following reasons?

    A. Violating a Supreme Court ruling that prohibited racial segregation on buses
    B. Heading a boycott of the Montgomery bus system in protest of segregation
    C. Acting as an accomplice in the assassination of Martin Luther King Jr.
    D. Refusing to give up her seat on a bus and violating segregation laws
    E. Leading a protest against forced busing for inner-city schools

AMERICAN MILITARY CASUALTIES, 1775 TO 1991

CONFLICT	TOTAL DEATHS	BATTLE DEATHS
Revolutionary War	4,435	4,435
War of 1812	2,260	2,260
Mexican War	13,283	1,733
Civil War (Union forces only)	364,511	140,414
Spanish-American War	2,446	385
World War I	116,516	53,402
World War II	405,399	291,557
Korean War	36,574	33,739
Vietnam War	58,220	47,434
Persian Gulf War	383	147

Source: Congressional Research Service

4. The chart above shows U.S. military deaths in major conflicts between 1775 and 1991. Which of the following is an accurate statement supported by the chart?

    A. The intractable nature of the Vietnam War and its long duration resulted in a significant number of U.S. casualties.
    B. Because of advances in firepower, World War I resulted in more U.S. casualties than any other war.

C. Battle deaths comprised a relatively small portion of the total U.S. casualties incurred during the American Revolution.

D. Civil War military deaths, including Northern and Southern casualties combined, exceeded American military losses in World War II.

E. U.S. battle deaths in the Mexican War exceeded battle deaths incurred during the War of 1812.

5. The concept of laissez-faire economics refers to the

A. overabundance of supply for a particular product

B. imposition of tight regulations on business practices

C. lack of government control over economic markets

D. excessive market demand for a service or product

E. reduction of competition between similar businesses

6. In 1894 activist Samuel Gompers wrote: "You may not know that the labor movement as represented by the trades unions, stands for right, for justice, for liberty. You may not imagine that the issuance of an injunction depriving men of a legal as well as a natural right to protect themselves, their wives and little ones, must fail of its purpose. Repression or oppression never succeeded in crushing the truth or redressing a wrong."

Which of the following would Gompers most likely accept as best characterizing American labor organizations?

A. Excellent models for labor relations governance to be followed by other nations

B. Difficult to establish and complicated and time-consuming to maintain

C. Driven by lofty goals that were undisputed by all but a few of the political elite

   D.   Misguided but necessary given the political pressures placed on big businesses

   E.   Important for protecting the rights of workers and improving their economic status

7.   Which of the following events marked the start of the Great Depression?

   A.   The U.S. stock market crash of 1929

   B.   The establishment of the Bretton Woods monetary system in 1945

   C.   The signing of the Treaty of Versailles in 1919

   D.   The origin of World War I in 1914

   E.   The collapse of the gold standard in 1971

8.   Which of the following was true of the Salem witch trials of 1692?

   A.   Abigail Williams was tried and found guilty of witchcraft.

   B.   The testimonies of the accusers in the trials were highly inconsistent.

   C.   Twenty individuals were executed as a result of the witch hunt.

   D.   Most of those accused of witchcraft in the trials were slaves.

   E.   Anne Hutchinson was one of the accusers who prompted the trials.

9.   The Fourteen Points speech was associated with which of the following?

   A.   Woodrow Wilson's peace negotiations at the end of World War I

   B.   Theodore Roosevelt's establishing the Roosevelt Corollary to the Monroe Doctrine

   C.   Ronald Reagan's participation in the Iran-Contra affair

   D.   Dwight D. Eisenhower's supporting the end of the Korean War

   E.   Richard Nixon's establishment of détente during the Cold War

10. The Second Great Awakening of the early 1800s contributed to which of the following?

   A. Shay's Rebellion
   B. The invention of the television
   C. The XYZ Affair
   D. The separation of church and state
   E. The temperance movement

Library of Congress

11. The cartoon above, created by Benjamin Franklin, makes which of the following points about the governments of the colonies pictured in 1754?

   A. They were not likely to survive the Revolutionary War.
   B. Their political effectiveness would be enhanced by unification.
   C. They were considered to be traitors to the British.
   D. They would benefit most from an alliance with the French.
   E. They had not established strong policies against the Native Americans.

12. The Louisiana Purchase was executed by the United States in 1803 as a transaction with

   A.   Britain
   B.   Spain
   C.   France
   D.   Mexico
   E.   Italy

13. Which of the following reflects the foreign policy doctrine implemented by President James Monroe in 1823?

   A.   The United States would use military force to combat terrorism at home and abroad.
   B.   The United States would reduce tariffs to increase trade with Europe.
   C.   The United States would use military might to protect slave trade routes to the West Indies.
   D.   The United States would contain the spread of Communism around the world.
   E.   The United States would intervene against attempts at colonialism in the Americas.

14. The origin of the U.S.-Soviet space race, which lasted from 1957 to 1975, was marked by which of the following?

   A.   The establishment of the first Soviet space station
   B.   The U.S. space shuttle *Challenger* launch
   C.   The U.S. *Apollo 11* moon landing
   D.   The Soviet launch of *Sputnik 1*
   E.   The flight of Russian cosmonaut Sergei Krikalev on a U.S. space shuttle

15. The Mexican War of 1846–1848 was prompted by which of the following doctrines?

   A. Monroe Doctrine
   B. Manifest Destiny
   C. Cowboy Diplomacy
   D. Brezhnev Doctrine
   E. Truman Doctrine

16. "It's going to be difficult for us to very long prosecute effectively a war that far away from home with the divisions we have here—and particularly the potential divisions…. And I don't see…that we have any…plan for victory—militarily or diplomatically."

The statement above was most likely made by which of the following?

   A. George Washington regarding the French and Indian War
   B. President James Madison regarding the War of 1812
   C. General Ulysses S. Grant regarding the Civil War
   D. President Lyndon B. Johnson regarding the Vietnam War
   E. President George H. W. Bush regarding the Gulf War

17. Public school reform in the 1830s was spearheaded by which of the following?

   A. Lucretia Mott
   B. Horace Mann
   C. Dorothea Dix
   D. Elizabeth Cady Stanton
   E. William Lloyd Garrison

18. Which of the following brought about the Nullification Crisis of 1832?

    A.   South Carolina's objections to the imposition of high tariffs

    B.   The formation of the Confederate States of America

    C.   South Carolina's declaration of secession from the Union

    D.   The ratification of the Articles of Confederation

    E.   Virginia's reactions to the outcome of the Mexican War

BRITISH IMPORTS FROM COLONIAL AMERICA, 1770

PRODUCT	SOURCE
Apples	Delaware
Cattle	Virginia
	North Carolina
	South Carolina
Furs	Maine
	New York
	Virginia
	North Carolina
	South Carolina
Grain	Pennsylvania
Iron	Massachusetts
	Pennsylvania
	Virginia
Peaches	Virginia
Tobacco	Virginia
	North Carolina
Wheat	Pennsylvania

Source: Routledge Atlas of American History

19. The chart above shows British imports from colonial America in 1770. Which of the following statements is supported by the chart?

    A.   British imports of furs from the colonies focused exclusively on suppliers based in the North.

B. The climate of the colonies was unsuited for the production of fruit and vegetable crops.

C. British contracts with Northern tobacco producers account for the largest portion of British tobacco imports.

D. Northern colonies were the most likely to produce and export livestock.

E. Tobacco products were primarily imported from the South, where they were produced by plantations that relied on slave labor.

20. "Well, I don't know what will happen now; we've got some difficult days ahead. But it really doesn't matter with me now, because I've been to the mountaintop.... And I've looked over, and I've seen the Promised Land. I may not get there with you. But I want you to know tonight, that we, as a people, will get to the Promised Land."

The statement above was made by

A. Marcus Garvey, arguing in support of Pan-African activism

B. Martin Luther King Jr., speaking in support of civil rights in Memphis

C. W. E. B. Du Bois, supporting the efforts of the NAACP

D. Malcolm X, advocating for African American rights in New York

E. Booker T. Washington, speaking on race relations in Atlanta

21. American antitrust legislation in the 1890s was backed by which of the following?

A. McCarthyism

B. Populist movement

C. Black Panthers

D. Militia movement

E. Tea Party movement

22. "This is God's curse on slavery!—a bitter, bitter, most accursed thing!—a curse to the master and a curse to the slave! I was a fool to think I could make anything good out of such a deadly evil."

The passage above is most likely excerpted from

A. Henry James's *The Turn of the Screw*
B. Herman Melville's *Moby Dick*
C. Harriet Beecher Stowe's *Uncle Tom's Cabin*
D. James Joyce's *Ulysses*
E. William Faulkner's *As I Lay Dying*

23. Each of the following fought in the American Revolutionary war EXCEPT

A. Mexico
B. France
C. the Dutch Republic
D. Britain
E. Spain

24. Which of the following Indian leaders instigated a rebellion that was defeated at the battle of Tippecanoe in 1811?

A. Geronimo
B. Tecumseh
C. Sitting Bull
D. American Horse
E. Crazy Horse

25. Which of the following presidents won the Nobel Peace Prize for mediating an end to the Russo-Japanese War in 1905?

A. Theodore Roosevelt

B.   Woodrow Wilson
C.   Andrew Johnson
D.   Warren Harding
E.   William McKinley

Diagnostic Test: Answer Key

1.	D	14.	D
2.	D	15.	B
3.	D	16.	D
4.	A	17.	B
5.	C	18.	A
6.	E	19.	E
7.	A	20.	B
8.	C	21.	B
9.	A	22.	C
10.	E	23.	A
11.	B	24.	B
12.	C	25.	A
13.	E		

Diagnostic Test: Explanations

1. The correct answer is D. Christopher Columbus sailed to the Americas in 1492, landing first in the Bahama Islands. His expedition included three ships: *Santa Maria*, *Pinta*, and *Niña*.

See Part 1 of the U.S. History Review.

2. The correct answer is D. The case of *McCulloch v. Maryland* established the supremacy of federal government over states' rights. It is important because it set a precedent that would permanently affect the legal relationship between the U.S. government and the individual states. A is incorrect because *Miranda v. Arizona* upheld the right of individuals to be protected against self-incrimination. B is incorrect because the unconstitutionality of school segregation was determined by *Brown v. Board of Education*.

See Part 2 of the U.S. History Review.

3. The correct answer is D. Rosa Parks is considered to be the mother of the civil rights movement. She was arrested in December 1955 for refusing to give up her seat on a bus in Montgomery, Alabama. She was tried and convicted for violating segregation laws that existed in Montgomery at the time.

See Part 5 of the U.S. History Review.

4. The correct answer is A. The statement in choice A is a true statement that is also supported by information in the chart. Compared to the losses faced by the United States in other wars, the deaths incurred in Vietnam were significant; only the Civil War and the two world wars show more casualties. The high losses in Vietnam were due to the long duration of the war and its intractable nature, so A is correct. B, C, and E are not supported by the chart.

See Part 5 of the U.S. History Review.

5. The correct answer is C. The concept of laissez-faire economics refers to the lack of government control over economic markets. This approach to the economy was widespread in the period before the New

Deal. B is incorrect because it is the opposite of the correct answer. E is incorrect because laissez-faire policies result in increased competition between similar businesses, not reduced competition.

See Part 1 of the U.S. History Review.

6.   The correct answer is E. Samuel Gompers was head of the American Federation of Labor and was a strong advocate of labor unions and workers' rights. He saw labor unions as important for protecting the rights of workers and improving their economic status. This view is reflected in his claim that labor unions stand "for right, for justice, [and] for liberty." A is incorrect because the passage does not provide any indication of Gompers' views regarding labor union models for other nations. C is incorrect because the passage does not suggest that the goals of labor unions were largely undisputed.

See Part 3 of the U.S. History Review.

7.   The correct answer is A. The start of the Great Depression was marked by the U.S. stock market crash of 1929. In the crash, U.S. investors lost significant amounts of money in short periods of time. Choices B and E are incorrect, because the Great Depression occurred in the 1930s, before these events. Choices C and D are incorrect because these events preceded the Great Depression by more than ten years.

See Part 4 of the U.S. History Review.

8.   The correct answer is C. Twenty individuals were executed as a result of the Salem witch trials. Nineteen were found guilty at their trials, and one individual was killed for refusing to stand trial. A is incorrect because Abigail Williams was one of the teenage girls who accused various townspeople of witchcraft. B is incorrect because the accusers' testimonies generally supported one another and relied on similar types of evidence. D is incorrect because most of those accused were upstanding townspeople and members of well-known families. E is incorrect because Anne Hutchinson was tried for her religious views almost fifty years before the witch trials.

See Part 1 of the U.S. History Review.

9.   The correct answer is A. The Fourteen Points speech was associated with Woodrow Wilson's peace negotiations at the end of World War I. Wilson gave the speech to Congress in 1918, and the Fourteen Points became the basis for negotiations with Germany at the end of the war. The Treaty of Versailles, which ended the war, ultimately abandoned the Fourteen Points.

See Part 4 of the U.S. History Review.

10. The correct answer is E. The temperance movement of the 1800s was influenced by the Second Great Awakening, a period of religious revival that led to many social reforms. Temperance activists urged a reduction in alcohol consumption. A and C are incorrect because these occurred before the Second Great Awakening. D is a principle of American government that was influenced by the First Great Awakening in the mid-1700s.

See Part 2 of the U.S. History Review.

11. The correct answer is B. The "Join or Die" cartoon depicts the American colonies in a fragmented state. Benjamin Franklin developed the cartoon to make the point that the colonies could enhance their political effectiveness through unification. The cartoon was a commentary on the divisiveness that existed between the colonies at the time.

See Part 1 of the U.S. History Review.

12. The correct answer is C. The Louisiana Purchase was a transaction conducted with France in 1803. The United States purchased France's claim to the land, but the land itself was acquired over time from the territory's Native American inhabitants. France was the only nation that held claim to the territory at the time, so the remaining answer choices are incorrect.

See Part 2 of the U.S. History Review.

13. The correct answer is E. The Monroe Doctrine, implemented in 1823, declared that the United States would not tolerate European attempts to colonize territories in the Americas. It was directed primarily

at Spain to curtail imperialism in Latin America and protect American spheres of influence. B is incorrect because, in general, during Monroe's presidency, U.S. tariffs were relatively high. D is incorrect because it describes the policy of containment implemented during the Cold War.

See Part 2 of the U.S. History Review.

14. The correct answer is D. The launch of the Soviet's first artificial satellite, *Sputnik 1*, occurred in 1957 and marked the origin of the U.S.-Soviet space race. The space race would proceed until 1975, a reflection of intense competition between the two countries as an offshoot of the Cold War. Attempts by each country to outpace the other resulted in rapid advances in aerospace technology, which ultimately benefited international space exploration as a whole and laid a foundation for U.S.-Soviet scientific cooperation in the era of détente.

See Part 5 of the U.S. History Review.

15. The correct answer is B. The doctrine of Manifest Destiny expressed the belief that the United States had the right to expand its borders across North America from the Atlantic to the Pacific. This doctrine led the United States to annex Texas, resulting in a territorial dispute with Mexico that escalated into war. Mexico lost the war over Texas and suffered other territorial losses as well, including California.

See Part 2 of the U.S. History Review.

16. The correct answer is D. The statement was made by President Lyndon B. Johnson regarding the Vietnam War. U.S. participation in the Vietnam War lacked popular support and was met with much antiwar protest at home. Part of the concern regarding the war was its protracted nature; opponents also failed to see any justification for American involvement.

See Part 5 of the U.S. History Review.

17. The correct answer is B. Public school reform in the 1830s was carried out by Horace Mann, who began extensive reform in Massachusetts in 1837. All of the individuals in the incorrect choices were activists during the same time period as Mann. Lucretia Mott and

Elizabeth Cady Stanton were activists for women's rights; Dorothea Dix was an activist for the rights of the mentally ill; and William Lloyd Garrison was an antislavery activist.

See Part 2 of the U.S. History Review.

18. The correct answer is A. The Nullification Crisis of 1832 was brought about by South Carolina's passage of an Ordinance of Nullification in 1832. South Carolina objected to the high tariffs imposed by the federal government in 1828 and 1832 and declared these tariffs to be nullified within the state. B, C, and E are incorrect because these events occurred after the Nullification Crisis. D is incorrect because the ratification of the Articles of Confederation occurred decades before the Nullification Crisis and did not have a direct impact on it.

See Part 3 of the U.S. History Review.

19. The correct answer is E. The chart shows that British imports of tobacco crops came from two Southern colonies, Virginia and North Carolina. Tobacco plantations were operated by slave labor, so E is correct. A, B, C, and D contradict information presented in the chart, so these choices are incorrect.

See Part 1 of the U.S. History Review.

20. The correct answer is B. The quoted text is excerpted from a speech by Martin Luther King Jr. advocating for civil rights in response to violence that broke out over strikes by African American sanitation workers in Memphis. The famous speech, known as King's "I've been to the mountaintop" speech, was his last public speech, given the day before his assassination on April 4, 1968, in Memphis.

See Part 5 of the U.S. History Review.

21. The correct answer is B. Antitrust legislation in the 1890s was backed by the early Populist movement. This movement was composed of farmers and workers who decried government corruption and advocated for an anti–big business agenda. Though the movement faded

from prominence in a short period of time, its influence helped establish antimonopoly laws such as the Sherman Antitrust Act of 1890.

See Part 3 of the U.S. History Review.

22. The correct answer is C. The passage is excerpted from *Uncle Tom's Cabin*, an antislavery novel written by Harriet Beecher Stowe. The novel, published in 1852, was a rampant bestseller and was highly influential in mobilizing popular support for the abolitionist movement. It helped spread understanding of the injustices of slavery through the perspective of a faithful slave named Tom who suffered at the hands of his cruel master, Simon Legree.

See Part 3 of the U.S. History Review.

23. The correct answer is A. Mexico was not a combatant in the Revolutionary War. The United States maintained alliances with France, Spain, and the Dutch Republic during the war, so B, C, and E are incorrect. D is incorrect because Britain fought against the United States in the war.

See Part 1 of the U.S. History Review.

24. The correct answer is B. Tecumseh was a Shawnee chief who organized a rebellion in Ohio and Indiana. The rebellion was defeated in 1811 at the battle of Tippecanoe.

See Part 2 of the U.S. History Review.

25. The correct answer is A. President Theodore Roosevelt won the Nobel Peace Prize for mediating an end to the Russo-Japanese War in 1905. William McKinley held the presidency just before Roosevelt (1897–1901), and Woodrow Wilson (1913–1921) and Warren Harding (1921–1923) held the office of president after Roosevelt's term.

See Part 3 of the U.S. History Review.

U.S. History Review Part 1: The United States Becomes a Country (1492–1789)

The United States began as thirteen colonies that were settled by British colonists. The colonies soon overthrew British rule and set up an independent government. The first phase of this country's life is characterized by:

1. Settlement of the colonies
2. The war for independence
3. Territorial expansion
4. The establishment of government

Early Explorers and Settlement of the Continent

Christopher Columbus is usually thought of as the first explorer to reach the Americas in 1492. But evidence shows that other explorers had discovered the continent before then. Notably, Norse explorer **Leif Ericsson** reached Newfoundland around AD 1000.

Christopher Columbus reached the Bahamas during a voyage sponsored by Spain. Columbus sailed to the New World in an exploration party on three ships: the *Pinta*, *Niña*, and *Santa Maria*. His voyage launched a period of expanded exploration in the Americas known as the **Age of Exploration**.

The tables that follow present information regarding the early explorers. The tables are organized by date, by explorer, and by sponsoring country. When you encounter questions regarding the early explorers on the test, you may be asked about the time line of discoveries, the names of the explorers and their accomplishments, or the names of the countries that supported the expeditions. This information has been organized for you in the three tables that follow for easy review.

Accomplishments by Date

DATE	EXPLORER	SPONSOR	DISCOVERY/TERRITORY
1000	Leif Ericsson	Norse	Newfoundland
1492	Christopher Columbus	Spain	Americas: Bahamas, Cuba, Haiti
1497	John Cabot	England	Nova Scotia, Newfoundland
1498	Vasco da Gama	Portugal	India
1499	Amerigo Vespucci	Spain	South America
1501	Amerigo Vespucci	Portugal	South America
1513	Ponce de León	Spain	Florida
1513	Vasco Balboa	Spain	Pacific Ocean
1519	Ferdinand Magellan	Spain	Circumnavigation of the globe
1519	Hernando Cortez	Spain	Aztecs (Mexico)
1530	Francisco Pizarro	Spain	Incas (Peru)
1539	Hernando de Soto	Spain	Mississippi River
1540	Francesco Coronado	Spain	Grand Canyon
1542	Jacques Cartier	France	St. Lawrence River
1608	Samuel de Champlain	France	Great Lakes
1609	Henry Hudson	Netherlands	Hudson River

Accomplishments by Explorer

EXPLORER	SPONSOR	DATE	DISCOVERY/TERRITORY
Vasco Balboa	Spain	1513	Pacific Ocean
John Cabot	England	1497	Nova Scotia, Newfoundland
Jacques Cartier	France	1542	St. Lawrence River

EXPLORER	SPONSOR	DATE	DISCOVERY/TERRITORY
Christopher Columbus	Spain	1492	Americas: Bahamas, Cuba, Haiti
Francesco Coronado	Spain	1540	Grand Canyon
Hernando Cortez	Spain	1519	Aztecs (Mexico)
Samuel de Champlain	France	1608	Great Lakes
Vasco da Gama	Portugal	1498	India
Ponce de León	Spain	1513	Florida
Hernando de Soto	Spain	1539	Mississippi River
Leif Ericsson	Norse	1000	Newfoundland
Henry Hudson	Netherlands	1609	Hudson River
Ferdinand Magellan	Spain	1519	Circumnavigation of the globe
Francisco Pizarro	Spain	1530	Incas (Peru)
Amerigo Vespucci	Portugal	1501	South America
Amerigo Vespucci	Spain	1499	South America

Accomplishments by Sponsoring Country

In the 1500s the major players in New World exploration were England, France, the Netherlands, Spain, and Portugal. The Spanish focused heavily on the southern parts of North America, Mexico, and South America. The Spanish explorations were led by groups of explorers known as **conquistadors** who conquered the peoples they discovered. They treated the native populations cruelly, stole their gold, and forced them into slave labor.

Notable conquistadors were Cortez in Mexico and Pizarro in Peru. Cortez conquered the Aztec Indians in Mexico, and Pizarro conquered the Inca Indians in Peru.

SPONSOR	EXPLORER	DATE	DISCOVERY/TERRITORY
England	John Cabot	1497	Nova Scotia, Newfoundland
France	Jacques Cartier	1542	St. Lawrence River
France	Samuel de Champlain	1608	Great Lakes
Netherlands	Henry Hudson	1609	Hudson River

SPONSOR	EXPLORER	DATE	DISCOVERY/TERRITORY
Norse	Leif Ericsson	1000	Newfoundland
Portugal	Vasco da Gama	1498	India
Portugal	Amerigo Vespucci	1501	South America
Spain	Christopher Columbus	1492	Americas: Bahamas, Cuba, Haiti
Spain	Amerigo Vespucci	1499	South America
Spain	Ponce de León	1513	Florida
Spain	Vasco Balboa	1513	Pacific Ocean
Spain	Ferdinand Magellan	1519	Circumnavigation of the globe
Spain	Hernando Cortez	1519	Aztecs (Mexico)
Spain	Francisco Pizarro	1530	Incas (Peru)
Spain	Hernando de Soto	1539	Mississippi River
Spain	Francesco Coronado	1540	Grand Canyon

The Thirteen Colonies

The territory that eventually became the United States was colonized originally by the English. English settlers established colonies on the eastern coast of the United States. **Thirteen original colonies** were founded, with dates and groupings shown below:

Northern Colonies

- New Hampshire (1623)
- Massachusetts (1628)
- Rhode Island (1636)
- Connecticut (1635)

Middle Colonies

- New York (1613)
- New Jersey (1664)
- Pennsylvania (1681)
- Delaware (1638)

Southern Colonies

- Virginia (1607)
- Maryland (1632)
- North Carolina (1653)
- South Carolina (1670)
- Georgia (1733)

Colonization occurred mainly for religious and economic reasons. Some groups, such as the Pilgrims and Puritans, established colonies for religious reasons. The **Pilgrims** wished to separate from the Church of England, whereas the **Puritans** wished to "purify" the church; both groups came to escape religious persecution. Other groups came to find a better way of life. Britain was able to increase its presence in the Americas at this time because Spain had been defeated in a naval battle and was becoming less powerful.

Funding and Governance

Colonization efforts were funded by endeavors known as **joint-stock companies**. These companies allowed shareholders to invest their money and to reap a share of the profits. Joint stock companies alleviated the burden on the British government for financing colonization.

Colonies were set up under three main types of governing structures. Each colony was established under a **charter** granted by the British government. **Proprietary colonies** were granted to individuals by the British government; the owners would then appoint a governor for the colony. **Royal colonies** were owned by the British Crown, with a governor appointed by the king. **Self-governing** colonies selected their own governors. They were developed when the Crown granted a charter to a joint-stock company.

Important Colonies

Jamestown was the first successful American colony, established in Virginia in 1607. Though it was not the first colony established, it was the first to become permanent. John Smith, Pocohantas, and John Rolfe were important figures in the Jamestown settlement. **John Smith** helped the colony thrive by taking command and helping the settlers organize their food supplies. **Pocohantas** negotiated with Native Americans to spare Smith's life and decrease hostilities against the settlers. She married **John Rolfe**, who introduced **tobacco** to Virginia, thereby enabling the colony to thrive.

Plymouth Colony was established in 1620 by Pilgrims who came over on the *Mayflower*. The Pilgrims were Puritan **separatists** who viewed the Church of England as corrupt. They wished not just to purify the church but to separate from it altogether. Puritanism had developed as a branch of **Protestantism**, which itself was an offshoot from the Catholic Church. Protestants in England broke with the Catholicism of the Anglican Church. The Puritans were a special branch of Protestants, and the Pilgrims were an even smaller group of Puritans who wished to separate from the Anglican Church completely.

Before landing in the New World, forty-one of the Pilgrim men on the ship signed a governing agreement called the **Mayflower Compact**. In this agreement, the Pilgrims contracted to govern themselves cooperatively and to follow the rules established by the majority. The Mayflower Compact was crucial because it established the first form of independent government in the colonies—agreed upon before the Pilgrims even reached land.

A third important colony, the **Massachusetts Bay Colony**, was established in 1630. This colony was established by Puritans who, unlike the Pilgrim separatists, wished to remain with the Anglican Church and improve it. They chose to relocate in the New World so they could practice their religion freely and create a society in which religion was more important than economic goals. The Massachusetts Bay settlers established a **theocracy** (rule by the church). Only church members had the right to vote.

The colony was governed by **John Winthrop**, who saw the settlement as a "city on a hill" that would abide by righteous precepts and serve as a model for others.

Colonial Life

In the late 1600s and 1700s the colonies matured. Regional differences affected the characteristics of daily life. Religion played a large role in the experience of the settlers, particularly for those in the North.

Relations with the Native American populations were fraught with conflict, and the strain ultimately led to war.

Regional Differences

Life in colonial America differed widely from region to region. The New England colonies in the North depended mainly on trade, and the inhabitants lived stable lives focused on work and religion. By contrast, the southern colonies relied on large-scale farming supported by an aristocratic **plantation culture**. Cash crops such as tobacco, rice, and indigo were produced largely through slave labor, which was less prominent in the North. The middle colonies displayed characteristics of both the North and the South, as they depended on a mix of farming and trade.

During the colonial era, settlers often gained passage to the New World by committing themselves to **indentured servitude**. Indentured servants made agreements to work on southern plantations in exchange for their freedom and in some cases a portion of land.

Indentured servitude fell out of favor with plantation owners, however, after **Bacon's Rebellion of 1676**. In this uprising, immigrant **Nathaniel Bacon** led a group of former indentured servants in a series of violent attacks on neighboring Native American tribes. The tribes were hostile to the settlers, and many pioneers felt the government failed to take adequate protective measures. After attacking the tribes, Bacon's rebels turned on colonial governor William Berkeley and burned the Jamestown capitol. The rebellion was quelled but helped prompt the movement in the South toward large-scale slave labor.

Religion

Religious beliefs dramatically molded the lives of the Puritan settlers in the North. In particular, they helped develop the **Protestant work ethic** that became characteristic of American culture. Puritans believed that hard work was necessary to serve God, and members of the church were expected to devote themselves to industry. Laziness and wasting time were viewed as sinful. Individuals developed a commitment to

asceticism, a rigid way of life devoid of worldly pleasures. It was acceptable to gain wealth only if done through the mechanism of hard work, and one's wealth was to be accumulated as a sign of God's blessings rather than enjoyed. Those who labored diligently, amassed riches, and lived frugally were seen as serving the glory of God.

Religious dissent and persecution were also part of the Puritan culture. The Puritans were highly restrictive in their religious codes. Deviation from the church's precepts was not accepted in any form. Even though they themselves had fled England to escape religious persecution, the Puritans could not tolerate religious freedom in their own society because their government was dedicated to serving Puritan ideals.

The Puritans' strict practices and requirements motivated multiple incidents of religious dissent. Two notable figures, **Roger Williams** and **Anne Hutchinson**, publicly rejected Puritan philosophies and were eventually banished. Williams was a minister who advocated the separation of church and state. He was banished and later founded the Rhode Island colony, which was based on religious tolerance. Anne Hutchinson similarly challenged certain aspects of Puritan ideology that threatened John Winthrop's leadership; she was tried for heresy and banished as well, eventually settling in Rhode Island with her followers.

Puritan rigidity further resulted in the persecution of many individuals in the **Salem witch trials of 1692**. Other witch trials had occurred in the colonies prior to this time, but the Salem witch trials accused the most at once: twenty people were killed as a result. Nineteen of these were women who were tried and found guilty; the twentieth was an eighty-year-old man who refused to stand trial. The story of the Salem witch trials is retold in *The Crucible*, a 1953 play by Arthur Miller. It is believed that class and political conflicts were part of what motivated the accusations, many of which were leveled at individuals from upstanding Salem families.

Religious revival in the colonies occurred during the **Great Awakening** of the 1730s–1740s. During this period a resurgence of interest in religion swept through the colonies. Unlike the rigid messages of the Puritan ministers, who preached about discipline and self-control, the sermons of the Great Awakening attempted to arouse the emotions of the congregants, particularly regarding fear of divine retribution. Revival leader **Jonathan Edwards** preached fire-and-brimstone sermons urging parishioners to repent of their sins or risk eternal condemnation.

Native Americans

In 1607 the Native Americans vastly outnumbered the Jamestown settlers, and for much of this early period of colonization the settlements were essentially white enclaves surrounded by native tribal populations. Despite any reinforcements they might receive from the mother country, the settlers quickly realized they could be easily overrun by these tribes.

In this early era, however, there was no united resistance by the Indians against the white inhabitants. The tribes were scattered, independent groups that spoke unique languages. In fact, the introduction of metal tools and other European goods increased conflict between the different Indian groups.

TRADE AND ITS IMPACT

When the settlers first arrived in the colonies, the initial reaction of many Native Americans was shock. They had not been exposed to many of the things they were seeing, including ships, for example, and they did not understand what they were seeing. Some Indians attributed healing powers or other virtues to the white settlers. Other Indian groups resisted the white settlers by force. As settlements became more common, co-existing relationships centered around trade. The Europeans introduced many foodstuffs, metal tools, and livestock such as horses. The Native Americans exchanged gold, hides, furs, food, and women for these.

Many Europeans were motivated to colonize the New World in search of gold. They often encountered disease, armed resistance, and harsh conditions that decimated their populations. To make matters worse, often there was no gold to be found in the area of their explorations.

In 1600, Spanish explorers introduced the horse into Native American culture, and this changed the Native American way of life permanently. Before having access to horses, many tribes were sedentary and focused on farming. Hunting was arduous, and because transportation was by foot, the spoils of the hunt could only be as much as the warriors could carry. The introduction of the horse meant that warriors could bring back enough meat to preserve for longer periods. This, along with the introduction of guns by the settlers, motivated the tribes to become more nomadic. Horses also became a source of revenue for the Indian tribes who sold them. Horses soon spread from tribe to tribe on the continent.

ONGOING CONFLICTS

The history of Native Americans during the colonial period is characterized by involvement in three types of conflicts. First were the European-Indian conflicts themselves. Native Americans engaged in a string of battles, raids, massacres, and wars with the British, French, Dutch, and other European settlers. These conflicts included the following:

- The **Pequot War** (1636–1638) was carried out in Connecticut by the British against the Pequot tribe. Many Pequot were killed in the Mystic River massacre in the first organized British effort to clear native populations from the New England area.
- The **Dutch-Indian Wars** (1655–1664) were carried out under the leadership of Peter Stuyvesant.
- **King Phillip's War** (1675–1676) was carried out in New England under the leadership of the Indian chief Metacomet, who went by the name King Phillip. Under Metacomet–King Phillip's leadership, the Wampanoag launched a series of attacks on British colonists. The colonists eventually achieved victory by superior firepower and by destroying the Wampanoag's food supplies.

Along with Indian-European conflicts, tribal wars continued during this period between the Native Americans themselves. Native groups remained embroiled in hostilities with warring tribes, and white settlers learned to take advantage of the factions by developing strategic alliances with certain groups. The ongoing intertribal conflict also made Native American tribes more susceptible to a third type of conflict: the imperialist conflicts between the European powers. European governments provided incentives for Native American participation and made alliances with the tribes against other European imperial powers and their Native American allies.

FRENCH AND INDIAN WAR

One such war that Native Americans joined in was the **French and Indian War** (1754–1761), also known as the **Seven Year's War**, with France and England as the major combatants. The French enlisted the help of the **Abenaki** tribes, while the British allied with the **Iroquois**. In U.S. history, the conflict is called the French and Indian War to reflect the main enemies of the American colonists in the battles: France and the Native Americans. The British won the war and as a result gained Canada and Florida. These concessions were specified in the **Treaty of Paris**, which ended the war in 1763.

When the French and Indian War ended, a demarcation line known as the **Proclamation Line of 1763** was drawn. This line was intended to stabilize relations between the British and the Native Americans. It declared that no colonial settlements would be established west of the Appalachian Mountains, and it stretched from New York to Florida. The agreement was successful for a brief period, from 1763–1765. Eventually, however, funds for enforcing the settlement ban ran out, and British settlers moved westward.

Events Leading Up to the Revolutionary War

After the French and Indian War ended, the British government had to put up funds to protect the colonists from attacks by the French and Native Americans (and by the Spanish too). This protection was costly, and the British Crown imposed taxes on the colonists to pay for it.

The colonists had no voting say over whether any taxes were imposed on them, and this caused great outrage. The theme of the era was "**no taxation without representation!**" The colonists weren't directly represented in Parliament, where the legislative decisions were made. Many refused to obey the new tax laws, which they viewed as unfairly imposed.

Eventually, this controversy over the tax issue led to war. The colonists declared themselves independent of the British government and revolted. Here is a list of important prerevolutionary events:

- **Salutary neglect (1607–1763)**—This phrase refers to the policy maintained by the British concerning enforcement of laws in the colonies. Essentially it involved the failure to enforce laws, or a purposefully relaxed approach to enforcement. After living under salutary neglect for more than 150 years, the colonists did not easily accept the imposition of taxes and other controls by the British in the 1760s.

- **Stamp Act (1765)**—This act levied a tax on all printed materials. It was the first direct tax imposed on the colonists. In response to colonial protest, the Stamp Act was repealed in 1766.

- **Quartering Act (1765)**—With this act, colonists were required to provide lodging in their homes to British soldiers. This act expired in 1767, but another was passed in 1774, as part of the so-called Intolerable Acts.

- **Declaratory Act (1766)**—In this act, which was passed when the Stamp Act was repealed, Britain declared that it had the right to create legislation for the colonies.

- **Townshend Acts (1767)**—The British levied a tax on multiple luxury goods, including sugar, glass, paint, and tea. Passage of the Townshend Acts led to the Boston Massacre. The tea tax was particularly important, because it prompted the Boston Tea Party (see below).

- **Boston Massacre (1770)**—This event involved the first American deaths in the Revolutionary War, though the war had not officially started at the time. Turmoil broke out when a group of angry colonists gathered around a small contingent of British soldiers. The skirmish started as a minor incident and spiraled out of control as the crowd of colonists grew. The townsmen were angry over the Townshend Acts and other acts of British control. The British troops fired into the crowd, hitting eleven men. **Crispus Attucks**, a mixed-race sailor, was killed instantly and is viewed as the first casualty of the Revolution.

- **Boston Tea Party (1773)**—This event was a colonial uprising in which rebels dumped shiploads of tea into Boston Harbor. Colonists further acted to protest the tax on tea.

- **Intolerable Acts (1774)**—Also known as the **Coercive Acts**, these laws were passed by Britain in response to the Boston Tea Party. This set of acts punished the entire city of Boston for the rebellion, closing Boston Harbor until the losses from the Tea Party were paid for. The Intolerable Acts also included a second Quartering Act, requiring lodging for British troops, because the first quartering act had expired.

- **First Continental Congress (1774)**—The colonists responded to the Intolerable Acts by forming the First Continental Congress, a gathering of delegates who crafted a unified response to British aggression. One important act of the Continental Congress was to ban all imports from Britain. Another was to call for the Second Continental Congress.

The American Revolution

The Revolutionary War officially began in 1775. Its political origins were rooted in the controversies over British taxation. Militarily, the first shots of the war were fired at **Lexington, Massachusetts**, when British soldiers fired on American **Minutemen** (the name for rapidly deployable troops in the American militia). In 1775, the colonial forces were officially recognized as the **Continental army** by the **Second Continental Congress**, a group of delegates convened to manage the war effort. **George Washington** commanded the army. The French and Spanish (long-standing enemies of Britain) supported the colonists by sending arms, and in 1776, the **Declaration of Independence** was issued.

Important Events

Among the events to note about the war are the following:

- **Second Continental Congress (1775)**—This gathering of delegates followed the First Continental Congress and was convened to manage the war effort. It was responsible for passing the Declaration of Independence.

- *Common Sense*, **by Thomas Paine (1776)**—This tract was written by journalist Thomas Paine and published anonymously in 1776. It argued for the importance of independence from British rule. It was widely read and effective in swaying public opinion because it spoke to people in plain language that could be easily understood.

- **Declaration of Independence (1776)**—With this famous document, drafted mainly by Thomas Jefferson, the colonists declared themselves independent of Britain, and citizens of the United States. The most well-known phrase from the document describes its underlying beliefs:

> We hold these truths to be self-evident, that all men are created equal, that they are endowed by their Creator with certain unalienable Rights, that among these are Life, Liberty and the pursuit of Happiness.

- **Battle of Saratoga (1777)**—In this battle in New York, the British were sorely defeated. Their defeat prompted the French to join the war in support of the American forces. Spain and the Netherlands also joined as allies of France.

- **Battle of Yorktown (1781)**—The last major battle of the Revolutionary War, the battle of Yorktown resulted in a decisive victory for American and French troops over British general Charles Cornwallis.

Ending and Treaty

The Revolutionary War officially ended after the surrender of Cornwallis at Yorktown in 1781. The British government voted to discontinue the hostilities, and a treaty was negotiated to restore peace. The **Treaty of Paris (1783)** established the United States of America as an independent nation that was recognized as such by Britain. The treaty was negotiated by **Founding Fathers** John Adams, Benjamin Franklin, and John Jay.

Economics

Before we move on to the next period in the chapter that follows, it is worth taking some time to review certain economic principles affecting the growth of the new country. Three important economic forces of this period were capitalism, mercantilism, and imperialism.

Capitalism is the philosophy that economic value can be gained through the encouragement of business competition in a free market environment. It operates according to the **law of supply and demand**. In modern economic theory, the supply of an item is seen as directly related to the demand for that item; the interplay of these two forces determines the item's price. During the Revolutionary period, one influential proponent of capitalism was **Adam Smith**, a British economist whose book *Wealth of Nations* was published in 1776. Smith argues that the "invisible hand" of market forces can have a profound impact on economic progress. Later economists used the French term **laissez-faire** to refer to the hands-off capitalist policy of allowing market forces to encourage economic efficiency.

Mercantilism and imperialism were also important forces affecting the economic climate and were highly intertwined. **Mercantilism** was the belief that to grow economically, a nation's exports must exceed its imports. In the 1600s, the British mercantilist philosophy required the constant attainment of new external markets for trade, prompting large-scale colonization overseas. **Imperialism** was the name given to a nation's endeavors to conquer foreign territories and control them. Much of the exploration in the Americas during the colonial period was prompted by European imperialism.

In addition, certain inventions of the pre-Revolutionary period improved American economic progress. By 1765, the **Industrial Revolution** was underway. Three important advancements were the **spinning jenny**, the **steam engine**, and the **iron-making process**. **James Hargreaves** invented the spinning jenny, helping to automate the textile industry, and **James Watt** enhanced the design of the steam engine for factory use.

Review Questions

1. Which of the following explorers was the first to circumnavigate the globe?

    A. Henry Hudson in 1609
    B. Juan Ponce de León in 1513
    C. Ferdinand Magellan in 1519
    D. John Cabot in 1497
    E. Amerigo Vespucci in 1499

2. Which of the following types of colonies were land grants awarded to individuals by the British government?

    A. Self-governing colonies
    B. Proprietary colonies
    C. Reform colonies
    D. Royal colonies
    E. Joint-stock colonies

3. The government of the Massachusetts Bay Colony was an example of which of the following?

   A. Plutocracy
   B. Federalism
   C. Representative democracy
   D. Theocracy
   E. Separation of church and state

4. Which of the following acts were passed by the British to punish colonists for the Boston Tea Party?

   A. Intolerable Acts
   B. Stamp Act
   C. Quartering Act of 1765
   D. Townshend Acts
   E. Declaratory Act

5. Crispus Attucks is considered to be

   A. a Founding Father of the U.S. government
   B. responsible for the negotiation of the Treaty of Paris
   C. the first commander to win a Revolutionary War battle
   D. the instigator of the Boston Massacre of 1770
   E. the first casualty of the American Revolution

U.S. History Review Part 2: Early Government (1783–1848)

Establishing the Constitution

Once independence had been recognized, the Founding Fathers turned their hand to the task of creating a government. The U.S. Constitution was established in several phases during a time known as the **Critical Period** in U.S. history. This Critical Period (the 1780s) referred to the time after the Declaration of Independence and before the inauguration of George Washington, when the fate of the United States as a nation was not yet assured. Times were particularly uncertain from 1783 to 1789, the end of the war until Washington's inauguration.

Articles of Confederation

The **Articles of the Confederation** were the precursor to the U.S. Constitution. Ratified in 1781, the Articles were developed and passed before the war ended. They provided for a provisional government and had significant weaknesses, one of which was the inability of Congress to levy taxes. Under the Articles, the federal government essentially had no power, due to the Founding Fathers' distrust of centralized authority: any powers that were not expressly given to the government were reserved for the states. Despite its limitations, however, the provisional government enabled the United States to make it through the war.

The weaknesses of the Articles of Confederation soon showed themselves in practical application. One notable event was **Shays's Rebellion**, which the government was unable to quell. In 1786, in the middle of the Critical Period, the new country was experiencing an economic downturn. War had created income and jobs but was followed by inflation and depression. In the state of Massachusetts, years before the rebellion, a law was passed denying the poor the right to vote. Farms were being seized to pay off debts. Angry about their debt and high taxes, a thousand protesters joined with Continental army veteran **Daniel Shays** in a violent march on Boston. Boston merchants paid for an army to stop the revolt, but the shortcomings of the Articles of Confederation were clear.

U.S. Constitution

The Founding Fathers convened a **Constitutional Convention** in 1787 to solve the problems evident in the Articles and form a more effective government. Attending the convention were George Washington, John Dickinson, John Jay, Benjamin Franklin, Alexander Hamilton, and James Madison, among others. In drafting the Constitution, the participants encountered two main issues: first, how much representation should each state have in the legislature and, second, should slaves be counted as part of each state's population?

The **Constitution** was ratified in 1788 by a very narrow majority—only 53 percent. The process of **ratification** involved arguments put forth by constitutional supporters and detractors. Proponents of ratification, known as Federalists, argued that a strong central government would be beneficial and that the Constitution provided a sound governmental structure. Opponents of ratification, known as Antifederalists, argued that the Constitution gave the government too much power. The Federalists advanced their argument in a series of essays called the **Federalist Papers**, written mainly by Alexander Hamilton, John Jay, and James Madison.

After the Constitution was ratified, certain additions and changes were made. A total of twenty-seven amendments were added to the

Constitution over time. The first ten amendments were ratified in 1791 and comprise the Bill of Rights. They protect various individual rights and freedoms, as shown below.

THE BILL OF RIGHTS

NO.	AMENDMENT
1	Protects freedom of religion, speech, the press, right to assembly, and right to petition the government
2	Protects the right to keep and bear arms
3	Prohibits the quartering of soldiers in private homes without the owner's consent
4	Protects against unreasonable search and seizure
5	Protects the right to due process in a trial; protects against self-incrimination
6	Protects the right to a fair and speedy trial
7	Protects the right to trial by jury
8	Protects against excessive bail or fines and cruel and unusual punishment
9	Acknowledges that there are fundamental human rights not specified in the Constitution
10	Indicates that powers not delegated to the government (or denied to the states) are reserved for the states or the people

U.S. Government

The Constitution established various components as part of the structure of the U.S. government. The following are important to know for the SAT U.S. History Subject Test:

- **Federalism**—One of the principles that evolved as part of the U.S. government is the principle of federalism, expressed in the Federalists' platform. In a federalist system, power is shared between a central authority (the national government) and the authority of individual units (the states).

- **Separation of Powers**—The Constitution also ensured that the federal government would be based on a separation of powers. The principle of separation of powers ensures that no one branch of government has too much control. The U.S. government therefore contains three branches, each with different functions. The **legislative branch** makes the laws; the **executive branch** enforces the laws; and the **judicial branch** interprets the laws.

The executive branch of government is made up of the presidential office and the president's cabinet. The judicial branch is made up of the courts, including the Supreme Court and lower federal courts at different levels of jurisdiction. The **Supreme Court** is the highest court of the land and makes decisions that are binding on all lower courts.

The legislative branch, known as the **Congress**, is made up of two houses: the **Senate** and the **House of Representatives**. One of the questions faced by the Constitutional Convention was how to determine the number of congressional delegates allowed for each state. Would the number of delegates correspond to the states' populations? Or would each state have an equal vote?

This problem was resolved by creating a bicameral legislature consisting of two houses, each with a different type of representation. In the Senate, each state has the same number of delegates (two). Delegates to the House of Representatives are based on population, so larger states have more delegates in the House. This solution was engineered at the Constitutional Convention in what is known as the **Great Compromise of 1787**.

Another question raised at the Constitutional Convention concerned whether slaves would be counted in the population of a state when determining its congressional representation. Would slaves count as people or as property for these purposes? The southern states wanted slaves to be counted as people, while the northern states believed that this approach would give the southern states disproportional representation in the government. A compromise was reached that allowed three-fifths of all slaves to be counted as part of the population for the purposes of determining delegations. This compromise was known as the **Three-Fifths Clause**.

- **Checks and balances**—In the three branches of government, there are checks and balances built in to ensure that no one branch of government has a preponderance of power. Among the checks and balances that ensure smooth operation are the following:

  1. The president has a veto power over legislation passed by Congress, so Congress cannot solely control the laws.
  2. The president appoints judges to the Supreme Court and other federal positions. The influence of the president in choosing the judges has a significant impact on the outcomes of the ensuing judicial decisions.
  3. Congress approves the cabinet members appointed by the president.
  4. Congress can remove the president or Supreme Court judges from office.
  5. Congress must ratify treaties proposed by the president (and therefore has the power to reject treaties).
  6. The judicial branch interprets the laws passed by Congress and determines whether they are constitutional.

- **Separation of church and state**—As with the principle of the separation of powers, the framers of the Constitution ensured that the new government contained a separation of church and state. This was to help free politics from religious influences and to help maintain individual religious freedom.

Federalists and Republicans

The Federalist Party

The first period of government under the new Constitution was known as the **Federalist period**. Two Founding Fathers held the office of president during this time: **George Washington** (1789–1797) and **John Adams**

(1797–1801). During Washington's term, a policy debate occurred that would define the American political party system for a number of years. This debate pitted the **Federalists** (supported by Alexander Hamilton) against the **Democratic-Republicans** (represented by Thomas Jefferson).

LOOSE VERSUS STRICT CONSTRUCTIONISM

The central element of difference between the two parties was their view of the role of the central government. Proponents of the Federalist Party were known as **loose constructionists** who interpreted the intent of the Constitution more liberally. In the loose constructionist view, any power not expressly reserved for the states should go to the central government. Among other points, Hamilton and the Federalists advocated a central national bank and protective tariffs to bolster the new country's industry.

The Democratic-Republican Party, by contrast, opposed the Federalists on these points. They were known as **strict constructionists**, and they interpreted the intent of the Constitution conservatively. In the strict constructionist view, any power not expressly delegated to the central government should fall to the states. The strict constructionists remembered the tyranny of British rule and looked to avoid this with a weaker central government and stronger **states' rights**. They opposed the idea of a central national bank and protective tariffs, instead supporting free trade.

The differences between the two parties are summarized in the table below:

FEDERALISTS	DEMOCRATIC-REPUBLICANS
Represented by Alexander Hamilton	Represented by Thomas Jefferson
Loose interpretation of the Constitution	Strict interpretation of the Constitution
Supported strong central government	Opposed strong central government; supported states' rights
Supported establishing a national bank	Opposed establishing a national bank

FEDERALISTS	DEMOCRATIC-REPUBLICANS
Supported protective tariffs (to bolster manufacturing)	Opposed protective tariffs; supported free trade
Supported the idea of raising taxes to pay off state debts	Opposed the idea of raising taxes to pay off state debts

President Washington sided with the views of the Federalists, so Hamilton's policies were chosen. They were implemented during Washington's presidency and were effective in creating stability and growth for the new country.

FOREIGN POLICY

During his term in office, Washington established the foreign policy of the country as neutral vis-à-vis other nations. Washington believed that **neutrality** was the most prudent course of action for the new nation. In 1793, Washington issued a **Proclamation of Neutrality** in response to the question of whether the United States should assist France in its conflict with Britain during the time of the French Revolutionary Wars. The proclamation was followed by the **Neutrality Act of 1794**, which declared that the United States would remain neutral.

THE WHISKEY REBELLION

Another accomplishment of Washington's term was to quell the **Whiskey Rebellion** of 1794. This uprising occurred in Pennsylvania when farmers rebelled against the tax Hamilton had imposed on alcohol. Washington raised an army that crushed the rebellion with military force. In 1786, the government under the Articles of Confederation had been unable to respond effectively to Shays's Rebellion, so it was important for Washington's government to show a decisive use of force and the ability to maintain social order. The public strongly supported this act of Washington's government; it was viewed as highly successful even though the government still had difficulty collecting the tax from those who refused to pay.

The Republicans

John Adams followed George Washington as the second president of the United States, and then the Democratic-Republicans held control of office for twenty-eight years. **Thomas Jefferson** was elected as third president after Adams and served from 1801–1809. After Jefferson, three more Democratic-Republicans served: **James Madison** (1809–1817); **James Monroe** (1817–1825); and **John Quincy Adams** (1825–1829). John Quincy Adams was the son of the second president, John Adams.

JUDICIAL REVIEW

Thomas Jefferson described his election as the "**Revolution of 1800**" because he believed that it represented a significant shift in political ideals. Two important events during his term were the establishment of the principle of judicial review and the Louisiana Purchase. **Judicial review** was established by the legal ruling in the 1803 case of *Marbury v. Madison*. This decision set the precedent that the Supreme Court could rule on the constitutionality of laws.

LOUISIANA PURCHASE

The **Louisiana Purchase** was made by Jefferson in 1803. This purchase, which doubled the nation in size, involved the acquisition of the territory from the French for $15 million. Jefferson was concerned over whether the purchase might be unconstitutional, but he went ahead with it and strengthened the support of western farmers for the Democratic-Republican Party. The United States did not purchase the land from the French, only the territorial claim to the land. The land itself belonged to the Native American tribes residing there and was obtained from the tribes over time through purchases and military force.

THE WAR OF 1812

The roots of the **War of 1812** were established during Jefferson's term and inherited by James Madison. During the Napoleonic Wars in Europe, the United States maintained its policy of neutrality. However, the British and French seized American ships and plundered them for supplies. In addition, the British captured Americans and forced them to serve in the British navy.

At home, U.S. politicians known as **War Hawks** were advocating for the United States to declare war on Britain. Among the War Hawks were statesmen **John Calhoun** and **Henry Clay**, who believed war might help the United States regain its honor with respect to Britain. They also had sights on the acquisition of Canada and believed the war would help reduce hostilities with the Native Americans. The War Hawks suspected that Britain was inciting Native American attacks on U.S. citizens. In 1811, in an attempt to weaken one **Shawnee** tribe, the United States attacked the tribe at the **battle of Tippecanoe**. The group was led by the warrior **Tecumseh** and his brother, who was known as the Prophet. Tecumseh's Shawnees did join forces with Britain in the War of 1812 and fought against the Americans.

The war went poorly for the United States and ended in a stalemate. However, it had two significant results. First, it caused the Federalists to permanently lose power as a U.S. political party. Second, it caused a strong increase in American nationalism.

These results occurred not because of a decisive U.S. victory in the war but because of a surprising twist. When the **Treaty of Ghent** was signed in 1814, its intent was to maintain the status quo with Britain. Before news of the treaty signing had reached the United States, however, a battle was won unexpectedly by troops under the command of **Andrew Jackson**. Even though it occurred after the war had officially ended, Jackson's victory at the **battle of New Orleans** left the impression that the United States had won the war.

Before the war's end, a group of Federalist Party members met in Connecticut at the **Hartford Convention** and developed several proposed amendments to the Constitution. These amendments included a requirement of a two-thirds' majority in Congress for a declaration of war. The Federalists brought the amendments to Washington just as news of Jackson's victory was breaking. With American morale soaring, the Federalists were seen as traitors and secessionists. They lost power permanently as a result.

The outcome of the war sparked a surge of nationalism that would highly influence subsequent presidencies. In particular, a set of economic policies known as the **American system** was proposed to promote U.S. economic self-sufficiency. This system was developed by Henry Clay and included a series of high tariffs to strengthen American industry.

THE ERA OF GOOD FEELINGS

Monroe's term followed Madison's in 1817. For eight years, the country enjoyed a period of relatively stable peace, termed the **Era of Good Feelings**. Three major landmarks of the Monroe presidency were the establishment of federalism, the intensifying of sectionalism, and the application of nationalism in foreign policy.

Federalism was established in the 1819 ruling of *McCulloch v. Maryland*. In this case, Chief Justice John Marshall ruled on whether the state of Maryland had the right to impose a tax on a branch of the national bank. Marshall ruled that federal law superseded state law and that the state had no right to interfere with the operations of the bank by taxing it. This ruling established the supremacy of federal law over states' rights.

Sectionalism intensified during this era with the **Missouri Compromise of 1820**. Missouri applied for statehood at a time when the number of slave states and free states in the country was equal. Controversy ensued over whether to admit another slave state and tip the balance. Maine applied for statehood around the same time, and Henry Clay helped negotiate a solution: Maine would be admitted as a free state and Missouri as a slave state, maintaining the existing balance.

Nationalism was applied in foreign policy through the exercise of the **Monroe Doctrine**, established in 1823. This doctrine asserted the influence of the United States in the Americas. In response to European imperialism, Monroe declared that any attempt at colonization by European powers within the Americas would be seen as an act of aggression. The

United States would intervene militarily to thwart such attempts. At the same time, the United States pledged to refrain from intervening in European affairs unless American interests were directly at stake.

A CORRUPT BARGAIN

The last of the Democratic-Republicans to hold office was John Quincy Adams, son of George Washington's successor, John Adams. Elected in 1824, John Quincy Adams was one of four contenders in the presidential race, which for the first time saw competition between multiple candidates. Splits in the Democratic-Republican Party led four statesmen to run: Adams, Andrew Jackson, Henry Clay, and William Henry Crawford.

Jackson won the most popular votes in the race, but he did not win the majority. So the decision went to the House of Representatives. Clay had received the fewest votes, and he withdrew from the race. As Speaker of the House, however, he had a large influence over the outcome. Clay strongly opposed Jackson, and Crawford was in bad health, so Clay chose to support Adams, who won the campaign. Adams and Clay met before the election, and Adams agreed to appoint Clay to the position of secretary of state in exchange for his support. Jackson decried this arrangement as a "**corrupt bargain**" and denounced Adams and Clay.

Adams attempted to shrug off the critique, but practically speaking, it stymied his presidential efforts. He and Clay worked together to implement elements of Clay's American System, proposing bills for roads, canals, and other projects, but these improvements were rejected by Congress. Adams's election paved the way for Jackson to create an entirely new party and a new party system in his first term in office.

Jacksonian Democracy

The election of Andrew Jackson in 1829 to the presidency marked the beginning of what was known as the **second party system**. Two new political parties arose: the **Democratic Party**, headed by Jackson, and the **Whig Party**, led by Henry Clay. The Democratic Party arose from Thomas Jefferson's Democratic-Republican Party—of which Jackson had been a member—but it upheld distinctly different ideals. Unlike Jefferson's platform, which was pro-artistocracy, Jackson's ideology supported **universal suffrage for white men**. In other words, he advocated that all white men should have voting rights, not just landowners.

The Whig Party opposed the Democrats on essentially every major political point. Some historians argue that the Whig platform was dedicated to Democratic opposition as its main ideological principle. In addition to Clay, the Whig Party included Daniel Webster, William Henry Harrison, Zachary Taylor, and Abraham Lincoln.

Antebellum Period

Social Reforms

During the **antebellum** (pre–Civil War) period in the United States, social reforms abounded. One factor motivating these reforms was the **Second Great Awakening**, a religious revival that swept across the states with great fervor. Like the First Great Awakening of the colonial period, this revival sparked renewed interest in salvation, and many religious denominations expanded their membership.

The Second Great Awakening also encouraged social reforms. Reform movements of the time included:

- **Temperance**—Temperance efforts urged Americans to reduce alcohol consumption. Some advocated eliminating alcohol altogether.
- **Prison and institution reform**—This movement was spearheaded by **Dorothea Dix**, an advocate for the poor, the mentally ill, and prison inmates.
- **Education reform**—Massachusetts educator **Horace Mann** led this reform movement, which improved public schools.
- **Women's rights**—Activists such as **Susan B. Anthony**, **Elizabeth Cady Stanton**, and **Lucretia Mott** worked to assure women's rights

and particularly women's suffrage, or the right to vote. The **Seneca Falls Convention of 1848** was convened by this movement.

- **Transcendentalism**—Transcendentalism was an ideological movement that maintained faith in humanity's divine nature. The movement was inspired by the European philosophy of romanticism. Transcendentalist proponents included authors **Nathaniel Hawthorne** (*The Scarlet Letter*); **Ralph Waldo Emerson** (*Self-Reliance*); and **Henry David Thoreau** (*Walden*). Thoreau's *Walden* detailed his two-year commitment to simple living in the remote location known as Walden Pond.

- **Abolition**—Abolition sought to abolish (or end) slavery. For a detailed discussion of the movement and its activists, see below.

Native Americans

Two developments during Jackson's presidency resulted in the large-scale resettlement of Native Americans. One was the **Indian Removal Act of 1830**. Jackson signed this act into law after gold was discovered on Cherokee land in Georgia. Jackson intended to relocate the Cherokee to Oklahoma, and a case was brought to the Supreme Court contesting the legislation. Chief Justice John Marshall ruled in favor of the Cherokee people, but Jackson refused to enforce the Supreme Court's decision.

The **Trail of Tears** was the name given to the long route taken by the Cherokee and other tribes from 1935 to 1938. Altogether over forty-five thousand Cherokee, Seminole, Chickasaw, Choctaw, and Creek were relocated. Conditions were arduous, and thousands died en route. The exact number of deaths is disputed, but four thousand Cherokee deaths (25 percent) were confirmed out of the fifteen thousand Cherokees moved.

Economic Differences

An understanding of the antebellum period must take into account the economic differences between the northern, southern, and western states. Northern economies depended on industry, southern economies relied on agriculture, and western economies centered around commercial farming. These differences, along with inventions particularly relevant to each region, are summarized in the table below.

REGIONAL ECONOMIES

WEST	NORTH	SOUTH
Livelihood		
Commercial farming	Industry	Agriculture
Fur trade	Manufacturing	Cash crops: tobacco, cotton
Key Inventions		
Mechanical reaper	Steamboat	Cotton gin
Cyrus McCormick	Robert Fulton	Eli Whitney
	Interchangeable parts	
	Eli Whitney	

Manifest Destiny

Despite sectional differences, the country was connected in this era more closely than ever before. Advances in transportation and communication flourished. Transportation was aided by the construction of the **Erie Canal**, which was a primary mode of industrial transportation from 1825 to 1850. Improvements in the **steam engine** made steamship travel more efficient, which benefitted shipping. **Railroad** transportation expanded in the 1830s as well. The **electronic telegraph** was developed at this time by **Samuel Morse** (1837), along with a telegraph language called **Morse Code**.

These advances allowed Americans to live out a doctrine before the Civil War known as **Manifest Destiny**. Under Manifest Destiny, Americans believed they had a God-given right to expand across the North American continent from coast to coast. The **California Gold Rush of 1848** in part inspired this expansion, as prospectors headed west to seek their fortunes. President James K. Polk was a strong supporter of Manifest Destiny, and the country saw significant growth during his administration.

The **Mexican War** (1846–1848) was one example of Manifest Destiny in practice. The United States annexed Texas, a territory in dispute with Mexico, and Mexico promptly declared war. The United States won the war and obtained several more territories as a result: Utah, Nevada, California, and parts of other western states.

Review Questions

1. In response to the question of whether the United States should assist France in its conflict with Britain during the time of the French Revolutionary Wars, the United States passed which of the following?

   A. Neutrality Act of 1794
   B. Declaratory Act of 1766
   C. Missouri Compromise of 1820
   D. Monroe Doctrine of 1823
   E. Thirteenth Amendment

2. Which of the following had the most influence on social reform movements of the early 1800s?

   A. Transcendentalism
   B. Laissez-faire economics
   C. Second Great Awakening
   D. Capitalism
   E. First Great Awakening

3. Which of the following was most strongly supported by the Democratic-Republican Party under Washington's presidency?

   A. Strong central government
   B. Protective tariffs
   C. Loose constructionism
   D. National bank
   E. States' rights

4. At the Constitutional Convention, the question of how slaves should be counted for purposes of determining a state's representation in Congress was decided by the

    A. Great Compromise of 1787
    B. three-fifths clause
    C. *Common Sense* pamphlet
    D. Anti-Federalist code
    E. First Amendment

5. Which of the following occurred during the Critical Period in U.S. history?

    A. Jim Crow laws were put into effect.
    B. The U.S. Constitution was established.
    C. American slaves were freed.
    D. The *Dred Scott* case was decided.
    E. The Stamp Act was passed.

U.S. History Review Part 3: Division, Unification, and Growth (1848–1914)

Slavery and Abolition

"I think we must get rid of slavery, or we must get rid of freedom."

—*Ralph Waldo Emerson*

Slavery

Slaves came to the United States through the **transatlantic slave trade**, also known as the **Atlantic slave trade**. African slave dealers captured African slaves through raids on rival tribes or by kidnapping. African kings also sold criminals into slavery. These captives were traded to European slave dealers for goods. Some kings refused to participate and were enslaved or killed themselves.

After their capture and sale, slaves were transported by ships on long and often deadly journeys to the New World. Slave ships were in deplorable condition, and slave traders lost many slaves as a result. Those individuals who did survive were sold at auction and maintained in captivity.

The first permanent slave in the American colonies was owned by a black man, **Anthony Johnson**, a former indentured servant. Johnson convinced the court that **John Castor**, a black man, was his permanent servant, and the court upheld Johnson's claim. This 1655 incident introduced permanent slavery into the American colonies.

The United States banned the import of slaves in 1808, but the practice of slavery continued. Slaves were held largely on southern plantations that produced **cotton, tobacco, rice, sugar, or hemp**. In 1860, about four million slaves inhabited the United States, half of whom worked on cotton plantations. The majority of slaveholders were wealthy aristocrats. Only about 25 percent of Southerners owned slaves, and only a small portion of those owned more than five. Yet plantation owners maintained significant political control in the South as representatives in government.

Slaves who came to the United States were converted to Christianity. They developed an oral tradition with a highly spiritual culture. They lived in poverty, endured hard work, and often experienced abusive treatment. Runaways received severe punishment if they were caught, but runaways were common.

Abolition

The **abolition** movement sought to stop slavery. Abolition in the United States had support from other abolitionist movements that were arising throughout the world. In the United States, abolitionists were divided into two groups: moderates and immediatists. **Moderates** wished to bring a gradual end to the institution of slavery, so as to ensure the cooperation of Southern slave owners. **Immediatists** were less concerned with the cooperation of slave owners and more concerned about the perils of slavery. They called for the immediate emancipation of all slaves. **William Lloyd Garrison** was an immediatist, and he used his newspaper, the *Liberator*, as the voice for his antislavery message. In 1833, Garrison cofounded the **American Antislavery Society** with fellow immediatists Theodore Dwight Weld, Arthur Tappan, and Lewis Tappan.

In addition to Garrison, well-known abolitionists included **Frederick Douglass, Harriet Tubman, Harriet Jacobs**, and **Sojourner Truth**, all of whom had been former slaves. Certain female suffragists worked diligently for the abolition cause as well. Perhaps the most impactful white female abolitionist was author **Harriet Beecher Stowe**, who wrote *Uncle Tom's Cabin* in 1852. This book condemned the evils of slavery through the story of an acquiescent slave, Tom, and his evil master, Simon Legree. *Uncle Tom's Cabin* quickly became a bestseller and galvanized the North's antislavery sentiment on the eve of the Civil War.

The Civil War and Reconstruction

Events Leading Up to the Civil War

The Civil War occurred in response to internal divisions over the institution of slavery. Among the major events leading up to the war were:

- **The Missouri Compromise (1820)**—Discussed above under Monroe's administration, this 1820 legislation resolved a dispute between the proslavery and antislavery factions in Congress by regulating slavery in the western region of the country. It addressed the question of whether Missouri should be admitted as a slave state.

  - The agreement prohibited slavery in the former Louisiana Territory, except within the boundaries of Missouri. Maine was admitted as a free state to maintain the balance between free and slave states that had existed prior to Missouri's application.

- **Tariff of Abominations (1828)**—This tariff was passed to help Northern industry thrive but was perceived as discriminatory by Southern states. South Carolina threatened to nullify the tariff, but nullification was avoided.

- **Nat Turner's Rebellion (1831)**—This slave rebellion occurred in Virginia and was led by a slave, Nat Turner. Approximately sixty white persons were killed in the rebellion, causing great tension in the South. Many innocent slaves were injured or killed as part of the public reaction, and fifty-six accused participants were formally executed by the state.

- **Tariff of 1832**—This tariff reduced tariffs imposed by the act of 1828, but it was rejected by the Southern states. South Carolina nullified the tariff under the leadership of Senator John C. Calhoun.

- **Nullification Crisis of 1832**—Precipitated by federal tariffs that unevenly affected economic conditions in various regions of the country, this crisis came to a head when South Carolina declared the tariffs null and void within its borders. South Carolina's action intensified the debate between proponents of states' rights and supporters of a strong federal government. Further conflict was averted when Congress passed a new tariff that South Carolina deemed acceptable, and the United States' government rejected the principle of nullification.

- **Compromise of 1850**—This compromise involved a package of legislation designed to defuse a four-year confrontation between the slave states and the free states. California was admitted as a free state, and the issue of slavery in New Mexico, Nevada, Arizona, and Utah was to be determined by popular vote—a concept known as **popular sovereignty**. The **Fugitive Slave Law** was passed, requiring citizens to help capture runaway slaves.

  The compromise temporarily avoided civil war by preventing the Southern states from seceding from the Union at the time. However, the Fugitive Slave Law ultimately increased tensions.

- **Kansas-Nebraska Act (1854)**—This act repealed the Missouri Compromise of 1820 and allowed the question of slavery to be determined by popular sovereignty in Kansas and Nebraska.

- **Bleeding Kansas (1854–1858)**—This title refers to a series of conflicts that concerned whether Kansas should be a free state or a slave state. The Kansas-Nebraska Act had allowed both states to determine the issue by popular vote, and violence broke out between proslavery and antislavery factions in Kansas. Kansas was admitted as a free state in 1861.

- *Dred Scott* **Decision (1857)**—In this landmark legal case, a slave named Dred Scott sued for his freedom and that of his wife and daughters. The U.S. Supreme Court ruled against him, claiming that no one of African ancestry could become a U.S. citizen or file a lawsuit in federal court.

Abraham Lincoln

Abraham Lincoln was president of the United States from 1861 to 1865. Lincoln ran on an abolition platform that garnered the support of abolitionists in the North. Largely self-educated, Lincoln led the country during the Civil War, restored the Union by defeating the Confederate states, and is credited with abolishing slavery. He was assassinated shortly after the end of the war by an actor, **John Wilkes Booth**, who shot the president while Lincoln was attending a play with his wife.

Another influential politician of the prewar period was **Stephen A. Douglas**. Douglas ran against Lincoln unsuccessfully in the 1861 presidential campaign after having defeated Lincoln in 1858 for an Illinois seat in the U.S. Senate. Douglas was the incumbent, and he contested Lincoln in a series of seven debates known as the **Lincoln-Douglas debates**, in which slavery was the primary issue. Although Lincoln lost the senate race, the debates brought him national prominence and highlighted the issues he faced in running for the presidency two years later.

Unification and Emancipation

As tensions over slavery mounted, the Southern states **seceded from the Union** in 1860. They declared themselves the **Confederate States of America**, and a temporary government was set up under the leadership of **Jefferson Davis**. The first military attack of the war was made by the Confederate army at Fort Sumter in 1861. This Charleston, South Carolina, fort was controlled by Union forces and guarded an important Confederate harbor. Although both sides had hoped to avoid military confrontation, the Confederacy decided to take control of the fort when they learned that it was soon to be resupplied.

Neither the Union nor the Confederate armies had a well-designed strategy going into the war. As a result, the war dragged on as each side repeatedly altered its course. This war was the first to employ **trench warfare**, which also made the war last longer and increased casualties on both sides. Soldiers in trenches were able to have sufficient protection from enemy fire while at the same time having the ability to hit oncoming soldiers in an advance, so trench warfare made large-scale infantry advances ineffective.

The **Emancipation Proclamation** was issued during the war in 1862. The Emancipation Proclamation did not free all the slaves or put an end to slavery; it merely freed slaves in the Confederate states that were fighting against the Union. It did, however, turned slavery into the main issue of the war. It also made it legal for freed slaves to enlist in the Union army; approximately two hundred thousand former slaves joined the war effort.

The Confederate commander, **Robert E. Lee**, attempted to gain the support of European countries in the conflict, but his attempts were not successful. Ultimately, the North was victorious; the Confederacy surrendered to Union commander **Ulysses S. Grant** in April 1865. By the time the war ended, public opinion strongly supported a cease-fire. The Civil War had the most losses of any American war, with over six hundred thousand deaths. One example of the extent of the destruction was **Sherman's March to the Sea in 1864**, during which the Union army systematically destroyed everything in its path.

Reconstruction

President Lincoln was assassinated shortly after the war's end, and the presidency was assumed by **Andrew Johnson**. The institution of slavery was abolished as a whole by the **Thirteenth Amendment**, passed after the war's end in 1865. This was the first amendment passed as part of the period known as **Reconstruction**, when the government imposed policies to restore order in the South. A detailed summary of the amendments is provided below.

RECONSTRUCTION AMENDMENTS SUMMARY

AMENDMENT	COMPONENT	DESCRIPTION
Thirteenth Amendment, 1865		Abolished slavery
Fourteenth Amendment, 1866	Citizenship Clause	Declared that blacks were citizens
	Due Process Clause	Protects individual rights to fairness in criminal proceedings
	Equal Protection Clause	Guarantees equal protection under the law
Fifteenth Amendment, 1870		Granted blacks the right to vote

Reconstruction went through several stages, and though it accomplished many things, it was generally considered to be ineffective. Three phases of the period can be distinguished roughly:

- **Phase One: Stalemate under Lincoln**—Immediately after the war, Lincoln was relatively lenient in crafting a plan for the South. Congress wanted a stricter program, so progress was deadlocked.

- **Phase Two: Leniency under Johnson**—After Lincoln's assassination, responsibility fell to Johnson to put a plan in place. He imposed a lenient plan similar to that proposed by Lincoln.

- **Phase Three: Strict Plan under the Republicans**—Congress passed a stricter Reconstruction plan despite Johnson's opposition. Military rule was established in the former Confederate states.

The Reconstruction governments under Republican control were soon seen as corrupt, however. The Republicans lost power in Congress, and Reconstruction ended in 1877.

The legacy of Reconstruction is mixed. Slaves were technically free, and the Union had been restored, but there was little real equality for black citizens, who faced rampant discrimination. The **Ku Klux Klan**, comprised of white supremacists, organized to resist black rights through violent scare tactics, and **black codes** were enforced in the South as a means of keeping the new citizens subjugated. **Jim Crow laws** were passed in the 1880s to impose segregation for blacks and whites or to prevent blacks from having access to certain public facilities. **Poll taxes** were introduced, making it costly (and therefore impossible) for black citizens to exercise their right to vote. The *Plessy v. Ferguson* decision of 1896 upheld the constitutionality of "separate but equal" facilities, and many blacks continued to live at subsistence level, with **sharecropping** arrangements that required them to give large parts of their harvests to their landlords in exchange for the right to use the land.

The Industrial Revolution

Manufacturing

During the late 1800s, manufacturing output rose exponentially due to inventions that increased productivity. The concept of **mass production** was developed, and factories began to produce on a large scale. Instead of producing items by hand, methods were developed to enable more **automation** of the production process. One notable method was the **assembly line**, made famous through the manufacturing of the **Ford Model T** automobile from 1908 to 1913. Automaker **Henry Ford** financed the refinement of the assembly line process to fulfill his vision of mass producing a car inexpensive enough that every working man could afford it.

A list of inventions during the Industrial Revolution includes:

DATE	INVENTION
1851	Sewing machine (Isaac Singer)
1852	Elevator (Elisha Otis)
1858	Internal combustion engine (Jean Lenoir)
1862	Plastic (Alexander Parkes)
1866	Dynamite (Alfred Nobel)
1867	Typewriter (Christopher Sholes)
1876	Telephone (Alexander Graham Bell)
1878	Phonograph (Thomas Edison)
1879	Light bulb (Thomas Edison)
1884	Steam turbine (Charles Parson)
1903	Airplane (Wright brothers)

Transportation, Immigration, and Farm Reform

At the same time that inventions were improving manufacturing productivity, advances in transportation technology enabled goods and people to travel longer distances in shorter periods of time. The **streetcar** and **automobile** improved personal transportation, and the **transcontinental railroad** revolutionized shipping. For the first time, starting in the 1860s, a connected system of railroads enabled passengers and goods to cross the country from coast to coast. **Railroad companies** became gigantic conglomerates and influenced politics as well as industry.

Improvements in industry required more than just automation and enhanced transportation. They also required people—more specifically, **labor**—to do the work. For this the United States saw a great increase in **immigration** from all parts of the globe. As it had been during colonial times, the United States was seen as a land of opportunity, but now the requirements of a pioneering spirit were not quite as steep. Immigrants flocked to U.S. ports in record numbers from the late 1800s through the turn of the century. Before 1890, immigrants came primarily from northern and western Europe; after 1890, emigration from eastern Europe and China surged.

The United States was likened to a **melting pot**, where peoples from all backgrounds came together and combined to create a unique culture. Later, in the 1970s, a second perspective on immigration arose, known as the **salad bowl** view. In this view, instead of melting with others and losing their distinct characteristics, immigrants were seen as maintaining their unique qualities but contributing to a greater culture, as do the separate ingredients of a salad.

As industry grew and became more profitable, an opposite trend characterized the farming sector. Many of the factors that enhanced urban industry caused problems for farmers. The growth of railroads led railroad companies to develop **monopolies** and fix prices on shipping. Often the prices were high and disadvantageous to farmers, who could not afford to pay to ship their goods. A high tariff and low prices for farm goods also combined to cause farmers hardship. Farmers banded together to push for reform in an agrarian movement that became known as the **Grange movement**. Efforts of Grange advocacy were effective in establishing the **U.S. Department of Agriculture (USDA)** in 1885.

Imperialism

The United States became a major **imperialist power** at the turn of the twentieth century. Its interests were mainly in Latin American and Asia. As we saw in part 1, the United States had its start as an imperialist colony of Britain, and the decision to overthrow British rule established the United States as a country. Why, then, would the United States adopt the same policies it had fought so hard to reject?

Causes

The causes of U.S. imperialism are generally traced to four factors:

1. **Strong Navy**—Americans believed there was a need for a strong navy to maintain the country's economic prowess and protect its shipping lanes. A book by Capt. Alfred T. Mahan, *The Influence of Sea Power upon History*, was very influential in spreading this notion.

2. **New Markets**—The United States saw the need to expand overseas

to obtain raw materials for production and to find new markets for its goods.

3. **Moral Responsibility**—Many believed in the notion of a moral responsibility to "spread civilization" to other parts of the world. *Our Country*, an ideological work by minister Josiah Strong, helped to promote the idea of an ethical imperative for colonization.

4. **Leadership**—Imperialism was prompted by the fact that the United States elected presidents on this platform. William McKinley (1897–1901) was one such president; his election amid much imperialist controversy reflected the tide of public opinion.

These factors prompted five major events that characterize the **Imperialist Era.**

Events

The most notable imperialist event of the time period is the **Spanish-American War**. Lasting only four months in 1898, this conflict was crucial because it established the United States as ruler of an empire. Cuba was an imperial colony of Spain, and it rebelled against Spain in a war for independence. The United States supported the war to protect its investments in Cuba.

The **Treaty of Paris** in 1898 gave the United States an empire. **Guam**, **Puerto Rico**, and the **Philippines** came under U.S. control as a result of the war. The United States also annexed **Hawaii** at this time. Further, the United States maintained the right to intervene in **Cuba** via the **Platt Amendment,** which became part of the Cuban constitution.

Other important events at the turn of the century include:

- The establishment by **Secretary of State John Hay** of an **Open Door** trading policy with **China** (1899), which gave the United States and all European countries equal access to trade with China and unrestricted access to China's ports.
- The construction of the **Panama Canal** (1904–1914) to connect the Atlantic and Pacific waterways.

- The establishment of the **Roosevelt Corollary to the Monroe Doctrine** (1904), offered by President **Theodore Roosevelt**, who used the slogan "Speak softly, and carry a big stick" to characterize American efforts to protect U.S. interests in Latin America through a series of military interventions.

- President **William Howard Taft's** failed attempts to continue imperialism through **dollar diplomacy**, which involved investments rather than the use of force.

Big Business and Economic Growth

As the United States expanded through imperialism during the late 1800s, it also grew economically at home. **Big businesses** developed and flourished in what was known as the **Gilded Age**, because of the great deal of wealth accumulated, often through unscrupulous means.

So-called **robber barons** were American businessmen and financiers who amassed significant wealth by unethical practices during this period. Many exploited workers and engaged in questionable stock market tactics. Well-known robber barons included **Andrew Carnegie**, **John D. Rockefeller**, **Cornelius Vanderbilt**, and **J. P. Morgan**.

Political attempts to address the corruption of big businesses focused on two types of reforms: (1) antitrust legislation and (2) labor organizations.

Antitrust Legislation

Antitrust legislation are laws that attempt to curtail the growth of big businesses to ensure they do not become trusts, or groups of highly integrated, centrally controlled companies that exist as monopolies in a given industry. **Monopolies** are companies that grow so large that they dominate a market and hedge out any competitors. Because the U.S. economy is based on the **capitalist** principle of **free market competition**, monopolies present a threat to business efficiency and can hurt the consumer as well. Since they are the only companies selling a particular good or service, they have the freedom to set prices as they choose, without regard for competition, as the railroad companies did with shipping rates before the Grange movement.

The Sherman Antitrust Act of 1890 was passed to outlaw monopolies, but it was very loosely enforced. Big businesses continued to influence politics and many aspects of the economy, including maintaining crowded, unsanitary working conditions that violated workers' rights.

Labor Organizations

This period saw the emergence of **labor unions** that advocated improvements in working conditions and protection of workers' rights. National organizations sprang up to coordinate the efforts of local unions. One of the first nationwide labor unions in the United States was the **American Federation of Labor** (AFL), founded in 1886 by an alliance of craft unions. AFL unions played a significant role in industrial cities, where they coordinated the actions of their members through a central office. The unions used strikes to pressure specific industrial sectors to hire union workers.

The AFL was headed by vocal union activist and organizer **Samuel Gompers**. As founder and president of the AFL, Gompers promoted cooperation among the craft unions that made up the organization, favored collective bargaining over strikes, and encouraged union members to take an active role in political elections.

Muckrakers and Yellow Journalism

Social criticism was widespread during this period because of the work of the **muckrakers**, U.S. journalists who exposed crime and corruption in American industry and politics from the 1890s through the 1930s. The muckrakers' disclosures often resulted in social reforms, including legislation aimed at addressing corporate monopolies, insufficient safety standards, unfair labor practices, and other social injustices.

Muckrakers practiced a type of inflammatory writing known as **sensationalism** or **yellow journalism**. Writers of this style used emotional tones and incendiary speech to arouse people's emotions and to incite public ire. Well-known muckrakers of the period include **Ida Wells**, **Upton Sinclair** (*The Jungle*), and **Jacob Riis** (*How the Other Half Lives*). In addition, a battle raged between two yellow journalism newspapers, Joseph Pulitzer's *New York World* and William Randolph Hearst's *New York Journal*, from 1895 to 1898.

Progressive Era (1890–1920)

The **Progressive Era** was a period of social reform that lasted from the 1890s to the 1920s. Activists in the Progressive movement worked to weaken the power of political bosses and machines and promoted the use of scientific methods in medicine, the social sciences, government, and industry. The women's suffrage movement achieved its long-sought goal in 1920 when the **Nineteenth Amendment** to the Constitution granted women in every state the right to vote.

The Progressive agenda had its roots in the **Populist movement** of the 1890s, which arose out of the activism of farmers. The movement gave birth to a political party called the **Peoples Party** that advocated economic help to farmers, particularly an increase in the money supply. Elements of the Populist platform later became incorporated as part of the Progressive reforms.

One particularly influential politician of the Progressive Era was **Robert M. La Follette**. He founded the **Progressive Party** and ran for president as the Progressive Party candidate in 1924. Though he lost the election and never served as president, he significantly influenced U.S. politics as a Wisconsin senator from 1906 to 1924. His impact was similar in scope to that of Henry Clay and John C. Calhoun of the antebellum era. La Follette had strong, independent views and often broke with the views of prominent politicians at the time. He was a staunch advocate of reform, particularly women's rights, antimonopoly legislation, and fighting against corruption in big business and government.

From 1920 to 1933, the **Eighteenth Amendment** to the Constitution prohibited the manufacture and sale of alcoholic beverages in the United

States. This period, known as **Prohibition**, reduced the total amount of liquor consumed in the country, but it also fueled illegal liquor sales through underground clubs known as **speakeasies** and gave rise to **organized crime**. Prohibition ended in 1933, when the **Twenty-First Amendment** repealed the Eighteenth Amendment.

Although advances in civil rights were not significant in this period, two activists laid the groundwork for later progress in the 1950s and '60s. **Booker T. Washington** was an African American educator born into slavery in 1856. Washington acquired an education after emancipation, and in 1881 became the first president of the Tuskegee Institute, a historically black university, which thrived under his leadership. Washington was an influential spokesman for African Americans in the post-Reconstruction era, advising them to work toward racial equality by learning vocational skills, striving for financial independence, and acquiring an understanding of the U.S. legal system.

W. E. B. Du Bois was an African American civil rights activist and educator who was a contemporary of Booker T. Washington. He was the first African American to earn a PhD at Harvard University, and he became head of the **National Association for the Advancement of Colored People (NAACP)** in 1910. Du Bois helped found the NAACP in 1909, and the organization continues to this day. Its mission is to eliminate racial discrimination and to ensure political, educational, social, and economic equality for all people, regardless of race.

Though both Du Bois and Washington advanced black rights, the men disagreed on many grounds. Notably, Washington advocated accommodating the Jim Crow segregation laws in the South, while Du Bois rejected this notion.

A final cultural phenomenon to note was the widespread belief in **Social Darwinism**, the application of Charles Darwin's theories of biological evolution and natural selection to the study of human society. In the late 1800s, sociologists used the term to describe the theory that certain groups or individuals gain advantages over others because of genetic or biological superiority.

Review Questions

1. Which of the following activists was most likely to argue that blacks should accept Jim Crow segregation laws?

    A. Malcolm X
    B. W. E. B. Du Bois
    C. Rosa Parks
    D. Booker T. Washington
    E. Martin Luther King Jr.

2. Which of the following put forth the statement, "Speak softly and carry a big stick"?

    A. Theodore Roosevelt
    B. William McKinley
    C. William Taft
    D. Grover Cleveland
    E. Herbert Hoover

3. The novel *Uncle Tom's Cabin*, published in 1852, was written by

    A. Harriet Jacobs
    B. Frederick Douglass
    C. William Lloyd Garrison
    D. Sojourner Truth
    E. Harriet Beecher Stowe

4. Samuel Gompers made his chief political contribution as founder and head of which organization?

    A. Hull House
    B. American Federation of Labor
    C. NAACP
    D. Planned Parenthood
    E. American Temperance Society

5. Which of the following represents the term given to corrupt big business owners during the Gilded Age?

    A. Flappers
    B. Shermanites
    C. Sharecroppers
    D. Robber Barons
    E. Scalawags

U.S. History Review Part 4: World Involvement (1914–1947)

During the period from 1914 to 1947, the United States took part in two world wars. This experience, in addition to internal growth, established the United States as a major world power. The United States also emerged from World War II as the most powerful economic nation.

World War I

World War I (1914–1918) was a global war in which Great Britain, France, Russia, Belgium, Italy, Japan, the United States, and other allies defeated Germany, Austria-Hungary, Turkey, and Bulgaria. The spark that ignited the war was the assassination of Archduke Franz Ferdinand, heir to the Austro-Hungarian throne, by a Serbian nationalist group. In response, Austria-Hungary declared war on Serbia. Subsequently, the conflict was escalated by a tangle of alliances binding Russia to Serbia and France, France to Britain, Britain to Japan, and Germany to Austria-Hungary.

Woodrow Wilson was the twenty-eighth president of the United States (1913–1921) and the country's leader during the war. Despite trying to maintain U.S. **neutrality** in relation to the conflict in Europe, he asked Congress to declare war in April 1917 after German submarines began sinking U.S. merchant ships. Germany's policy of **unrestricted submarine warfare** posed a serious threat to U.S. commercial shipping.

Wilsonian Idealism

Wilson gave a famous speech, known as the **Fourteen Points Speech**, to Congress in 1918 as the war was nearing its end. The speech called for a just peace and an end to secret diplomacy, which was believed to be one of the primary factors that escalated the conflict into war. The speech reflected **Wilson's idealism** and became the basis for the terms of the German surrender.

When the **Treaty of Versailles** was negotiated to end the war, however, the British and French insisted on harsh terms for Germany. In particular, France demanded **war reparations** from Germany to pay for the destruction the war had wreaked. Wilson's fourteen points were essentially abandoned in the final treaty, and a harsh peace with Germany was imposed.

League of Nations

After the war, Wilson pushed to form the **League of Nations** in the hope of preventing such large-scale devastation in the future. A precursor to the United Nations, the league was the first international organization formed for the purpose of maintaining world peace. It was established in 1920 after the end of the war. At its height, from September 1934 to February 1935, it had fifty-eight members, but the United States was not among them. Although Wilson received the **1919 Nobel Peace Prize** for his efforts to establish the league, he was unable to convince the U.S. Senate to ratify its covenants. This **failure of ratification** was primarily due to Republican opposition in the U.S. Senate.

The Roaring Twenties

During the period from 1920 to 1933, the **Eighteenth Amendment** to the Constitution prohibited the manufacture and sale of alcoholic beverages in the United States. This time period was known as **Prohibition** and had its roots in the **Temperance** movement of the antebellum period. Although Prohibition reduced the total amount of liquor consumed in the country, it fueled illegal liquor sales through underground clubs known as **speakeasies** and gave rise to **organized crime**. Prohibition ended in 1933, when the **Twenty-First Amendment** repealed the Eighteenth Amendment.

Despite the restrictions of Prohibition, the Roaring Twenties brought with it increasing social liberalism and a gaiety that had not existed since the years before the war. Young women in particular began to rebel and become more outspoken in this period. Women known as **flappers** symbolized the age with fringed dresses, boyish haircuts, and long cigarette holders. Students in college became more daring and open to parties, illegal drinking, and new types of dancing. A **sexual revolution** occurred during the period that allowed both men and women to be more open regarding sex.

The **Harlem Renaissance** was a cultural movement centered in New York City's Harlem neighborhood and spanning the 1920s and 1930s. The movement was characterized by a surge in literature, art, and music created by African Americans, as well as a new sense of racial pride. The Harlem Renaissance also influenced a group of black writers who lived in Paris but were originally from French-speaking African and Caribbean colonies. Notable figures of the Harlem Renaissance included authors **Langston Hughes, James Weldon Johnson, Zora Neale Hurston** (*Their Eyes Were Watching God*), and Claude McKay.

African American culture flourished throughout the country during this period, not just in Harlem. **Jazz music** began to become more popular in key cities, starting first in New Orleans and then spreading across the country. Soon white Americans were enjoying the genre, which became so popular that the decade is also called the **Jazz Age**. Influential jazz musicians of the period included trumpet player **Louis Armstrong** and singer **Bessie Smith**.

The **Scopes Monkey Trial** of 1925 reflected the increasing controversy in the country between **creationism**, or the theory that humans were created by God, and **evolutionism**—**Charles Darwin's** hypothesis that humans evolved over time. **William Jennings Bryan**, an influential politician and attorney of the period, pressed for schools to make it unlawful to teach evolution. When the state of Tennessee passed such a law, the **American Civil Liberties Union (ACLU)** issued a pledge to support any teacher who would challenge the legislation with a legal case.

John Scopes violated the law and the case went to court; **H. L. Mencken** was a well-known journalist and social commentator who reported on the proceedings. At the end of a carnival-like trial, Scopes changed his plea to guilty and was fined. He was convicted, but the Supreme Court ultimately ruled that Tennessee's anti-evolution law was unconstitutional. The impact of the trial was to increase respect for scholastic freedom and to protect scientific inquiry from encroachment by state law.

President **Herbert Hoover** also reflected an important cultural element of the period in a campaign speech in 1928. This speech, known as Hoover's "**rugged individualism**" speech, emphasized the importance for Americans of individualism and **self-reliance**. Hoover was a self-made man who had become a millionaire by age forty. He had been orphaned as a child and earned his fortune through his own ingenuity. Though Hoover was a complex president and was criticized for many faults—among them being a lack of compassion for the significant effects faced by the poor during the Depression—he inspired many with his emphasis on industry and strength of character as American ideals.

The Great Depression

The **Great Depression** was a severe economic depression that occurred in the decade before World War II and affected almost every country in the world. Originating in the United States, the Depression started with a decline in stock prices that began around September 4, 1929, and came to the attention of the rest of the world with the **stock market crash of October 29, 1929** (a day known as **Black Tuesday**). The Great

Depression was the most widespread, serious, and longest-lasting economic crisis of the twentieth century.

In a stock market crash, when investors start to sell and stock prices plummet, this causes more investors to seek to sell their failing stocks. The panic launches a declining spiral that takes on a life of its own. As the Depression set in after the stock market crash, the same type of phenomenon happened with banks, as depositors came in droves to withdraw their cash. This **run on the banks**, as it was called, put too much pressure on the bank cash system, and many banks failed.

Western economies learned a great deal from the Great Depression. Circumstances sank exceptionally low because of two main factors. First, the Great Depression was a difficult situation with many complicated causes, and second, it was not handled well in its initial years.

Causes

The causes of the Great Depression were multifaceted. The trigger event, the Stock Market Crash, occurred because too many investors purchased through a method called "buying on margin." **Buying on margin** involves purchasing stocks with borrowed funds. Investors who make gains then repay the borrowed money from their profits, plus interest. Investors who are not successful, however, compound their losses—owing what they've lost, plus interest, to their creditor.

While individuals used this practice in their investing, so did banks and businesses. When these large investors lost money in the crash, they found themselves near bankruptcy with no means to pay their debts. Banks could not cover their deposits or pay employees, and systematic layoffs ensued.

Other factors prompting the descent into the Great Depression were excessive supplies of goods and agricultural unrest fueled by falling prices. During the time leading up to the Depression, many manufacturers had stockpiled inventories of goods and were continuing to overproduce. Consumers with no hope and no paychecks weren't buying much, so supply surged past demand. A long-term drought in the Midwest destroyed agricultural productivity and provoked farmer unrest. Desperate to raise crop prices with no means of doing so, many farmers lost their property to evictions and foreclosures.

These overlapping factors combined to produce stark results. While the rich lost substantial amounts of their wealth, reducing their net worth significantly almost overnight, working- and middle-class people lost their jobs, their life savings, and their homes. The effect on the post–World War I United States was devastating.

Response

President Hoover's initial response to the crisis worsened it. Hoover's campaign had centered around the concept of "rugged individualism." He was reluctant to develop assistance programs because he did not want citizens to depend on government help. In addition, Hoover did not realistically acknowledge the extent of the Depression and its widespread effects. In 1930 he stated that the Depression was over. He eventually changed course and began to implement certain programs, but it was too late. Hoover also implemented the wrong policies, or those with unanticipated results. The **Smoot-Hawley Tariff** of 1930 was intended to ease economic difficulties by protecting U.S. business, but it made the situation worse. European countries resented the tariff and reduced their purchase of U.S. exports.

The New Deal

Franklin Delano Roosevelt was elected easily in the 1932 contest against Hoover, with hopes that he could help the country recover. As president during the second half of the Great Depression and throughout World War II, Roosevelt became a dominant political figure both at home and abroad from 1933 to 1945. He is best known for creating programs that stimulated the country's economic recovery and for overseeing the country's military and civilian efforts during the war. His popularity in office is attested to by the fact that he is the only person to run for and be elected president four times.

In the 1930s, Roosevelt instituted a group of economic programs designed to help the United States recover from the Great Depression. These programs, known collectively as the **New Deal**, included legislation promoting labor unions, a public works initiative (the Works Progress Administration) designed to create jobs, and legislation creating Social Security. In actuality, Roosevelt developed two New Deals, known as the first and second New Deals, to respond to criticisms from all camps on the political spectrum. The New Deal programs and acts included:

RELIEF PROGRAMS

Civilian Conservation Corps (CCC)	States received grants to manage work programs
Public Works Administration (PWA)	Created jobs by building roads and housing
Works Progress Administration (WPA)	Generated jobs and employed artists and photographers

RECOVERY PROGRAMS

Agricultural Adjustment Act (AAA)	Paid subsidies to farmers; farmers agreed to cut production
Federal Housing Administration (FHA)	Provided insurance for mortgages
Tennessee Valley Authority (TVA)	Provided jobs and electricity

REFORM ACTS

Glass-Steagall Banking Act	Created Federal Deposit Insurance Corporation (FDIC), which guaranteed deposits made by bank customers
Securities Exchange Act	Regulated the stock market
Social Security Act	Provided retirement benefits to workers and families

World War II

After establishing the New Deal to put the United States on more stable economic footing, President Roosevelt oversaw U.S. involvement in the

Second World War. **World War II** (1939–1945) was a global conflict involving all of the world's most powerful nations. The war was fought by two alliances known as the Allies (consisting of Great Britain, France, the Soviet Union, the United States, China, and other allies) and the Axis (consisting of Germany, Italy, and Japan). The conflict began when Germany invaded Poland as a first step toward establishing a vast European empire.

Prewar **Nazi Germany**, under the leadership of **Adolf Hitler**, had expansionist aims that were not recognized by the allied powers at the time. From a diplomatic perspective, it was believed by many statesmen that global military conflict could have been avoided in World War I if prewar negotiations had been approached with more diplomacy. In 1914, there existed a tight system of alliances that gave little leeway for alternative courses of action once aggression commenced. Hostilities that might otherwise have been quelled short of war in 1914 led to a global conflagration because of bellicose military personalities and a lack of diplomatic restraint.

The Allies were determined to learn from the mistakes of World War I and to avert war if at all possible. Though some statesmen (Britain's **Winston Churchill**, for example) staunchly opposed accepting Germany's prewar expansionist territorial claims, on the whole it was believed that a **policy of appeasement** would help restore "**peace for our time**." This was the statement made by British prime minister **Neville Chamberlain** after prewar negotiations conceded to Hitler's demands. In fact, the Allies were wrong, and Hitler's expansionistic aims continued to grow. By the eve of war, it was clear that only military victory would deter the Nazi war machine from its attempt at territorial domination.

The United States was drawn into the war when Japan attacked the U.S. naval base at **Pearl Harbor** in Hawaii on December 7, 1941. U.S. involvement made World War II a full-out global war. The Allied powers were victorious, but the devastation was enormous.

In addition to involving more than twenty million military casualties, the war caused massive numbers of civilian deaths, exceeding forty million. Germany slaughtered approximately six million Jews, and the United States killed hundreds of thousands of people by dropping atomic bombs on the Japanese cities of Hiroshima and Nagasaki. It was the deadliest war in history.

The Atomic Bomb and the End of the War

Harry Truman (1945–1953) succeeded Roosevelt when FDR died during his fourth term and was in office at the time the atomic bomb was deployed. Truman inherited a tremendous responsibility in taking office as the war was nearing its end. "I felt like the moon, the stars, and all the planets had fallen on me," he said.

The **atomic bomb** was developed through the efforts of a scientific endeavor known as the **Manhattan Project**. The Manhattan Project was administered through the U.S. Army Corps of Engineers, with assistance by Britain and France. It was developed in part because of warnings given by prominent U.S. scientists, including **Albert Einstein**, that Nazi Germany might be in the process of developing its own atomic arsenal. The Manhattan project produced two types of bombs: a **fission bomb** (known as **Little Boy**) that used uranium, and an **implosion bomb (Fat Man)** that used plutonium.

Both types of bombs were used to bring the war with Japan to an end. The Little Boy fission bomb was dropped on **Hiroshima** on August 6, 1945; three days later, the Fat Man implosion bomb was detonated over **Nagasaki**.

The decision to deploy the bombs was highly controversial. Ultimately, the bombs were dropped because of the likelihood that they would secure an unconditional surrender from Japan. Japan's culture and fighting ethic led people to believe that the country would never surrender under any imaginable circumstances. The Japanese military commonly used suicide missions (**kamikazes**), and Japanese soldiers were determined to fight to the death.

Approximately ten days before the Hiroshima bombing, the Allies sent an **ultimatum** to Japanese emperor **Hirohito** calling for Japan's surrender. Japan did not respond to the ultimatum. It was argued by the

U.S. command that use of the bombs would wreak destruction significant enough to secure Japan's surrender and bring an end to the war.
Those responsible contended that ending the war then would later save
the lives of at least a million American soldiers and significant numbers
of Japanese troops and civilians.

The devastation of the bombings was beyond description. Japan surrendered immediately, but at a staggering cost. Use of the bombs raised
ethical questions about the limits of warfare that remain salient today.

Impact of the War

As a result of World War II, the United States emerged as the most powerful economy in the world. The countries of Europe had been ruined by
the war because of the military campaigns on their own soil. By contrast,
with the exception of Pearl Harbor, the U.S. engagement in the war had
occurred mainly on foreign ground. The war brought jobs and increased
U.S. industry, particularly the defense industry, which required muni-
tions, tanks, planes, and other military equipment to be manufactured.
The war also employed women outside the home, paving the way for
later social reforms. **Rosie the Riveter** was a wartime symbol of a woman
with her sleeves rolled up, lending a hand to the war effort.

Rosie the Riveter WWII Poster
National Museum of American History, Smithsonian Institution

After the war ended, recovery commenced with the help of the Marshall Plan. Named for U.S. Secretary of State George Marshall, the **Marshall Plan** (1947–1951) was a large-scale economic and reconstruction program designed to help the countries of Europe recover from World War II. During the program's four years of operation, the United States contributed approximately $13 billion in economic and technical assistance to the war-torn countries of Europe.

Review Questions

1. The United States and its allies fought against which of the following during World War II?

    A.   France, Britain, and the Soviet Union
    B.   Germany, Japan, and Italy
    C.   China and the Soviet Union
    D.   Germany, Serbia, and Russia
    E.   Germany and Austria-Hungary

2. The Manhattan Project was responsible for the development of

    A.   the atomic bomb
    B.   the Social Security Act of 1935
    C.   the Bretton-Woods monetary system
    D.   the German U-boat
    E.   modern chemical warfare

3. Which of the following prompted U.S. entry into World War I?

    A.   The formation of the League of Nations
    B.   The bombing of Pearl Harbor
    C.   Germany's invasion of Poland
    D.   The assassination of Archduke Franz Ferdinand
    E.   Germany's policy of unrestricted submarine warfare

4. Each of the following individuals is matched with the appropriate initiative EXCEPT

    A. Woodrow Wilson and the 1919 Nobel Peace Prize
    B. George Marshall and the Marshall Plan
    C. Franklin Roosevelt and the New Deal
    D. Woodrow Wilson and the League of Nations
    E. Dwight D. Eisenhower and the Works Progress Administration

5. During World War II, which of the following was responsible for the end of the war with Japan?

    A. The Stimson Doctrine
    B. The Truman Doctrine
    C. The Treaty of Versailles
    D. The bombing of Hiroshima and Nagasaki
    E. The Scopes Trial

U.S. History Review Part 5: Leadership (1947–Today)

O nly a small portion of the questions on the SAT U.S. History Subject Test is likely to involve the period from 1950 to the present. What follows is a discussion of the most significant historical events from this period, with particular emphasis on the Cold War and events prior to 1970.

The Cold War

Origins

At the end of World War II, as the participants were negotiating the peace, a series of events occurred causing tension between the USSR and the United States. This conflict continued in the years after World War II and became known as the **Cold War**.

At the **Yalta Conference** (1945) at the end of the war, the Allies planned the military occupation of Germany. The capital city of Berlin was divided into four **occupation zones**, each controlled by one of the Allies. The Soviet Union occupied East Germany and the nearby countries in Eastern Europe. Soviet occupation soon turned into military dictatorship. Under Joseph Stalin's leadership, the Soviets imposed Communist governments on Eastern Europe and created an alliance known as the **Soviet bloc**.

British statesman Winston Churchill declared that an **iron curtain** separated the countries of east and west. The division was between eastern Communism, on the one hand, and Western democracy, on the other. Soviet **Communism** was a political system that involved control of resources by the central government. In contrast to Western democracy, which involved a mix of federal and state governments, the Communist central government reigned supreme.

Soviet Communism was an economic system as well as a political system. In addition to maintaining tight political control, the Communist Party maintained ownership of all property and businesses. It differed strongly from Western **capitalism**, where property was owned privately by businesses and individuals.

NATO AND THE WARSAW PACT

Concerned over the spread of Communism, the United States and its allies joined together to form the **North Atlantic Treaty Organization (NATO)**, an intergovernmental military alliance whose member countries agreed to defend one another in the event of an external attack on any member nation. NATO's formation prompted the Soviets to establish a similar alliance, known as the **Warsaw Pact**. The original members of each alliance are shown in the table below.

NORTH ATLANTIC TREATY ORGANIZATION (NATO)	WARSAW PACT
United States, Canada, Great Britain, France, Italy, Belgium, Luxembourg, Portugal, the Netherlands, Denmark, Norway, Iceland—1949	Soviet Union, Czechoslovakia, Hungary, Poland, Romania, Bulgaria, Albania, East Germany—1955
Greece, Turkey—1952	
West Germany—1955	

CONTAINMENT

During the Cold War, the United States adopted a policy of **containment**—military, economic, and diplomatic strategies intended to curtail the spread of Communism and prevent a "domino effect." Under the **domino effect**, if one country in a region came under the influence of Communism, the surrounding countries would follow suit. The policy of containment was associated primarily with the administration of President **Harry Truman** (1945–1953). The **Truman Doctrine**, declared in 1947, made clear that the United States would provide aid to Greece and Turkey to protect them from Communist takeover.

Major Events That Affected Cold War Tensions

Among the most significant events of the Cold War were the following:

- The **Korean War** (1950–1953): The United States defended South Korea when it was invaded by North Korean forces. North Korea was supported by Communist China and the Soviet Union.

- The **Vietnam War** (1954–1975): This prolonged military conflict was eventually between the Communist forces of North Vietnam, supported by China and the Soviet Union, and the non-Communist forces of South Vietnam, supported by the United States. The U.S. government saw its involvement in the war as a way to prevent Communism from gaining a foothold in Southeast Asia.

- In 1956, the United States imposed the **Eisenhower Doctrine** to stop the spread of Communism in the Middle East.

- The U.S.-Soviet **space race** began in 1957 with the launch of the Soviet satellite **Sputnik**.

- The **Berlin Wall** was erected by East Germany in 1961, establishing a permanent barrier between the eastern (Communist) and western (democratic) sectors of the German city of Berlin.

- In 1961 the United States narrowly averted war with the Soviet Union during the **Cuban Missile Crisis**. The Soviets had stationed missiles in Cuba, and the United States blockaded Cuba in response. A military clash was avoided when the Soviets agreed to withdraw the missiles in exchange for a U.S. agreement not to invade Cuba. The United States also agreed to remove missiles then in Turkey.

- President Richard Nixon initiated a policy of **détente** (1971–1979) with the Soviet Union. Relations improved significantly for a number of years.
- In 1979 the USSR launched an **invasion of Afghanistan**. Tensions heightened in the 1980s under U.S. president Ronald Reagan.

Important Figures During the Cold War

Aside from the political leaders mentioned in this section, other influential U.S. figures in the Cold War included Senator Joseph McCarthy, George Kennan, and Henry Kissinger. **Joseph McCarthy** was a U.S. Senator who in 1950 began holding public congressional hearings in which he accused military officials, journalists, and other public figures of being Communist spies and sympathizers. McCarthy stirred up a great deal of fear with his anti-Communist propaganda, and the term McCarthyism came to be used for accusations of treason made without sufficient evidence. McCarthy's ruthless tactics and his inability to prove his claims led the Senate to censure him in 1954.

George Kennan was an American diplomat who highly influenced the development of the Marshall Plan and particularly the U.S. policy of containment. Stationed in Moscow at the onset of the Cold War, Kennan shared his perspective on Soviet intentions in a dispatch called the **Long Telegram** (1946). Kennan argued that the Soviets were inherently expansionist and would always be at war with capitalism. He later shifted his views as he saw evidence of Soviet openness to negotiation, but his recommendations at that point were downplayed.

Henry Kissinger was secretary of state under Richard Nixon and Gerald Ford. He was instrumental in creating détente with the Soviet Union and improving relations with the People's Republic of China.

End of the Cold War

The end of the Cold War occurred with the **collapse of the Berlin Wall** in 1989. Soviet Communism had proved to be a dismal failure, economically speaking. The countries of Eastern Europe were highly disadvantaged compared to their Western counterparts because Communism offered few incentives for economic growth. Pressures for change led Soviet leader **Mikhail Gorbachev** to initiate a policy of political openness (**glasnost**) and liberalization (**perestroika**). These policies incited Soviet citizens to demand further reforms, and soon rebellions occurred throughout Eastern Europe.

The celebratory destruction of the Berlin Wall, which was televised around the world as East Berliners poured into West Berlin and danced among the rubble, signaled an end to an era of distrust and political opposition. The United States emerged from the Cold War as the single **superpower** in a new position of leadership and responsibility.

Vietnam and Counterculture

The Vietnam War had a significant impact on the development of **counterculture** in the United States. Two major aspects of the war led American citizens to question—and ultimately object to—U.S. involvement in Southeast Asia. The first aspect concerned the level of loss in the war. The conflict was drawn out and lasted far longer than the U.S. public expected. The second problematic component concerned the country's entry into the war.

Lyndon B. Johnson engaged the United States in the war by affirming the **Gulf of Tonkin Resolution** in 1964. This resolution gave the president the right to act without the approval of Congress, and U.S. troops were committed without a formal declaration of war.

Military action was expected to be limited, but in reality, it was not. Public sentiment turned against the war and protests mounted. **Anti-Vietnam protesters** decried the war on several grounds. First, the war was protracted. Second, it involved a great deal of attrition for U.S. military forces, and it was costly as well. Third, it had not been authorized by Congress. Many viewed the war as unwinnable, and they were not persuaded by Johnson's justifications for continuing to support South Vietnam.

The military difficulty faced by the American forces was largely due to the nature of **guerilla warfare** in Vietnam, which was unpredictable and involved a series of surprise attacks. U.S. soldiers were unaccustomed to this style of fighting and had little experience in jungle warfare. Troop morale plummeted as the death toll increased. Victory appeared to be unattainable.

Protests against the Vietnam War ultimately led to American withdrawal, but with no appreciable gains for the losses incurred during a decade of involvement. After the United States withdrew, the North Vietnamese conquered South Vietnam, and the country was unified under Communist rule.

During this time, **hippies** in the United States became a significant social force as part of the counterculture. Many hippies protested the Vietnam War, using slogans such as "Make Love, Not War." The hippie movement was characterized by drug use, **free love**, and an emphasis on peace and communal living. In the mid-1960s, the **Haight-Ashbury** district in San Francisco became the center of a drug culture where hippies known as **Flower Children** gathered to enjoy music acts such as the **Grateful Dead**, **Janis Joplin**, and **Jefferson Airplane**. Other highly influential rock 'n' roll acts of the 1960s counterculture included **The Beatles**, **Jimi Hendrix**, **The Doors**, and **The Rolling Stones**.

Civil Rights

The **civil rights movement** made progress in the 1950s and 1960s toward protecting the rights of African Americans. **Segregation** was made unlawful, and the rights of African Americans to equal treatment were protected, at least on paper. Gains were made through a series of steps that involved two landmark legal cases and the passage of important two pieces of legislation.

Brown v. Board of Education was a landmark U.S. Supreme Court decision declaring that state laws establishing separate public schools for black and white students were unconstitutional. The court's unanimous decision, handed down on May 17, 1954, asserted that "separate

> "People always say that I didn't give up my seat because I was tired… The only tired I was, was tired of giving in."
>
> —*Rosa Parks*

educational facilities are inherently unequal." Consequently, racial segregation was ruled to be a violation of the equal protection clause of the Constitution's Fourteenth Amendment, and the judgment paved the way for further civil rights activism.

In 1956 a second decision led to further reinforcement of the unconstitutionality of segregation, when the Supreme Court declared that segregation on Alabama buses was illegal. The case was sparked by **Rosa Parks**, a seamstress who refused to give up her seat on a bus in Montgomery to make room for white passengers. Parks was arrested and tried for violating the segregation laws. Public outrage over her arrest led to **boycotts of the busing system in Montgomery**, and the case was pursued in the courts until the Supreme Court ruled on the matter.

The Supreme Court's decisions and ensuing attempts at forced integration encountered enormous resistance. Dr. **Martin Luther King Jr.**, an activist who had taken a leadership role in the Montgomery bus boycott, led **nonviolent protests** and acts of **civil disobedience**, including a **March on Washington in 1963**, to support pending civil rights legislation. The **Civil Rights Act of 1964** and the **Voting Rights Act of 1965** made racial discrimination in the United States unlawful.

Women's Rights

The **women's rights movement** made strides in the 1960s and 1970s, partly because of gains in the area of civil rights. Women's rights groups pressed politically for equal rights through the **Equal Rights Amendment**, a proposed amendment to the U.S. Constitution prohibiting discrimination based on gender. Introduced in Congress in 1923, the amendment eventually passed both chambers of Congress in 1972 but failed to be ratified by the required number of states.

After the Supreme Court's 1973 **Roe v. Wade** decision struck down various state laws restricting abortion, further gains in women's rights were made. The Court argued that the right to privacy granted by a provision of the Fourteenth Amendment includes a woman's right to decide to have an abortion.

Betty Friedan is often credited with starting the **second wave of feminism** in the 1960s with the 1963 book *The Feminine Mystique*. Friedan questioned women's traditional roles in society. She noted that many women were unhappy as wives and mothers, even though their lives were stable and financially secure. Friedan advocated that women pursue education and meaningful work and not simply accept the roles of wives and mothers because society expected as much. Friedan later helped to found the **National Organization for Women (NOW)** and became its first president.

Postwar Presidents

At the age of forty-three, **John F. Kennedy** (1961–1963) was the youngest person to be elected to the presidency. Known for establishing the Peace Corps and advancing the civil rights of African Americans, he also authorized the Bay of Pigs invasion, which was a failed attempt to overthrow the government of Cuban president Fidel Castro. Kennedy was assassinated in Dallas, Texas, on November 22, 1963.

The **War on Poverty** was a series of domestic programs proposed by President **Lyndon B. Johnson** to combat poverty and improve living standards among the nation's poor. Johnson declared this war in his 1964 State of the Union address, a few weeks after becoming president after Kennedy's assassination. Among the programs deployed to fight the War on Poverty were Head Start, Vista, the Job Corps, **Medicare**, and **Medicaid**.

Richard Nixon (1969–1974) was the thirty-seventh U.S. president and the only president to resign from office. Nixon's accomplishments as president included ending U.S. involvement in the Vietnam War, establishing détente with the Soviet Union, and initiating diplomatic relations with China. He resigned to avoid impeachment for his role in the Watergate scandal and was subsequently pardoned by his successor, Gerald Ford.

Watergate was a 1972 political scandal. Five men broke into the headquarters of the Democratic National Committee with the intention of wiretapping the phones. After the burglars were arrested, it was discovered that they had been paid by the Committee to Reelect the President, that Nixon had known about the break-in, and that he had participated in the cover-up that followed. Facing near-certain impeachment and likely conviction, Nixon resigned from office on August 9, 1974.

Vice president **Gerald Ford** assumed the presidency when Nixon resigned and became the thirty-eighth president of the United States (1974–1977). Ford's best-known official act was granting Nixon a presidential pardon, which met with widespread negative reaction. Among the problems inherited by Ford from the Nixon administration were the economic effects of the **Oil Embargo of 1973**, in which Middle Eastern petroleum exporting companies refused to sell oil to the West. The oil shortage caused an energy crisis that increased inflation and damaged the U.S. economy.

Succeeding Ford in office was **Jimmy Carter** (1977–1981), a strong **human rights** activist. He and his wife, Roslyn, founded the Carter Center for Human Rights after leaving the White House. During his term, Carter organized the **Camp David Peace Accords** to help ease tensions between Israel and Egypt. His presidency was characterized by **stagflation**, a combination of high inflation and low economic growth. Though Carter's efforts to bring an end to the **Iran Hostage Crisis**—including a failed rescue attempt—were not fruitful during his presidency, the hostages were released as soon as Carter left office. In 2002 Carter was awarded the Nobel Peace Prize for his work to advance human rights and the cause of peace.

Ronald Reagan served two terms in office from 1981–1989. Before running for the presidency, Reagan had been an actor and later served as governor of California. He survived an assassination attempt shortly after his inauguration. He championed economic policies know as **Reaganomics**, which called for lower taxes, less government spending, fewer governmental regulations (**deregulation**), and low inflation through federal control of the money supply. Reagan's administration was also marked by military operations in Grenada, Central America, Lebanon, and Libya and the end of the Cold War with the Soviet Union.

Reagan's presidency was followed by that of **George H. W. Bush** (1989–1993), whose son was later elected to the presidency. The senior Bush is best known for initiating a successful offensive known as the Gulf War (1991) and for his role in establishing the **North American Free Trade Agreement (NAFTA)**, which lifted trade restrictions between Canada, the United States, and Mexico.

Bill Clinton (1993–2001) was the first baby boomer to be elected president. He was considered a political centrist, and the country experienced economic growth during his presidency. Technology investments made significant gains during the **dot-com boom** of the 1990s, but losses of similar proportion ensued when the dot-com bubble burst. One of only two presidents to be **impeached**, Clinton was eventually acquitted by the U.S. Senate. First lady **Hillary Rodham Clinton** later became a senator for the state of New York and ran for the presidency against Illinois Senator Barack Obama in 2008. She lost the presidential bid but was appointed Obama's secretary of state.

George W. Bush (2001–2009) is the son of George H. W. Bush. His term was characterized by recession, increased national debt, and involvement in the Afghanistan and Iraq wars. He launched the **War on Terror** in response to the **9/11** terrorist attacks, which took the lives of over three thousand people.

Barack Obama (2009–) was the first African American to be elected president. A native of Hawaii, Obama represented Illinois in the U.S. Senate before becoming a presidential candidate. He received the Nobel Peace Prize in 2009.

Post–Cold War Foreign Policy

At the end of the Cold War, the United States' role on the world stage changed. During the Cold War, it was one of two superpowers engaged in a series of struggles with each other. After the Cold War, the United States maintained its position as a superpower but took a greater leadership role.

Major events in U.S. foreign policy after the Cold War include:

- **Iran Hostage Crisis:** This diplomatic crisis occurred between the United States and Iran during the Carter administration. The crisis began on November 4, 1979, when a group of Islamic militants seized the U.S. Embassy in Tehran and took sixty-six Americans hostage in retaliation for America's long-standing support of the recently overthrown government of the Shah of Iran. Thirteen hostages were released later that month; one more was released in July 1980; but fifty-two were held for 444 days—until a few minutes after President Ronald Reagan's inauguration on January 20, 1981.

- **Iran-Contra Affair:** This 1983 event was a scandal of the Reagan administration, similar in impact to Nixon's Watergate affair. The cover-up concealed the use of funds for military aid that had not been authorized by Congress. The United States sold arms to the Iranians and used some of the proceeds to fund military operations against Communists in Central America. In exchange for the arms sale, the Iranians used their influence with Lebanon to secure the release of several U.S. hostages. Iran was under an arms embargo at the time, and the news of secret operations conducted without congressional approval caused a great uproar. The ensuing investigation did not find conclusive evidence regarding the president's knowledge of the operations.

- The **Gulf War** (August 2, 1990–February 28, 1991): This conflict was waged against Iraq by a coalition force representing thirty-four nations and led by the United States. Authorized by the United Nations and spearheaded by the United States under President

George H. W. Bush, the offensive successfully repelled Iraqi forces from Kuwait.

- **9/11 Terrorist Attacks**: On September 11, 2001, nearly three thousand Americans were killed when Islamic terrorists crashed hijacked aircraft into the Twin Towers of the World Trade Center in New York and the Pentagon. Astonished Americans watched on television when the second tower was hit and the two buildings crumbled to the ground. The site of the attacks in New York, known as **Ground Zero**, has been memorialized as the location of the largest terrorist assault on U.S. soil. The Islamic group **al Qaeda**, a militant fundamentalist organization, claimed responsibility for the attacks. A fourth plane, apparently headed for Washington, DC, was diverted when passengers attempted to wrest control of the plane from the hijackers and crashed in a field in Pennsylvania.

- **Afghanistan War**: In response to the September 11, 2001, attacks, the United States launched military operations in Afghanistan with the intention of dismantling al Qaeda and ending its ability to use Afghanistan as a base of operations for terrorist activities.

- **Iraq War**: This military campaign began on March 20, 2003, when a multinational force led by troops from the United States and the United Kingdom invaded Iraq. Before the invasion, the U.S. and British governments asserted that Iraq had weapons of mass destruction that could threaten the security of these nations and their allies. After the invasion, the U.S.-led Iraq Survey Group concluded that Iraq had no active programs for developing nuclear, chemical, or biological weapons at the time of the invasion. Some members of President George W. Bush's administration accused Iraqi president Saddam Hussein of harboring terrorists associated with al Qaeda, but no evidence of a connection was ever found.

Review Questions

1. The Cold War represented a conflict between which of the following?

   A. The USSR and the Balkan states
   B. Communist and Socialist nations
   C. The Entente powers and the Central powers
   D. NATO and the Warsaw Pact
   E. The Axis powers and the Alliance powers

2. The 9/11 attacks on the United States were conducted by members of which of Islamic terrorist group?

   A. Hezbollah
   B. Hamas
   C. Islamic Jihad
   D. Fatah al-Islam
   E. al Qaeda

3. The Watergate scandal damaged the credibility of which U.S. president?

   A. Richard Nixon
   B. George W. Bush
   C. Bill Clinton
   D. Jimmy Carter
   E. Gerald Ford

4. Which of the following Supreme Court decisions struck down various state laws restricting abortion?

   A. *Brown v. Board of Education*
   B. *Roe v. Wade*
   C. *Plessy v. Ferguson*

D.   *Miranda v. Arizona*

E.   *McCulloch v. Maryland*

5.   Civil rights activists supporting the philosophy of Dr. Martin Luther King Jr. would be likely to use each of the following strategies EXCEPT

A.   nonviolent demonstrations

B.   sit-ins

C.   looting

D.   boycotts

E.   picketing

Answers to Review Questions

Part 1

1. The correct answer is C. Ferdinand Magellan became the first explorer to circumnavigate the globe in 1519. Henry Hudson sailed on the Hudson River in 1609. Juan Ponce de León explored Florida in 1513. John Cabot explored Nova Scotia and Newfoundland in 1497. Amerigo Vespucci explored South America in 1499.

2. The correct answer is B. Proprietary colonies were land grants to individuals from the British government. The owners appointed a governor for the colony who reported to the king. Royal colonies were owned and controlled by the king. Self-governing colonies chose their own governors and arose when the king granted a charter to a joint-stock company.

3. The correct answer is D. The government of the Massachusetts Bay Colony was an example of a theocracy. E is incorrect because it reflects the opposite of the correct answer. The Massachusetts Bay Colony was set up purposely to serve the goals of the Puritan church. Plutocracy is defined as rule by the wealthy, so A is incorrect. Federalism and representative democracy are principles of the current governing structure of the United States, but they were not part of the Massachusetts Bay Colony's government.

4.   The correct answer is A. The Intolerable Acts, also known as the Co-ercive Acts, were passed by Britain in 1774 as a response to the Boston Tea Party, which occurred in 1773. The acts were designed to punish the colonists for the uprising; Boston Harbor was closed until the cost of the damage was repaid and order was restored. All of the other acts mentioned occurred before the Boston Tea Party. The Quartering Act of 1765 was the first quartering act to be passed by the Crown; a second one was passed in 1774 and was included as part of the Intolerable Acts.

5.   The correct answer is E. Crispus Attucks is considered to be the first casualty of the American Revolution. He was a mixed-race sailor who was killed in the Boston Massacre by British fire. Soldiers fired on a crowd that had gathered to watch a skirmish, and Attucks was hit and killed instantly. D is incorrect because although Attucks was killed in the Boston Massacre, he is not credited with being the instigator of the event.

Part 2

1.   The correct answer is A. In response to the question of whether the United States should assist France in its conflict with Britain during the time of the French Revolutionary Wars, the United States passed the **Neutrality Act of 1794**, which declared that the United States would remain neutral. George Washington was a strong advocate of neutrality; his views on neutrality were opposed by Thomas Jefferson.

2.   The correct answer is C. The Second Great Awakening had the most influence on the social reform movements of the early 1800s. This event was a religious revival that swept across the states with great fervor. It influenced reforms in the area of temperance, prisons and institutions for the mentally ill, education, women's rights, transcendentalism, and abolition. E is incorrect because the First Great Awakening occurred in the 1730s and 1740s, during the colonial period.

3.   The correct answer is E. Under the leadership of Thomas Jefferson, the Democratic-Republican Party supported a weak central government

and championed states' rights. A, B, C, and D are incorrect because they all reflect elements of the Federalist Party ideology, which Jefferson opposed. Democratic-Republicans maintained a strict constructionist view of the Constitution.

4.   The correct answer is B. The question of how slaves should be counted for the purpose of determining a state's representation in Congress was decided by the three-fifths clause. Three-fifths of the slaves in a state were counted in the population total to determine the size of the state. A is incorrect because the Great Compromise of 1787 involved the decision to establish a bicameral legislature. Representation in one house would be based on the size of the state, while representation in the other house would be fixed at two delegates.

5.   The correct answer is B. The U.S. Constitution was established during the Critical Period, which occurred during the 1780s. This period referred to the time after the Declaration of Independence and before the inauguration of George Washington, when the fate of the United States as a nation was not yet assured. The Stamp Act occurred before the Critical Period; it was one of the events leading up to the Revolutionary War. A, C, and D are incorrect because they each happened after the Critical Period.

Part 3

1.   The correct answer is D. Booker T. Washington was most likely to argue in the late 1800s that blacks should accept Jim Crow segregation laws. W. E. B. Du Bois opposed this idea, so B is incorrect. Malcolm X, Rosa Parks, and Martin Luther King Jr. were all activists in the civil rights movement of the mid-1900s.

2.   The correct answer is A. Theodore Roosevelt put forth the statement, "Speak softly, and carry a big stick" in 1901. This ideology supported Roosevelt's issuing the Roosevelt Corollary to the Monroe Doctrine.

3.   The correct answer is E. The novel *Uncle Tom's Cabin* was written by white abolitionist Harriet Beecher Stowe. Harriet Jacobs, Frederick

Douglass, and Sojourner Truth were all former slaves who were also abolitionists, so A, B, and D are incorrect. William Lloyd Garrison was a white abolitionist who advocated the immediate emancipation of slaves, so C is incorrect.

4. The correct answer is B. Gompers was a labor organizer who founded the American Federation of Labor in 1886. Hull House was founded by Jane Addams, and the NAACP was founded by a group of activists that included W. E. B. Du Bois and Ida B. Wells.

5. The correct answer is D. Corrupt big business owners were referred to as robber barons during the Gilded Age. Prominent robber barons included Andrew Carnegie, John D. Rockefeller, Cornelius Vanderbilt, and J. P. Morgan. Flappers were young, freethinking women in the 1920s, and scalawags and sharecroppers were terms that were prominent during Reconstruction, before the Gilded Age.

Part 4

1. The correct answer is B. The United States and its allies fought against the Axis Powers—Germany, Italy, and Japan—during World War II. France, Britain, and the Soviet Union fought on the side of the United States in the war, so A is incorrect. Serbia, Russia, and Austria-Hungary were combatants in World War I, not in World War II. By the time of the Second World War, Russia had become Communist and was known as the Soviet Union.

2. The correct answer is A. The Manhattan Project was responsible for the development of the atomic bomb during World War II. President Franklin Roosevelt approved the program, which resulted in two atomic bombs that were dropped on Japan to end the war.

3. The correct answer is E. U.S. entry into World War I was prompted by unrestricted submarine warfare on the part of Germany. The United States had declared its neutrality prior to the start of the war, but it became involved when German submarines escalated attacks on American ships.

4.   The correct answer is E. The Works Progress Administration (WPA) was part of the New Deal administered by Franklin Roosevelt. Eisenhower was responsible for proposing the creation of the International Atomic Energy Agency to promote the peaceful use of atomic power.

5.   The correct answer is D. The bombing of Hiroshima and Nagasaki brought an end to the war with Japan in World War II. The United States had developed the atomic bomb during the war and used this weapon to secure an unconditional surrender from Japan. The Treaty of Versailles brought an end to World War I, and the Truman Doctrine stated that the United States would provide support to Greece and Turkey to prevent a Soviet Communist takeover during the Cold War.

Part 5

1.   The correct answer is D. The Cold War represented a conflict between NATO and the Warsaw Pact. The North Atlantic Treaty Alliance (NATO) consisted of the United States and its allies, including Britain, France, and other countries from Western Europe. The Warsaw Pact consisted of the Soviet Union and its allies, primarily the nations of Eastern Europe. A is incorrect because the nations in the Balkan region of Eastern Europe were members of the Warsaw Pact during the Cold War. The Entente powers and Central powers were combatants in World War I, and the Axis powers and Alliance powers fought one another in World War II.

2.   The correct answer is E. The 9/11 attacks were conducted by members of the Islamic terrorist group al Qaeda under the leadership of Osama bin Laden. Hezbollah, Hamas, Fatah al-Islam, and the Islamic Jihad are also terrorist groups, but they were not responsible for the attacks. Hezbollah and Fatah al-Islam are Lebanese terrorist groups, and Hamas and the Islamic Jihad are Palestinian terrorist groups.

3.   The correct answer is A. The Watergate scandal damaged the credibility of Richard Nixon, who resigned from office before allegations from the scandals led to his impeachment. Watergate involved a cover-up

by Nixon to hide his involvement in illegal activities designed to bolster his campaign for reelection. Gerald Ford was Nixon's vice president and took office when Nixon resigned.

4. The correct answer is B. The 1973 Supreme Court decision in the case of *Roe v. Wade* struck down various state laws restricting abortion. The Court argued that the right to privacy granted by a provision of the Fourteenth Amendment includes a woman's right to decide to have an abortion. *Brown v. Board of Education* occurred in 1954 and established that separate public schools for black and white students were unconstitutional. *Plessy v. Ferguson* (1896) ruled that segregated facilities provided for each race were constitutional as long as they were equal; this decision was reversed by *Brown*.

5. The correct answer is C. Civil rights activists supporting the philosophy of Dr. Martin Luther King Jr. would be likely to use nonviolent forms of civil disobedience. These include nonviolent demonstrations, sit-ins, boycotts, and picketing. Looting, choice C, is a violent activity that involves stealing goods or taking them by force.

Glossary

Abolition: The movement to abolish, or put an end to, human slavery.

Afghanistan War: In response to the September 11, 2001, attacks, the United States launched military operations in Afghanistan with the intention of dismantling al Qaeda, a militant Islamist organization, and ending its ability to use Afghanistan as a base of operation for terrorist activities.

American Federation of Labor: One of the first nationwide labor unions in the United States, the AFL was founded in 1886 by an alliance of craft unions. AFL unions played a significant role in industrial cities, where they coordinated the actions of their members through a central office. The unions used strikes to pressure specific industrial sectors to hire union workers.

American Revolution: The political upheaval during the late 1700s in which the thirteen North American colonies broke free from the British Empire and formed the United States of America. The colonies joined forces to defend their right to self-governance and to coordinate an armed conflict against the British. This conflict became known as the American Revolutionary War (1775–1783).

Articles of Confederation: The first document outlining how the U.S.

government would operate. Drafted in June 1776 by a committee appointed by the Second Continental Congress, the Articles of Confederation were sent to the states for ratification in November 1777. The ratification process was completed in March 1781. Under the Articles of Confederation, the states retained control of all governmental functions not expressly assigned to the national government.

Asceticism: A lifestyle characterized by abstinence from various types of worldly pleasures, usually with the purpose of focusing on religious and spiritual goals instead of pursuing sensual pleasures and the accumulation of wealth.

Bill of Rights: The first ten amendments to the U.S. Constitution. These provisions became Constitutional amendments on December 15, 1791, after being ratified by three-fourths of the states. As a set of limits on the power of the federal government in relation to the rights of individuals, the Bill of Rights protects fundamental liberties such as freedom of speech, a free press, freedom of association, freedom of assembly, and the right to keep and bear arms.

Boston Tea Party: A symbolic event in which colonists in Boston protested against a British tax on tea imported into the colonies. The colonists believed that only their elected representatives had the authority to levy taxes. On December 16, 1773, after Boston's royal governor refused to return three shiploads of taxed tea to Britain, a group of colonists boarded the ships and tossed the tea into Boston Harbor.

Brown v. Board of Education: A landmark U.S. Supreme Court decision declaring that state laws establishing separate public schools for black and white students were unconstitutional. The Court's unanimous decision, handed down on May 17, 1954, stated, "Separate educational facilities are inherently unequal." Consequently, racial segregation was ruled a violation of the equal protection clause of the Fourteenth Amendment, and the judgment paved the way for the civil rights movement (1955–1968).

Calhoun, John C.: An outspoken political thinker and politician during the first half of the 1800s. Calhoun believed that states had the right to nullify any federal legislation they considered unconstitutional. A native of South Carolina, Calhoun defended slavery and opposed the Compromise of 1850.

Checks and balances: The model for the structure of the U.S. government. Developed in ancient Greece, this model divides government into branches, each with separate and independent powers and areas of responsibility so that no branch has more power than the other branches. The U.S. Constitution divides the federal government into three branches: executive, legislative, and judicial. In addition, the United States adopted the principle of separation of church and state.

Civil War (1861–1865): The deadliest war in American history, this conflict occurred when eleven Southern slave states seceded from the Union, formed the Confederate States of America, and fought for independence from the U.S. government. After four years of bloody battles, the federal government, sustained by twenty Northern free states and five Border States, defeated the Confederate army. The Union was restored, and slavery was outlawed throughout the country.

Clay, Henry: A nineteenth-century statesman who served as Speaker of the U.S. House of Representatives, as a U.S. senator, and as secretary of state (1825–1829). Known as the "Great Compromiser," he pushed the Missouri Compromise through the House of Representatives in 1820 and designed the Compromise of 1850.

Clinton, Bill: Forty-second president of the United States (1993–2001). The first baby boomer elected to this office, Clinton was considered a political centrist, and the country experienced economic growth during his presidency. One of only two presidents to be impeached, he was eventually acquitted by the U.S. Senate.

Compromise of 1850: A package of legislation passed in September 1850 and designed to defuse a four-year confrontation between the Southern slave states and the Northern free states. The compromise, drafted by Whig Party leader Henry Clay and brokered by Democratic Senator Stephen A. Douglas, temporarily avoided civil war by preventing the Southern states from seceding from the Union at the time.

Containment policy: A U.S. policy consisting of military, economic, and diplomatic strategies intended to curtail the spread of Communism and prevent a "domino effect" (the theory that if one country in a region came under the influence of Communism, then the surrounding countries would follow suit). The policy, associated primarily with the Truman administration (1945–1953), was developed in response to the Soviet Union's attempts to expand Communist influence in Eastern Europe, China, and Southeast Asia.

Emancipation Proclamation: An executive order issued by President Abraham Lincoln, proclaiming the freedom of all slaves who lived in the Confederacy. The order, issued January 1, 1863, during the Civil War, immediately freed approximately fifty thousand slaves and specified that the rest would be freed as the Union army advanced into the Confederate states. The proclamation did not apply to Union states that still permitted slavery.

Equal Rights Amendment: A proposed amendment to the U.S. Constitution prohibiting discrimination based on gender. Introduced in Congress in 1923, the amendment eventually passed both chambers of Congress in 1972, but it fell three votes short of ratification before its June 30, 1982 deadline.

FDIC: The Federal Deposit Insurance Corporation is a U.S. government corporation that provides insurance guarantees of the safety of deposits in its more than seven thousand member banks. The FDIC was created by the Glass–Steagall Act, which was signed into law by Franklin D. Roosevelt in 1933. Since FDIC insurance was initiated in January 1934, no depositor has lost any insured funds as the result of a bank failure.

Federalism: A system of government in which sovereignty is constitutionally divided between a central governing authority and the political units within it (such as states or provinces). Under the U.S. system, the power to govern is shared between the federal government and the governments of the fifty states.

Federalist Papers: A series of eighty-five essays advocating ratification of the U.S. Constitution. The essays were written by Alexander Hamilton, James Madison, and John Jay. Because the essays explain the philosophy and motivations behind the proposed system of U.S. government, they still serve as a primary resource for interpreting the U.S. Constitution.

Ford, Gerald: Thirty-eighth president of the United States (1974–1977). Ford assumed the presidency when Richard Nixon resigned after being implicated in the Watergate scandal. Ford's best-known official act was granting Nixon a presidential pardon.

Gompers, Samuel: As founder and president of the American Federation of Labor, Gompers promoted cooperation among the craft unions that made up the organization, favored collective bargaining over strikes, and encouraged union members to take an active role in political elections.

Great Awakening: The term refers to a series of U.S. religious revivals, the first of which occurred from 1734 to the late 1740s. The phenomenon was characterized by widespread revival meetings led by evangelical Protestant ministers, a heightened interest in religion, increasing numbers of evangelical church members, and the formation of new religious denominations.

Great Depression: A severe economic depression that occurred in the 1930s and affected almost every country in the world. Originating in the United States, the Depression started with a decline in stock prices that began around September 4, 1929, and came to the attention of the rest of the world with the stock market crash of October 29, 1929 (a day known as Black Tuesday). The Great Depression was the most widespread, serious, and longest-lasting economic crisis of the twentieth century.

Gulf War: A war waged against Iraq from August 2, 1990, to February 28, 1991, by a coalition of thirty-four nations led by the United States. The conflict was authorized by the United Nations after Iraqi troops invaded and occupied Kuwait in August 1990. Coalition forces successfully expelled all Iraqi forces from Kuwait in February 1991.

Hamilton, Alexander: A proponent of ratification of the U.S. Constitution, one of the authors of the Federalist Papers, and a leader of the Federalist Party. As the first secretary of the treasury (1789–1795), he devised President George Washington's economic policies, creating a strong tariff system and a national bank. Hamilton was killed in a duel by political rival Aaron Burr in 1804.

Harlem Renaissance: A cultural movement centered in New York City's Harlem neighborhood and spanning the 1920s and 1930s. The movement was characterized by a surge in literature, art, and music created by African Americans as well as a new sense of racial pride. The Harlem Renaissance also influenced a group of black writers who lived in Paris but were originally from French-speaking African and Caribbean colonies.

Indentured servants: Unlike slaves, indentured servants were young unskilled laborers who were legally obligated to work for an employer for a specified number of years in return for transportation to the colonies, room and board, training, and other essentials. These servants, primarily Europeans, did not receive wages. Both males and females, they typically became farm workers or household servants.

Iran Hostage Crisis: A diplomatic crisis between the United States and

Iran during the Carter administration. The crisis began on November 4, 1979, when a group of Islamic militants seized the U.S. Embassy in Tehran and took sixty-six Americans hostage in retaliation for America's long-standing support of the recently overthrown government of the Shah of Iran. Thirteen hostages were released later that month; one more was released in July 1980; but fifty-two were held for 444 days—until a few minutes after the inauguration of Ronald Reagan on January 20, 1981.

Iraq War: A military campaign that began on March 20, 2003, when a multinational force led by the United States and the United Kingdom invaded Iraq. Before the invasion, the U.S. and British governments asserted that Iraq possessed weapons of mass destruction that threatened their security and their allies. After the invasion, the U.S.-led Iraq Survey Group concluded that Iraq had no active programs for developing nuclear, chemical, or biological weapons at the time of the invasion. Some members of the Bush administration also accused Iraqi president Saddam Hussein of harboring terrorists associated with al Qaeda, but no evidence of a connection was ever found.

Jackson, Andrew: Seventh president of the United States (1829–1837). A wealthy slaveholder from Tennessee, Jackson was also a general who defeated the British at the battle of New Orleans in 1815. As president, Jackson advocated limited federal government but expanded presidential powers. His supporters created the modern Democratic Party.

Jim Crow laws: These state and local laws, in effect from 1876 to 1965, legalized systematic discrimination against African Americans. The laws authorized racial segregation in all public facilities—public schools, public transportation facilities, and restaurants—and even sanctioned separate rest rooms and drinking fountains for whites and blacks. The U.S. military was also segregated. Although Jim Crow laws supposedly assured separate but equal status for African

Americans, they typically allowed African Americans to be subject-
ed to inferior treatment and conditions, institutionalizing numerous
social, educational, and economic disadvantages and making it difficult for African Americans to vote.

Kennedy, John F.: Thirty-fifth president of the United States (1961–
1963). At the age of forty-three, Kennedy was the youngest person
elected to the presidency. Known for establishing the Peace Corps
and advancing the civil rights of African Americans, he also authorized the Bay of Pigs invasion, a failed attempt to overthrow the
government of Cuban president Fidel Castro. Kennedy was assassinated in Dallas, Texas, on November 22, 1963.

King, Martin Luther, Jr.: An American clergyman, orator, and civil rights
leader who pushed for racial equality through nonviolent means. King
became a national figure during the 1955 Montgomery, Alabama,
bus boycott that protested the relegation of African Americans to
backseats on public transportation. He is perhaps best remembered
for his eloquent "I have a dream" speech, delivered at the 1963 March
on Washington. He received the Nobel Peace Prize in 1964, and four
years later he was assassinated in Memphis, Tennessee.

Korean War: A military conflict (June 1950–July 1953) between the
Republic of Korea, supported by the United Nations, and the Democratic People's Republic of Korea, supported by the People's Republic of China and the Soviet Union. From 1910 until the end
of World War II, Japan ruled the Korean Peninsula. After Japan
surrendered to the Allies in 1945, the peninsula was divided along
the thirty-eighth parallel, with U.S. troops occupying the southern
part and Soviet troops occupying the north. Eventually, the North
instituted a Communist government, tensions mounted along the
border, and war broke out on June 25, 1950, when North Korean
forces invaded South Korea.

League of Nations: A precursor to the United Nations, the League of
Nations was the first international organization formed for the purpose

of maintaining world peace. It was established in 1920 after the end of World War I. At its height, from September 1934 to February 1935, it had fifty-eight members, but the United States was not among them. Although President Woodrow Wilson received the 1919 Nobel Peace Prize for his efforts to establish the League of Nations, the U.S. Senate did not ratify the covenant spelling out the organization's goals.

Lincoln, Abraham: Sixteenth president of the United States (1861–1865). His campaign for the presidency focused on ending slavery. He was a self-educated man who led the country during the Civil War, restored the Union by defeating the Confederacy, and is credited with abolishing slavery. He was assassinated shortly after the end of the war.

Lincoln-Douglas Debates of 1858: A series of seven debates between Abraham Lincoln, the Republican candidate for the Illinois senate, and incumbent Senator Stephen A. Douglas, the Democratic Party candidate. Slavery was the primary issue of the debates. Although Lincoln lost the race, these debates brought him into national prominence and highlighted the issues he later faced after winning the presidency two years later.

Louisiana Purchase: In 1803, President Thomas Jefferson essentially doubled the size of the United States by purchasing more than eight hundred thousand square miles of France's claim to the Louisiana Territory. The purchase, which cost $15 million, encompassed land from the Mississippi River to the Rocky Mountains and from the Gulf of Mexico to Canada. Jefferson's primary reason for acquiring the territory was to prevent France and Spain from being able to block U.S. access to the port of New Orleans.

Manifest Destiny (1845–1860): A mid-nineteenth-century American policy based on the belief that the United States had not only the right but also the duty to expand its territory across North America, from the Atlantic to the Pacific.

Marbury v. Madison: This 1803 U.S. Supreme Court decision marked the first time a court invalidated a law by declaring it unconstitutional. This is considered a landmark legal case because it established the concept of judicial review: the idea that courts may nullify (render invalid) the actions of another branch of government. The decision helped to define the checks and balances of the U.S. system of government.

Marshall Plan (1947–1951): A large-scale economic and reconstruction program named for U.S. Secretary of State George Marshall and designed to help the countries of Europe to recover from World War II. During the program's four years of operation, the United States contributed approximately $13 billion in economic and technical assistance to European countries that had joined the Organization for European Economic Cooperation.

McCarthy, Joseph: A U.S. Senator who in 1950 began holding public congressional hearings in which he accused military officials, journalists, and other public figures of being Communist spies and sympathizers. His ruthless tactics and his inability to prove his claims led the Senate to censure him in 1954.

McCulloch v. Maryland: This 1819 U.S. Supreme Court decision broadened the powers of Congress by ruling that states may not interfere with the federal government's constitutionally valid exercise of power. In support of its decision, the Court cited the necessary and proper clause of the Constitution, which allows the federal government to pass laws not expressly provided for in the Constitution.

Mercantilism: An economic theory based on the belief that a nation's prosperity depends on maintaining a favorable balance of trade. Implicit in the theory is the idea that a national government should advance this goal by encouraging exports (through subsidies) and discouraging imports (through tariffs). Mercantilism dominated Western European economic policies in the 1600s and 1700s and is ideologically linked with colonialism and imperialism, both of which involve establishing and maintaining unequal economic, cultural, and territorial relationships based on domination and subordination.

Mexican War: This armed conflict between the United States and Mexico (1846–1848) started after the United States annexed Texas in 1845. At the time, Mexico still considered Texas to be part of its territory in spite of the 1836 Texas Revolution. When the war ended, the United States took possession of Texas, New Mexico, and California in exchange for $15 million, and the Rio Grande became the border between the two countries.

Miranda v. Arizona: A 1966 U.S. Supreme Court decision requiring that a person under arrest must be informed of his or her right to remain silent and to consult legal counsel. Otherwise, the Court ruled, statements the defendant made while being interrogated are not admissible at trial. This decision has had a significant effect on U.S. law enforcement by making these provisions, known as Miranda rights, part of regular police procedures.

Missouri Compromise: This 1820 legislation resolved a dispute between the proslavery and antislavery factions in Congress by regulating slavery in the western region of the country. The agreement prohibited slavery in the former Louisiana Territory, except within the boundaries of the proposed state of Missouri.

Monroe Doctrine: On December 2, 1823, President James Monroe introduced a policy proclaiming that any further attempts by European countries to establish colonies on U.S. soil or to interfere with the states would be considered acts of aggression threatening U.S. peace and safety. The doctrine also stated that, in turn, the United States had no intention of interfering with the internal affairs of European countries or their existing colonies.

Muckrakers: This term was first used to describe U.S. journalists who exposed crime and corruption in industry and politics from the 1890s through the 1930s. The muckrakers' disclosures often resulted in social reforms, including legislation aimed at addressing corporate monopolies, insufficient safety standards, unfair labor practices, and other social injustices.

NAACP: The National Association for the Advancement of Colored People, founded in 1909, is the country's oldest and largest civil rights organization. Its mission is to eliminate racial discrimination and to ensure political, educational, social, and economic equality for all people, regardless of race.

NATO: The North Atlantic Treaty Organization is an intergovernmental military alliance whose member countries agree to defend one another in the event of an external attack on any single member nation. The alliance was formed in 1949 during a period of political conflict between Communist countries and Western powers. By the end of the twentieth century, the organization had expanded to include some Eastern European countries that formerly had been under Communist control.

Neutrality Act of 1794: Federal legislation making it illegal for an American citizen to commit any act of war against a country that's at peace with the United States. The law's purpose was to ensure that the United States remained neutral in relation to a conflict between England and France. The legislation has been amended several times and is still in force.

New Deal: A group of economic programs initiated by President Franklin D. Roosevelt during the 1930s to help the United States recover from the Great Depression. The programs included legislation promoting labor unions, a public works initiative (the Works Progress Administration) creating jobs, and legislation creating Social Security.

Nixon, Richard: Thirty-seventh president of the United States (1969–1974) and the only president to resign from office. Nixon's presidential accomplishments include ending U.S. involvement in the Vietnam War and initiating diplomatic relations with China. He resigned to avoid impeachment for his role in the Watergate scandal, and he was subsequently pardoned by his successor, Gerald Ford.

Nullification Crisis of 1832: Precipitated by federal tariffs that unevenly affected economic conditions in various regions of the country, this crisis came to a head when South Carolina declared the tariffs null and void within its borders. South Carolina's action intensified the debate between proponents of states' rights and supporters of a strong federal government. Further conflict was averted when Congress passed a new tariff that South Carolina deemed acceptable, and the United States' government rejected the principle of nullification.

Obama, Barack: Forty-fourth president of the United States (2009–). Obama is the first African American to win election to this office. A native of Hawaii, Obama represented Illinois in the U.S. Senate before becoming a presidential candidate. He received the Nobel Peace Prize in 2009.

Plessy v. Ferguson: An 1896 U.S. Supreme Court case that upheld the constitutionality of state laws sanctioning racial segregation so long as the facilities provided for each race were equal. This "separate but equal" doctrine remained the underpinning of legalized segregation until it was nullified by the Supreme Court's 1954 decision in *Brown v. Board of Education*.

Polk, James K.: Eleventh president of the United States (1845–1849). A fervent proponent of Manifest Destiny, Polk led the United States to victory in the war with Mexico, adding Texas, New Mexico, and California to the nation. In addition, he reached an agreement with the British that established the forty-ninth parallel as the country's northern border.

Progressive Era: A period of social reform from the 1890s to the 1920s. Activists in the Progressive movement worked to weaken the power of political bosses and machines and promoted the use of scientific methods in medicine, the social sciences, government, and industry.

The women's suffrage movement achieved its long-sought goal in 1920 when the Nineteenth Amendment granted women in every state the right to vote.

Prohibition: The period from 1920 to 1933 during which the Eighteenth Amendment prohibited the manufacture and sale of alcoholic beverages in the United States. Although Prohibition reduced the total amount of liquor consumed in the country, it fueled illegal liquor sales through underground clubs known as speakeasies and gave rise to organized criminal activity. Prohibition ended in 1933, when the Twenty-First Amendment repealed the Eighteenth Amendment.

Protestants: After some Western European Christians in the mid-1500s broke away from the Roman Catholic Church, their movement became known as the Protestant Reformation. Among the numerous Protestant denominations that evolved after the Reformation was a sect known as the Puritans, who viewed pleasure and luxury as sinful and wanted to cleanse the Church of England of these transgressions. Regarded as fanatics, many Puritans came to North America to escape religious persecution. Religious life in the colonies was dominated by Protestant groups of various creeds, and anti-Catholic feeling was common.

Puritans: A group of Protestants that viewed the Church of England as corrupt and wished to "purify" it. Many Puritans who came to North America settled in Massachusetts. See *Protestants*.

Puritan work ethic: The belief that hard work is an inherent obligation of human beings that demonstrates their religious devotion. The concept emerged from the teachings of John Calvin, a French theologian who broke with the Catholic Church in 1533 and whose precepts formed the basis of a Protestant theological system known as Calvinism.

Reagan, Ronald: Fortieth president of the United States (1981–1989). Before running for the presidency, Reagan was an actor and later served as governor of California. He survived an assassination attempt shortly after his inauguration. In addition to his economic policies (see *Reaganomics*), his administration was marked by military operations in Grenada, Central America, Lebanon, and Libya and better relations with the Soviet Union.

Reaganomics: A nickname for the economic policies championed by President Ronald Reagan. The philosophical assumptions behind these policies included lower taxes, less government spending, fewer governmental regulations, and low inflation achieved through federal control of the money supply.

Reconstruction: A series of policies implemented during and after the Civil War. Aimed at restoring national unity and ending slavery, Reconstruction policies began with Lincoln's Emancipation Proclamation in 1863 and were applied to the Confederate states as they fell to the Union army and returned to federal government control.

Robber barons: American businessmen and financiers who amassed wealth during the late 1800s by unethical means such as exploiting workers and engaging in questionable stock-market tactics.

Roe v. Wade: A 1973 U.S. Supreme Court decision that struck down various state laws restricting abortion. The Court argued that the right to privacy granted by a provision of the Fourteenth Amendment includes a woman's right to decide to have an abortion.

Roosevelt, Franklin Delano: Thirty-second president of the United States (1933–1945). As president during the Great Depression and World War II, Roosevelt became a dominant political figure both at home and abroad. He is best known for creating programs that stimulated the country's economic recovery (see *New Deal*) and for overseeing the country's military and civilian efforts during the war. Roosevelt was the only person to run for and be elected president four times; he died while in office.

Roosevelt, Theodore: Twenty-sixth president of the United States

(1901–1909). As the country's vice president under President William McKinley, Roosevelt took over the presidency after McKinley was assassinated. Roosevelt's administration was marked by corporate trust busting aimed at protecting workers and consumers, and he was the moving force behind construction of the Panama Canal. He claimed to conduct foreign relations by the motto "Speak softly and carry a big stick."

Salem Witch Trials: A series of court proceedings held in colonial Massachusetts in 1692 and 1693 for the purpose of prosecuting people accused of witchcraft. Precipitated by religious extremism and fueled by the local government's encroachment on individual liberties, the trials resulted in twenty-nine convictions. Nineteen of those found guilty were hanged, and several others died in prison.

Scott, Dred: An African American slave who sued for his freedom and that of his wife and daughters in the 1857 case *Dred Scott v. Sandford*. The U.S. Supreme Court ruled against him, claiming that no one of African ancestry could become a U.S. citizen or file a lawsuit in federal court.

Secession: In 1861, eleven Southern states seceded, or withdrew, from the Union, forming the Confederate States of America and triggering the Civil War. The Confederate states returned to the Union during the era of Reconstruction.

Second Great Awakening: This period of religious growth occurred in the early 1800s, almost a century after the First Great Awakening. Like its predecessor, the movement was characterized by Protestant revival meetings and the formation of new denominations. The most popular new denominations were the Methodists, Baptists, and Presbyterians.

Slave trade routes: From the mid-1600s through the mid-1800s, millions of people from western and central Africa were captured and sold as slaves. Most of the slaves were transported to North and

South America by slave traders who brought them across the Atlantic Ocean by ship.

Slavery: Between the early 1600s and the mid-1800s, approximately twelve million Africans were brought to North and South America to be sold as property and forced to work without wages or individual freedom. Most American slaves worked on Southern plantations that produced high-value cash crops such as sugar, rice, cotton, coffee, and tobacco. The agrarian economy of the Southern states was based on slave labor.

Social Darwinism: The application of Charles Darwin's theories of biological evolution and natural selection to the study of human society. In the late 1800s sociologists used the term to describe the theory that certain groups or individuals gained advantages over others because of genetic or biological superiority.

Tecumseh: A Shawnee chief who, along with his brother (known as "The Prophet"), attempted to unite Native Americans against the encroachment of white settlements. Tecumseh and the Prophet were attacked by the U.S. government at the 1811 battle of Tippecanoe in the Indiana Territory, an ambush designed to crush Shawnee activity. Tecumseh fought with the British during the War of 1812 and was killed in the October 1813 battle of the Thames.

Trail of Tears: Between 1831 and 1838 the U.S. government forced five Native American tribes—Choctaw, Seminole, Creek, Chickasaw, and Cherokee—to leave their homelands in the Southeast and relocate to eastern Oklahoma, known at the time as Indian Territory. Because many tribal members died from disease or starvation as they walked to their new destinations, the route became known as the Trail of Tears.

Uncle Tom's Cabin: An antislavery novel written by American abolitionist Harriet Beecher Stowe. Published in 1852, the novel became the second-best-selling book of the nineteenth century—after the

Bible. The novel and numerous dramatic performances based on its story were credited with furthering the abolitionist cause.

Vietnam War: A prolonged military conflict (1954–1975) between the Communist forces of North Vietnam, supported by China and the Soviet Union, and the non-Communist forces of South Vietnam, supported by the United States. The U.S. government saw its involvement in the war as a way to prevent Communism from gaining a foothold in Southeast Asia. U.S. military advisers appeared on the scene as early as 1950, and U.S. combat troops arrived in 1965. Military operations during the conflict also extended into the neighboring countries of Laos and Cambodia. The war ended when the North Vietnamese captured Saigon, South Vietnam's capital city, on April 30, 1975.

War of 1812 (1812–1815): A military conflict initiated by the United States against the British. The United States justified the war for several reasons, including the desire to take over some British-held territory in the Northwest, anger at trade obstructions resulting from a war between the British and the French, impressments of U.S. merchant sailors by the British Navy, and resentment of Britain's support of the Native American tribes Tecumseh had united in opposition to additional U.S. expansion. Andrew Jackson's historic victory at the battle of New Orleans happened two weeks after a treaty officially ended the war.

War on Poverty: A series of domestic programs proposed by President Lyndon B. Johnson to combat poverty and improve living standards among the nation's poor. Johnson declared this war in his State of the Union address in 1964, a few weeks after the Kennedy assassination. Among the programs deployed to fight the war on poverty were Head Start, Vista, the Job Corps, Medicare, and Medicaid.

Washington, Booker T.: An African American educator who was born into slavery in 1856, acquired an education after emancipation, and in 1881 became the first president of Tuskegee Institute, a historically black university, which thrived under his leadership. Washington was an influential spokesman for African Americans in the post-Reconstruction era, advising them to work toward racial equality by learning vocational skills, striving for financial independence, and acquiring an understanding of the U.S. legal system.

Washington, George: The first president of the United States (1789–1797). As commander in chief of the American forces, he solidified U.S. independence by defeating the British during the Revolutionary War. In 1787 he presided over the Second Constitutional Convention, whose participants drafted the U.S. Constitution. As president, he established numerous precedents, including the custom of making an inaugural speech and relying on cabinet members as advisers. Washington resigned from the presidency after serving two terms, admonishing Americans to avoid partisanship, regionalism, and involvement in foreign conflicts.

Watergate: A term referring to a political scandal that led to the resignation of President Richard Nixon. On June 17, 1972, five men broke into the headquarters of the Democratic National Committee at the Watergate Hotel and Office Complex in Washington, DC, with the intention of wiretapping the phones. After the burglars were arrested, it was discovered that they had been paid by the Committee to Reelect the President, that Nixon had known about the break-in, and that he had participated in a cover-up. Facing near-certain impeachment and likely conviction, Nixon resigned from office on August 9, 1974.

Wilson, Woodrow: Twenty-eighth president of the United States (1913–1921). The only U.S. President to hold an earned PhD, Wilson was the country's leader during World War I and at the time Prohibition was introduced. Despite trying to maintain U.S. neutrality in relation to the Great War in Europe, he asked Congress to declare war in April 1917 after German submarines began attacking U.S. merchant ships. When the war ended, Wilson pushed to form the

League of Nations in the hope of preventing such large-scale devastation in the future. Although he received the Nobel Peace Prize for establishing and promoting the League of Nations, he was unable to convince the U.S. Senate to ratify its covenants.

World War I: A global war in which Great Britain, France, Russia, Belgium, Italy, Japan, the United States, and other allies defeated Germany, Austria-Hungary, Turkey, and Bulgaria (1914–1918). The war began after the assassination of Austrian archduke Franz Ferdinand, heir to the Austro-Hungarian throne, by a Serbian nationalist group. In response, Austria-Hungary declared war on Serbia. Subsequently, a tangle of treaties and secret alliances binding Russia to Serbia and France, France to Britain and its Commonwealth, Britain to Japan, and Germany to Austria-Hungary escalated the conflict. Although the United States tried to remain neutral, it eventually entered the war after Germany's policy of unrestricted submarine warfare posed a serious threat to U.S. commercial shipping. By the time the war ended, more than nine million soldiers had been killed.

World War II: A global war involving all of the world's most powerful nations from 1939 to 1945. The war was fought between the Allies (Great Britain, France, the Soviet Union, the United States, China, and other countries) and the Axis (Germany, Italy, and Japan). The conflict began when Germany invaded Poland as a first step toward establishing a vast European empire. The United States was drawn into the war when Japan attacked the U.S. naval base at Pearl Harbor, Hawaii, on December 7, 1941. In addition to involving more than one hundred million military personnel, the war caused massive numbers of civilian deaths. Germany slaughtered approximately six million Jews, and the United States killed hundreds of thousands of people by dropping atomic bombs on the Japanese cities of Hiroshima and Nagasaki. It was the deadliest war in history.

THE BIG PICTURE: HOW TO PREPARE YEAR-ROUND

Registering for the Test

Even if you don't plan to take the SAT U.S. History Subject Test for months, it's not too early to begin preparing. This section provides instructions for registering for the test, as well as information designed to improve your performance when you take the actual test. As your test day approaches, reviewing all the information in this book can go a long way toward helping you to remember what you've already learned. Having this material crystallized in your head will boost your confidence and help to minimize any stress you might be feeling in connection with taking the test.

When to Take the Test

Most SAT subject tests, including the one on U.S. history, are offered six times a year—in October, November, December, January, May, and June. Because of their admission deadlines, many colleges require you to take subject tests no later than December or January of your senior year in high school, but you'll need to take them sooner if you apply for early admission at any college. Some students choose to take the SAT U.S. History Subject Test toward the end of their junior year, when they're just finishing a yearlong class in this subject and the material is fresh in their minds. Students who are homeschooled can also take the SAT subject tests.

Because your high school undoubtedly offers a class in American history, the SAT U.S. History Subject Test may be offered at your school or in your school district.

How to Register for the Test

To take an SAT subject test, you must sign up with the College Board (the organization that administers these tests), fill out some forms, and pay a fee. The easiest way to register is online. For registration information, visit the College Board's Web site at www.collegeboard.com and click on the link for "SAT Subject Tests." If you have a credit card handy and decide to register online, you can choose your test date and test site immediately. Once you create an online account, you can print your test admission ticket, see your scores, and have your scores sent to the schools of your choice. The site is accessible twenty-four hours a day.

How to Prepare for the Test Year-Round

Long before your test date, you can adopt a number of behaviors that will boost your performance when test day rolls around. These behaviors include cultivating the habit of active listening, training yourself to take notes in class and from books efficiently, and learning how to use your notes to your greatest advantage.

Active Listening

Your ability to perform well on the test depends on your ability to retain relevant information, whether you glean it from classroom lectures, homework assignments, supplementary reading, or other resources.

Knowing how to take useful notes can maximize your ability to recall key information from all of these sources.

The first step in taking good notes in class is to practice active listening. This does not entail trying to write down every word your teacher utters. Here are three tips to help you to become adept at active listening:

- **Identify the key point of the lecture:** Before you write anything down, listen for the kernel of information that reveals the subject to be discussed. If you're lucky, the teacher will start with an introduction that describes the material to be covered. Once you're aware of what to focus on, you can structure you notes around that subject.

- **Listen for signals:** Certain words and phrases indicate how a lecture has been organized. Be mindful of words that act as signposts—for example, transitional words like "next" or "the following..." If the lecture includes lists, highlight the items listed with numbers or bullets.

- **Look at the teacher:** Rather than bury your nose in your notebook, pay attention to the teacher's gestures and facial expressions. These nonverbal cues can tell you what he or she considers most interesting or significant.

Taking Notes in Class

As soon as you've mastered active listening in class, turn your attention to taking effective notes. Trying to take down every word of a lecture is close to impossible, plus it's not very effective. Instead, follow these three guidelines:

- **Record the date and topic:** Having these two pieces of information in a prominent spot on the page will help you find specific sets of information when you go looking for them.

- **Jot down key ideas:** If you try to write down every word you hear or document every piece of information in a visual presentation, you'll get bogged down and fail to actively listen. Pay attention to what the teacher says and focus on the most important ideas.

- **Ask about anything you don't understand:** Classroom lectures can contain a lot of information, and even the best teachers sometimes move through the material too quickly or state things in a way that's not entirely clear. Don't bother taking notes on something you don't comprehend. Ask the teacher to explain what you don't understand so your notes will make sense when you come back to them at a later date.

Using Your Notes

The notes you take in class will be even more useful if you put them in a form that will be meaningful in the future. Here are three tips on how to maximize the value of your classroom notes:

- **Rewrite or type your notes as soon as possible after class:** If you have a free period at school or can spare some time that evening, take the opportunity to rewrite your notes or key them on a computer so they'll be tidy for future reference. Revisiting the information right away will help you to absorb it more completely and enable you to recall it better later.

- **Review the previous day's notes before class:** Because history is typically taught chronologically, going over what you've learned most recently will help you put the next set of information in the proper context.

- **Ask for help if you need it:** Your teacher may be willing to serve as a resource if you need additional information or clarification. If not, seek out other sources of information.

Taking Notes from a Book

Taking notes as you read your textbook, test-preparation books, or other supplementary sources can enhance your understanding of the things you learn in class and expand your knowledge of U.S. history generally. Here are eight tactics for taking notes from books.

- **Read before you write:** Don't start making notes the minute you start to read. Instead, look at the table of contents and notice how the book is organized, glance at the chapter titles and subheads, and then read enough text to get the gist of the information it contains.

- **Read to understand:** Your notes will be useless if you don't comprehend the material you're reading. Don't simply rewrite what's already been written; try to put new information in context and integrate it with what you already know.

- **Map out the main ideas:** Once you've been through the material and have a general understanding of what you've read, write down the main ideas that were presented. Leave some space under each idea so you can come back later and fill in the details. You may also want to leave extra space for your own ideas, comments, or questions.

- **Use your own words:** Avoid copying the text exactly as it appears in the book. Simply regurgitating passages word for word isn't likely to help you learn anything. On the other hand, paraphrasing the material will ensure that you're actively engaged in the learning process and will increase the likelihood that you'll retain the information.

- **Reread the material:** Once you've mapped out the main ideas you gleaned, read the material again, concentrating on the information you'll need to add to your list of main ideas.

- **Fill in the details:** After you've read the material a second time, you're ready to expand your notes with more comprehensive information. Remember to use your own words rather than copy text directly from the book.

- **Go over your notes:** Read through your notes, checking to make sure you've interpreted the main ideas accurately and incorporated an appropriate amount of supporting information. Above all, be sure your notes make sense. They won't be helpful to you later if you don't understand them.

- **Review your notes as you study for the test:** Store your typed or handwritten notes in a notebook or file folder so they're easy to find when you're ready to prepare for test day. Keeping them in chronological order will help you to remember the sequence of historical events.

Creating a Study Plan

Like many other high school students, your days may be heavily scheduled. In addition to classes and homework, you're probably involved in extracurricular activities and have other outside interests. You may also have chores at home or even a part-time job. These activities will impinge on the amount of time you can devote to test preparation, so you'll need to make the most of the time that's available.

The most efficient way to get the maximum benefit from a limited amount of preparation time is to create a study plan. This plan should be customized especially for you. It should be based on your specific needs and the amount of time you've allocated to preparing for the test. You won't necessarily use this book in the same way your fellow test takers will, and your study plan won't be identical to theirs.

The key to creating a personalized study plan is to pinpoint the areas in which your knowledge is spotty or deficient and to set aside enough time to beef up your grasp of those areas. Here are three fundamental steps for developing a personalized study plan:

- **Identify your weak points:** Start by taking a practice test. This will help you to become familiar with the test—how it's set up, how to recognize different types of questions, and how to pace yourself in order to get through the entire test. Assessing your performance on a practice test will enable you to establish priorities among the subject areas you need to review. Focus first on the subjects in which your performance on the practice test was weakest. If you don't feel ready to take a practice test, you might start by scanning the glossary and flagging the terms you find most daunting or difficult to remember.

- **Create a review plan and a schedule:** Just as you'll want to budget your time as you take practice tests and the actual test, you'll need to pace yourself through your test-preparation agenda. Determine how many hours you can devote to test preparation each week, and block out specific time slots with this intention. Put your timetable in writing and designate which topics you plan to review during each block of time you've set aside. Divide the time to ensure you can get through all the material you need to review.

- **Use the "Last-Minute Study Guide" or the "Comprehensive Strategies and Review" as a benchmark:** You'll want to concentrate on some content areas and some types of questions more than others, so skim the topics you know well and add time to focus on those you've identified as areas of weakness. In addition, designate some time to take practice tests and become proficient at the test-taking strategies described in this book.

- **Mobilize your self-discipline:** Stick to your study plan! No matter how much you're tempted to stray from the path you've outlined for yourself, discipline yourself to forge ahead on schedule. Make your test-prep schedule your highest priority and plan other activities around it—not the other way around.

Some students find that having a study partner helps them abide by a schedule. Sometimes a partner can help you study more effectively—you can exchange ideas and information and reinforce your knowledge by asking each other questions. Other students do better studying on their own. They may find having another person around distracting, diverting their attention from the topic at hand or interfering with their concentration. Figure out what works best for you so you can enforce your study plan and use your time most productively.

If self-discipline isn't your strong suit, remind yourself of your long-term educational goals. Think about how much U.S. history you've already learned and will be able to recall after some focused review, and remember that this test-prep period is only temporary. After the test is over, you can revel in your recaptured free time!

This book contains two practice tests. Visit mymaxscore.com to download your free third practice test with answers and explanations.

Practice Test 1

<u>Directions</u>: Choose the answer choice that best answers the question or completes the incomplete statement below.

1. The Bill of Rights refers to the

    A. importance of a central government
    B. first ten amendments to the Constitution
    C. abolition of slavery
    D. Electoral College
    E. checks and balances within the government

2. Maine was admitted to the United States as

    A. a slave state during the Missouri Compromise of 1820
    B. a free state after passage of the Kansas-Nebraska Act
    C. a free state at the end of the Spanish-American War
    D. a free state during the Missouri Compromise of 1820
    E. a slave state after passage of the Kansas-Nebraska Act

3. In capitalist theory, the law of supply and demand dictates that

    A. demand for an item typically increases as supply of the item increases
    B. the demand for an item decreases as the supply of the item decreases
    C. demand has a greater influence than supply in determining price
    D. supply is more important than demand in determining an item's price
    E. the interplay of supply and demand determines the price of an item

4. Which of the following was associated with the Roosevelt Corollary to the Monroe Doctrine?

    A. "Speak softly and carry a big stick"
    B. Rugged individualism
    C. Gunboat diplomacy
    D. Open-door policy
    E. "A house divided against itself"

5. The painting above, which shows a figure guiding settlers moving west, supports which of the following concepts?

    A. Protectionism
    B. Manifest Destiny

C. Neutrality
D. Isolationism
E. Sectionalism

6. Each of the following was true of the American Federation of Labor during the late 1800s EXCEPT

A. it was founded by activist Samuel Gompers
B. it favored collective bargaining over strikes
C. it was primarily active within Southern farming communities
D. it promoted cooperation among its member craft unions
E. it encouraged union members to take an active role in political elections

7. The concept of federalism refers to the

A. primacy of states' rights over the central government's power
B. establishment of checks and balances within the government
C. separation of church and state
D. sharing of power between the national government and the states
E. purposeful curtailing of central government power

8. In the 1930s, the Public Works Administration did which of the following as part of the New Deal?

A. Employed artists and photographers
B. Created jobs by building roads and housing
C. Provided jobs and electricity
D. Gave states grants to manage work programs
E. Regulated the stock market

9. Each of the following is an example of a nonviolent protest EXCEPT

    A. student sit-ins
    B. the Montgomery bus boycott
    C. Nat Turner's Rebellion
    D. picket lines
    E. the March on Washington in 1963

10. During the colonial period, New England colonies were character-
    ized by which of the following?

    A. Economic growth through commercial farming
    B. Economies based on agriculture
    C. Economic reliance on indentured servitude labor
    D. Aristocratic plantation cultures
    E. Economies based on trade

11. Which of the following was the precursor to the Populist Party?

    A. The Temperance movement
    B. The Knights of Labor organization
    C. The Grange movement
    D. The People's Party
    E. The Federalist Party

12. What did Stephen A. Douglas accomplish?

    A. He defeated Abraham Lincoln in the Illinois senate race in 1858.
    B. He spearheaded the political effort to repeal the Missouri
        Compromise.
    C. He led the state of South Carolina in seceding from the Union.
    D. He defeated Abraham Lincoln in the presidential campaign of 1861.
    E. He was head of the government created by the Confederate
        States of America.

13. *Roe v. Wade* was significant because it

   A.   established the primacy of federal power over states' rights
   B.   established that separate facilities for blacks were inherently unequal
   C.   established the doctrine of "separate but equal"
   D.   struck down various state laws restricting abortion
   E.   led to the implementation of busing to integrate public schools

14. Which of the following contributed most to the lengthening of the Civil War?

   A.   The assassination of Abraham Lincoln
   B.   Political impasses in Parliament
   C.   The utilization of trench warfare
   D.   The development of Lincoln's plan for Reconstruction
   E.   Sherman's March to the Sea in 1864

15. In 1773, colonists destroyed tea in Boston Harbor to protest against

   A.   deaths at the battle of Lexington
   B.   events of the Boston Massacre
   C.   British imposition of the Stamp Act of 1765
   D.   the Declaratory Act of 1766
   E.   passage of the Townshend Act of 1767

16. The Twenty-First Amendment to the U.S. Constitution was significant because it

   A.   established Prohibition
   B.   repealed the Eighteenth Amendment
   C.   repealed the Fifteenth Amendment
   D.   provided for the direct election of senators
   E.   outlawed the institution of slavery

17. The ideas expressed in Adam Smith's 1776 book, *Wealth of Nations*, lent support to all of the following EXCEPT

   A.   government ownership of all property

   B.   the theory of capitalism

   C.   the law of supply and demand

   D.   laissez-faire economics

   E.   the invisible hand of market forces

18. The presidency of James Garfield included which of the following?

   A.   Impeachment

   B.   The League of Nations

   C.   Prohibition

   D.   Reconstruction

   E.   Assassination

19. Which of the following debates was the subject of the Scopes trial of 1925?

   A.   Capitalism vs. Communism

   B.   Evolution vs. creationism

   C.   Imperialism vs. dollar diplomacy

   D.   Immediate emancipation vs. gradual emancipation

   E.   Segregation vs. integration

20. The presidential administration of George Washington was characterized by which of the following?

    A. Distrust of a strong central government
    B. Emphasis on a strict constructionist interpretation of the
        Constitution
    C. Adherence to Federalist Party policies as proposed by Alexander
        Hamilton
    D. Implementation of an aggressive foreign policy of territorial
        expansion
    E. Avoidance of protective tariffs to encourage free trade

21. "And the great owners, who must lose their land in an upheaval,
    the great owners with access to history, with eyes to read history
    and to know the great fact: when property accumulates in too few
    hands it is taken away. And that companion fact: when a majority
    of the people are hungry and cold they will take by force what they
    need. And the little screaming fact that sounds through all history:
    repression works only to strengthen and knit the repressed."

In the passage above, the time period to which the author refers was

    A. the Jazz Age
    B. the Harlem Renaissance
    C. the Roaring Twenties
    D. the Great Depression
    E. the Progressive Era

Project Gutenberg

22. The twentieth-century cartoon above supports which of the follow-
    ing conclusions about the League of Nations?

    A. It was doomed to failure.
    B. It suffered from lack of direction by Woodrow Wilson.
    C. Ratification by the United States was guaranteed.
    D. It was likely to be a success.
    E. It did not command adequate international attention.

23. Large conglomerates such as U.S. Steel were developed during
    which of the following?

    A. The Cold War
    B. The Great Depression
    C. The Roaring Twenties
    D. The Progressive Era
    E. The Gilded Age

24. "There is no wilderness where I can hide from these things, there is
    no haven where I can escape them; though I travel to the ends of the

earth, I find the same accursed system—I find that all the fair and noble impulses of humanity, the dreams of poets and the agonies of martyrs, are shackled and bound in the service of organized and predatory Greed!"

This passage was most likely written by which of the following?

A. A muckraker at the turn of the twentieth century
B. A British loyalist in colonial America
C. A Communist sympathizer during the Cold War
D. A Southern plantation owner in the antebellum period
E. A U.S. soldier during World War I

25. Which of the following contributed to the banishment of Anne Hutchinson from the Massachusetts Bay Colony in 1638?

A. She attempted to start a new colony based on religious tolerance.
B. She preached "fire and brimstone" sermons publicly.
C. She advocated the separation of church and state.
D. She was accused of being a witch, tried, and found guilty.
E. She challenged aspects of Puritan religious ideology.

26. The *Liberator* newspaper was published by William Lloyd Garrison for which reason?

A. To call for the repeal of poll taxes
B. To spread his abolitionist message
C. To support the activities of women suffragists
D. To call for an end to segregation
E. To denounce Jim Crow laws

27. "Clearly, no longer can a dictator count on East-West confrontation to stymie concerted United Nations action against aggression. A new partnership of nations has begun. And we stand today at a unique and extraordinary moment. The crisis in the Persian Gulf, as grave as it is, also offers a rare opportunity to move toward an historic period of cooperation...in which the nations of the world, east and west, north and south, can prosper and live in harmony."

The statement above was most likely made by which of the following?

    A.   Gerald Ford, in a speech to the U.S. Senate

    B.   Bill Clinton, in a televised interview with the press

    C.   Barack Obama, in a State of the Union address

    D.   George H. W. Bush, in an address to a joint session of Congress

    E.   Richard M. Nixon, in an address to the House of Representatives

28. "From my earliest recollection, I date the entertainment of a deep conviction that slavery would not always be able to hold me within its foul embrace; and in the darkest hours of my career in slavery, this living word of faith and spirit of hope departed not from me, but remained like ministering angels to cheer me through the gloom."

—Frederick Douglass, 1845

The passage above suggests that Frederick Douglass would probably have supported all of the following EXCEPT

    A.   the granting of citizenship to blacks

    B.   the Fourteenth Amendment

    C.   the Emancipation Proclamation

    D.   secession from the Union

    E.   the abolition of slavery

29. All of the following reformers are correctly paired with the reform issue with which they were most involved EXCEPT

    A. Horace Mann...public school reform

    B. Harriet Beecher Stowe...abolition

    C. Jane Addams...transcendentalism

    D. John Dewey...education reform

    E. Lucretia Mott...women's suffrage

30. Which of the following developed as part of the Second Party System in the 1820s?

    A. The Whig Party, headed by Henry Clay

    B. The Democratic Party, headed by Thomas Jefferson

    C. The Democratic-Republican Party, headed by Andrew Jackson

    D. The Republican Party, headed by John Quincy Adams

    E. The Progressive Party, headed by Daniel Webster

31. Which of the following presidents went through impeachment proceedings related to his participation in the Monica Lewinsky scandal?

    A. Richard Nixon

    B. Gerald Ford

    C. George H. W. Bush

    D. Barack Obama

    E. Bill Clinton

32. The energy crisis of 1973 occurred for which of the following reasons?

    A. Arab nations ran short of oil supplies for exports.
    B. Arab nations cut off oil supplies to nations that had supported Israel during the Arab-Israeli War.
    C. The United States experienced an extreme coal shortage due to increased international demand.
    D. Israel initiated an oil embargo against the United States due to its position in the Arab-Israeli War.
    E. U.S. attempts to develop advanced nuclear reactors failed for technological reasons.

33. The battle of Yorktown in 1781 was significant because

    A. it marked the beginning of the Revolutionary War
    B. it prompted the French to join the Revolutionary War
    C. it was the last major battle of the American Revolution
    D. it prompted Spain to join the Revolution as an ally of France
    E. it demonstrated the strategic skills of British General Cornwallis

34. "To leave office before my term is completed is abhorrent to every instinct in my body. But as President I must put the interests of America first. America needs a full-time President and a full-time Congress, particularly at this time with problems we face at home and abroad."

The statement above was made by

    A. Bill Clinton
    B. Andrew Jackson
    C. Richard M. Nixon
    D. Lyndon B. Johnson
    E. Woodrow Wilson

35. Abraham Lincoln's plan for Reconstruction was characterized by

    A. collaboration with a united Congress
    B. military occupation of Southern cities
    C. a harsher plan than that recommended by Congress
    D. leniency for the South compared to Congress' plan
    E. strict enforcement of congressional recommendations

36. Blacks were granted the right to vote by which of the following amendments, passed during Reconstruction?

    A. The Fifteenth Amendment
    B. The Fourteenth Amendment
    C. The Nineteenth Amendment
    D. The Thirteenth Amendment
    E. The Seventeenth Amendment

37. Which of the following presidents held office during the Federalist period of U.S. government?

    A. George Washington and James Monroe
    B. George Washington and John Adams
    C. George Washington and Thomas Jefferson
    D. Alexander Hamilton and Thomas Jefferson
    E. Thomas Jefferson and John Quincy Adams

38. Which of the following was best known for her "Ain't I a Woman?" speech, given at the 1854 Ohio Women's Rights Convention?

    A. Harriet Jacobs
    B. Harriet Beecher Stowe
    C. Harriet Tubman
    D. Sojourner Truth
    E. Susan B. Anthony

39. Which of the following was true of Nat Turner's Rebellion?

    A. The incident involved British guards firing into a crowd of onlookers, hitting eleven men.
    B. The incident led colonial settlers to reduce the use of indentured servants.
    C. The incident led to a legal case in which Nat Turner sued for his freedom.
    D. The incident introduced permanent slavery into the American colonies.
    E. Many innocent slaves were injured or killed as part of the public's reaction.

40. In the late 1800s, which of the following published the book *Our Country*, popularizing the view that Americans had a moral responsibility to spread civilization around the world?

    A. Ida Wells
    B. Edward Bellamy
    C. Josiah Strong
    D. Zora Neale Hurston
    E. Langston Hughes

41. The Articles of Confederation provided for which of the following?

    A. Congressional power to regulate foreign trade
    B. A provisional government during the American Revolution
    C. Congressional ability to levy taxes
    D. A strong central government with far-reaching powers
    E. Congressional power to regulate interstate commerce

42. Which of the following was true of religious leader John Winthrop?

    A. His religious philosophy called for separation from the Protestant Church.

B.   He was the founder of the Jamestown Colony, established in 1607.

C.   He established a colony in Rhode Island based on religious tolerance.

D.   He had a vision for the Plymouth Colony as a "city on a hill."

E.   He was the founder of the Massachusetts Bay Colony, established in 1630.

43. Publication of Alfred T. Mahan's book *The Influence of Sea Power upon History* was significant because

A.   it urged for a strong navy and motivated U.S. imperialism

B.   it was directly responsible for the U.S. decision to enter World War II

C.   Theodore Roosevelt used it as justification for his "Big Stick" policy

D.   Herbert Hoover was highly influenced by the book during his administration

E.   it motivated the U.S. decision to launch the Persian Gulf War

"My heart is a stone: heavy with sadness for my people; cold with the knowledge that no treaty will keep whites out of our lands; hard with the determination to resist as long as I live and breathe. Now we are weak and many of our people are afraid. But hear me: a single twig breaks, but the bundle of twigs is strong."

44. The quotation above most clearly expresses the views of

A.   William Lloyd Garrison, abolitionist

B.   Frederick Douglass, former slave

C.   Tecumseh, Shawnee leader

D.   Josiah Strong, minister

E.   John Smith, Jamestown settler

45. Advocates of Prohibition argued that

    A. African Americans should work toward total racial equality
    B. moderate consumption of alcohol was acceptable in speakeasies
    C. African Americans should accommodate the Jim Crow laws of
        the South
    D. institutions for the mentally ill should be subject to reforms
    E. alcohol consumption should be banned entirely in the United
        States

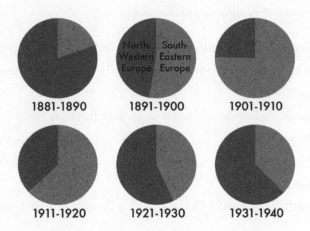

46. Which of the following statements about immigration to the United
    States in the period from 1901 to 1910 is supported by the graphs
    above?

    A. Immigration from southeastern Europe stayed relatively con-
        sistent compared to immigration from southwestern Europe
        over the previous twenty-year period.
    B. Immigration from northwestern Europe surged compared to
        immigration from northwestern Europe over the previous
        twenty-year period.
    C. Immigration from southeastern Europe plummeted compared
        to immigration from southeastern Europe over the previous
        twenty-year period.

    D. Immigration from southeastern Europe surged compared to immigration from southeastern Europe over the previous twenty-year period.

    E. Immigration from northwestern Europe stayed relatively consistent compared to immigration from northwestern Europe over the previous twenty-year period.

47. Which of the following best reflects Thomas Jefferson's position regarding the imposition of protective tariffs during the Federalist period?

    A. Jefferson supported protective tariffs to improve agrarian efficiency.

    B. Jefferson supported protective tariffs to bolster manufacturing.

    C. Jefferson was opposed to the imposition of protective tariffs.

    D. Jefferson was neutral on the issue of imposing protective tariffs.

    E. Jefferson agreed with Hamilton's position regarding the role of tariffs.

48. Which of the following represents an ideal of Andrew Jackson's Democratic Party that differentiated it from its precursor?

    A. Universal suffrage for white men

    B. Individual rights

    C. Women's suffrage

    D. The abolition of slavery

    E. Protection from self-incrimination

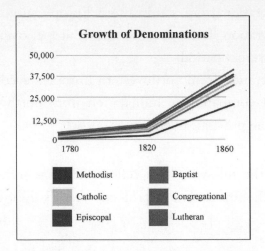

49. The chart above most likely reflects the influence of which of the following?

   A. The transcendentalist movement
   B. The First Great Awakening
   C. The Civil War
   D. The abolition movement
   E. The Second Great Awakening

50. "I am cognizant of the interrelatedness of all communities and states. I cannot sit idly by in Atlanta and not be concerned about what happens in Birmingham. Injustice anywhere is a threat to justice everywhere. We are caught in an inescapable network of mutuality, tied in a single garment of destiny. Whatever affects one directly, affects all indirectly."

The passage above is most likely excerpted from a work by which of the following?

   A. Adolf Hitler
   B. Dr. Martin Luther King Jr.
   C. Upton Sinclair

D. John Steinbeck

E. F. Scott Fitzgerald

51. "We hold these truths to be self-evident, that all men are created equal, that they are endowed by their Creator with certain unalienable Rights, that among these are Life, Liberty and the pursuit of Happiness. That to secure these rights, Governments are instituted among Men, deriving their just powers from the consent of the governed."

The passage above comes from

A. the Articles of Confederation

B. *The Federalist Papers*

C. the U.S. Constitution

D. the Declaration of Independence

E. the Bill of Rights

52. The dot-com boom of the 1990s involved which of the following?

A. Agrarian reforms

B. Gold mining stocks

C. Technology investments

D. Silver supplies

E. The energy sector

53. The Treaty of Paris brought an end to

A. the Spanish-American War in 1899

B. World War I in 1918

C. the Cold War in 1989

D. World War II in 1946

E. the War of 1812 in 1814

54. Which of the following contributed to the banishment of Roger Williams from the Massachusetts Bay Colony?

    A.   Williams refused to participate in church-sanctioned activities.

    B.   Williams created a political alliance with Jonathan Edwards.

    C.   Williams was an avid follower of John Winthrop's ideas.

    D.   Williams was accused of practicing witchcraft.

    E.   Williams advocated the separation of church and state.

55. The construction of the Panama Canal established which of the following?

    A.   Improved relations between the United States and Central America

    B.   A connection between the Atlantic and Pacific waterways

    C.   A method of traversing the United States from the East to the West Coast

    D.   The first functional navigation system for circling the globe

    E.   An aerial route from the Atlantic Ocean to the Pacific Ocean

56. The concept of asceticism refers to the

    A.   stated intent of the Anglican Church to punish dissenters

    B.   belief in the importance of religious tolerance

    C.   philosophy of the Pilgrims who wished to separate from Protestantism

    D.   philosophy of a rigid way of life devoid of worldly pleasures

    E.   Puritan commitment to rid the Protestant church of corruption

57. "General Secretary Gorbachev, if you seek peace, if you seek prosperity for the Soviet Union and Eastern Europe, if you seek liberalization: Come here to this gate! Mr. Gorbachev, open this gate! Mr. Gorbachev, tear down this wall!"

The previous statement was most likely made by which of the following?

    A.   Harry Truman at the end of World War II

    B.   Joseph McCarthy during the Cold War

    C.   George Kennan at the onset of the Cold War

    D.   Henry Kissinger during the Cold War

    E.   Ronald Reagan before the end of the Cold War

58. The diplomatic efforts of George Kennan were significant because they

    A.   helped establish the U.S. policy of containment during the Cold War

    B.   helped Senator Joseph McCarthy prosecute alleged Communist sympathizers

    C.   helped the Soviet Union develop a comprehensive strategy against NATO

    D.   provided information that enabled the United States to win the Cold War

    E.   provided information that allowed the Allies to defeat Nazi Germany

59. Which of the following inspired the Civil War?

    A.   The establishment of the U.S. Constitution

    B.   The creation of the Articles of Confederation

    C.   The creation of the Continental Army

    D.   The creation of the Confederate States of America

    E.   The creation of the Declaration of Independence

60. "The problem lay buried, unspoken for many years in the minds of American women… Each suburban housewife struggled with it alone. As she made the beds, shopped for groceries, matched slipcover material, ate peanut butter sandwiches with her children, chauffeured Cub Scouts and Brownies, lay beside her husband at night, she was afraid to ask even of herself the silent question—'Is this all?'"

The passage above is most likely excerpted from a work by the noted feminist researcher and women's movement activist

    A.   Betty Friedan
    B.   Lucretia Mott
    C.   Gloria Steinem
    D.   Geraldine Ferraro
    E.   Hillary Rodham Clinton

COMPARISON OF THE UNION AND THE CONFEDERACY

	UNION	CONFEDERACY
Total population	22,100,000 (71%)	9,100,000 (29%)
Free population	21,700,000	5,600,000
Slave population, 1860	400,000	3,500,000
Soldiers	2,100,000 (67%)	1,064,000 (33%)
Manufactured items	90%	10%
Firearm production	97%	3%
Bales of cotton in 1860	Negligible	4,500,000
Bales of cotton in 1864	Negligible	300,000
Prewar U.S. exports	30%	70%

Source: 1860 U.S. Census and The Historical Statistics of the United States

61. Which of the following statements about the period from 1860 to 1864 is supported by the table above?

    A.   The slave population in the Confederacy grew significantly.

B.   Bales of cotton produced in the Confederacy decreased significantly.

C.   Exports from the Union states to European countries grew substantially.

D.   Firearm production in the Union states increased significantly.

E.   Manufactured items in the Confederacy increased significantly.

62. The War on Poverty designed by President Lyndon B. Johnson included

A.   the Social Security Act (SSA)

B.   the Works Progress Administration (WPA)

C.   Medicare and Medicaid

D.   the Persian Gulf War

E.   the Iraq War

63. Which of the following explorers discovered Florida in 1513?

A.   Ferdinand Magellan

B.   Hernando de Soto

C.   Amerigo Vespucci

D.   Vasco Balboa

E.   Ponce de León

64. Business monopolies are LEAST likely to be associated with

A.   high prices

B.   fixed prices

C.   free market competition

D.   market domination

E.   reduced business efficiency

65. In the antebellum period, which of the following was most likely dependent on the slave trade for economic survival?

   A.   A Boston shipping merchant
   B.   A plantation owner in Georgia
   C.   A traveling revival minister
   D.   A California fur trader
   E.   A women's suffragist in New York

66. The Iran-Contra affair was a scandal of which presidential administration?

   A.   Ronald Reagan
   B.   Jimmy Carter
   C.   Gerald Ford
   D.   Bill Clinton
   E.   George H. W. Bush

67. Which of the following played a crucial role in establishing détente with the Soviet Union during the Cold War?

   A.   Henry Kissinger
   B.   Ronald Reagan
   C.   George Kennan
   D.   Joseph Stalin
   E.   Joseph McCarthy

68. In the late 1800s, after being granted the right to vote, African Americans were still prevented from voting in practice due to

   A.   the Supreme Court ruling in *Plessy v. Ferguson*
   B.   the Supreme Court ruling in *Brown v. Board of Education*
   C.   Jim Crow laws
   D.   segregation laws
   E.   poll taxes

69. The Puritans migrated to North America primarily because

   A. they were barred from residing in England due to their religion
   B. they wished to escape religious persecution in England
   C. quotas prevented them from migrating to the Netherlands
   D. they wished to escape famine in Ireland
   E. they believed migration was necessary for their economic survival

70. Which of the following individuals is most closely associated with the concept of religious tolerance?

   A. John Calvin
   B. Abigail Williams
   C. Sojourner Truth
   D. Roger Williams
   E. Jonathan Edwards

University College London Digital Collections

71. Which of the following is the subject of the cartoon above?

   A. Communism
   B. Capitalism
   C. Evolution
   D. Abolition
   E. Dollar diplomacy

72. The Indian Removal Act was prompted by which of the following?

    A. The discovery of gold on Cherokee land in Georgia
    B. The suspicion that Shawnee troops were colluding with the British
    C. Internal tensions within the Chickasaw, Choctaw, and Creek tribes
    D. The need to increase revenues from the fur trade in western states
    E. The invention of the steamboat by Robert Fulton

73. Which of the following reflects the foreign policy of the United States during George Washington's presidency?

    A. The United States established an open-door policy with China.
    B. The United States colonized parts of the Caribbean.
    C. The United States engaged in imperialist competition with Europe.
    D. The United States intervened in foreign conflicts in Latin America only.
    E. The United States remained neutral in foreign affairs.

74. The battle of New Orleans was significant in the War of 1812 because it

    A. served to demoralize the U.S. public regarding the war
    B. gave the impression that the United States had won the war
    C. turned the tide of public opinion in favor of the war
    D. represented a decisive victory for British forces
    E. prompted the British to sign a treaty ending the war

75. Former slave Harriet Tubman was best known for her work involving which of the following?

    A. The novel *Uncle Tom's Cabin*
    B. *The Liberator* newspaper
    C. The underground railroad
    D. The women's suffrage movement
    E. The transcendentalist movement

76. "I went to the woods because I wished to live deliberately, to front only the essential facts of life, and see if I could not learn what it had to teach, and not, when I came to die, discover that I had not lived."

The quotation above is most likely excerpted from

    A. John Steinbeck, *The Grapes of Wrath*
    B. Zora Neale Hurston, *Their Eyes Were Watching God*
    C. Nathaniel Hawthorne, *The Scarlet Letter*
    D. Henry David Thoreau, *Walden*
    E. Jacob Riis, *How the Other Half Lives*

77. The historical efforts of Elizabeth Cady Stanton contributed most to

    A. establishing Prohibition in the 1920s
    B. passage of the Nineteenth Amendment
    C. passage of the Equal Rights Amendment to the Constitution
    D. securing the repeal of the Eighteenth Amendment in 1933
    E. the founding of the NAACP in 1910

78. During the colonial period, tobacco was instrumental to which of the following?

    A. Merchants in the port city of Boston, who exported tobacco as a staple crop
    B. Shawnee leader Tecumseh, who used tobacco trades to gain tribal allegiance
    C. Native American tribes, which introduced tobacco to the settlers
    D. The New England colonies, whose economies relied on tobacco sales
    E. Jamestown Colony, which flourished economically due to tobacco sales

79. Which of the following presidents was awarded the 1919 Nobel Peace Prize for his contributions to establishing the League of Nations?

    A. Woodrow Wilson
    B. Calvin Coolidge
    C. William Howard Taft
    D. Warren G. Harding
    E. James Garfield

80. Shays's Rebellion of 1786 and the Whiskey Rebellion of 1794 differed in that only one involved

    A. expressions of protest against British forces
    B. violence on the part of rebel citizens
    C. the use of military force to quell the uprising
    D. suppression by U.S. government forces
    E. widespread public support for the rebels

81. During the late 1800s, which of the following helped inspire the coining of the term Robber Barons?

    A. Andrew Carnegie
    B. Alexander Hamilton
    C. Theodore Roosevelt
    D. George Kennan
    E. Herbert Hoover

82. The work of Jacob Riis in the late 1800s was significant because it

    A. enabled the automation of the manufacturing industry
    B. led to the invention of an improved process for making steel
    C. promoted the use of scientific methods in medical research
    D. exposed crime and corruption in American during the Gilded Age
    E. provided an important justification for corporate monopolies

"The bar is in full swing, and floating rounds of cocktails permeate the garden outside, until the air is alive with chatter and laughter, and casual innuendo and introductions forgotten on the spot, and enthusiastic meetings between women who never knew each other's names. The lights grow brighter as the earth lurches away from the sun, and now the orchestra is playing yellow cocktail music, and the opera of voices pitches a key higher."

83. The time period that the author refers to in the passage above is most likely the

A. World War I era
B. Great Depression
C. Jazz Age
D. World War II era
E. Cold War

84. Each of the following was a factor motivating U.S. imperialism in the early 1900s EXCEPT

A. the election of pro-imperialist presidents
B. the perceived need for a strong navy
C. the sense of moral responsibility to spread civilization
D. the need to expand overseas to obtain raw materials
E. the need to protect U.S. agrarian interests

85. "'A house divided against itself cannot stand.' I believe this government cannot endure, permanently, half slave and half free. I do not expect the Union to be dissolved—I do not expect the house to fall—but I do expect it will cease to be divided. It will become all one thing or all the other."

The statement above was made by

    A.   Jefferson Davis, concerning the Confederate army

    B.   Abraham Lincoln, concerning secession from the Union

    C.   John C. Calhoun, regarding the Kansas-Nebraska Act

    D.   Stephen A. Douglas, regarding the issue of slavery

    E.   Andrew Johnson, regarding the Emancipation Proclamation

86. The Jim Crow laws passed in the 1880s were significant because they

    A.   imposed segregation for blacks and whites

    B.   abolished the institution of slavery

    C.   prohibited discrimination based on race

    D.   reduced economic discrimination against former slaves

    E.   gave black men the right to own property

87. The Treaty of Versailles that ended World War I included which of the following?

    A.   Adherence to Wilson's Fourteen Points

    B.   Repayment by Japan for the damage caused at Pearl Harbor

    C.   Provisions for the establishment of the Yalta Conference

    D.   Provisions for the establishment of the NATO alliance

    E.   A harsh peace for Germany that required war reparations

88. Which of the following was a significant movement focused on African American literature and art in the 1920s?

    A.   The Jacksonian Era

B.   The Big Band Era
C.   The Jazz Age
D.   The Harlem Renaissance
E.   The Prohibition era

Library of Congress

89. The cartoon above illustrates popular reaction to which of the following?

A.   The Missouri Compromise of 1820
B.   The concept of popular sovereignty
C.   The *Dred Scott* decision
D.   The Tariff of 1832
E.   The Compromise of 1850

90. Which of the following authorized the Vietnam War?

A.   The Ground Zero Authorization Act
B.   The Iran-Contra Resolution
C.   The War on Terror Act
D.   The Bay of Pigs Resolution
E.   The Gulf of Tonkin Resolution

91. The muckrakers were best known for which of the following styles of writing?

    A.   Transcendentalism

    B.   Romanticism

    C.   Realism

    D.   Sensationalism

    E.   Historical fiction

92. Economic policies during the administration of Ronald Reagan were characterized by each of the following EXCEPT

    A.   reduced government spending

    B.   lower taxes

    C.   high inflation

    D.   deregulation

    E.   federal control of the money supply

93. Which of the following was a provision written into the Cuban constitution granting the American government the right to intervene in Cuba?

    A.   The Teller Amendment

    B.   The Platt Amendment

    C.   The Open-Door Policy

    D.   The Roosevelt Corollary

    E.   The Taft Amendment

94. The contributions of Wisconsin Senator Robert M. La Follette included each of the following EXCEPT

    A.   opposing antimonopoly legislation

    B.   opposing the League of Nations

    C.   running for president as the Progressive Party candidate

D. advocating for women's rights
E. fighting against corruption in big business

Practice Test 1: Answer Key

1. B	22. A
2. D	23. E
3. E	24. A
4. A	25. E
5. B	26. B
6. C	27. D
7. D	28. D
8. B	29. C
9. C	30. A
10. E	31. E
11. C	32. B
12. A	33. C
13. D	34. C
14. C	35. D
15. E	36. A
16. B	37. B
17. A	38. D
18. E	39. E
19. B	40. C
20. C	41. B
21. D	42. E

43. A	69. B
44. C	70. D
45. E	71. C
46. D	72. A
47. C	73. E
48. A	74. B
49. E	75. C
50. B	76. D
51. D	77. B
52. C	78. E
53. A	79. A
54. E	80. D
55. B	81. A
56. D	82. D
57. E	83. C
58. A	84. E
59. D	85. B
60. A	86. A
61. B	87. E
62. C	88. D
63. E	89. B
64. C	90. E
65. B	91. D
66. A	92. C
67. A	93. B
68. E	94. A

Practice Test 1: Explanations

1. The correct answer is B. The Bill of Rights refers to the first ten amendments to the Constitution. These amendments protect individual rights, including the freedoms of speech, the press, and assembly; the right to bear arms; due process; trial by jury; and protection against cruel and unusual punishment. The Tenth Amendment also protects states' rights: any power not delegated to the federal government nor denied to the states is reserved for the states.

The Electoral College and checks and balances within government were addressed by the Constitutional Convention before the Constitution was ratified. Therefore, D and E are incorrect.

See Part 2 of the U.S. History Review.

2. The correct answer is D. Maine was admitted to the United States as a free state by the Missouri Compromise of 1820. Missouri was admitted as a slave state at this time, so A is incorrect.

See Parts 2 and 3 of the U.S. History Review.

3. The correct answer is E. In capitalist theory, the law of supply and demand dictates that the interplay of supply and demand determines the price of an item. In this view, as the demand for an item increases, the supply of that item decreases and the price of the item increases. Conversely, as the demand for an item decreases, the supply of that item increases and the price of the item decreases. A and B are therefore incorrect.

See Part 1 of the U.S. History Review.

4. The correct answer is A. The Roosevelt Corollary to the Monroe Doctrine was associated with the phrase "Speak softly and carry a big stick," so A is correct.

B is incorrect because it was associated with Herbert Hoover, and D is incorrect because it was associated with China, while the Roosevelt Corollary was associated with Latin America.

See Part 3 of the U.S. History Review.

5. The correct answer is B. This painting by John Gast supports the concept of Manifest Destiny, or the belief that Americans had the God-given right to expand across North America from coast to coast. Manifest Destiny was assisted by inventions such as the expansion of the railroad, which is shown in the painting.

See Part 2 of the U.S. History Review.

6. The correct answer is C. The AFL was primarily active in industrial cities, not farming communities. Under the leadership of Gompers, the AFL promoted cooperation among the craft unions that made up the organization, favored collective bargaining over strikes, and encouraged union members to take an active role in political elections.

See Part 3 of the U.S. History Review.

7. The correct answer is D. The concept of federalism refers to the sharing of power between a central authority (the national government) and the authority of individual units (the states). B and C are incorrect because, although these concepts are part of the U.S. government structure, they do not relate specifically to federalism.

See Part 2 of the U.S. History Review.

8. The correct answer is B. The Public Works Administration (PWA) was a New Deal program that created jobs building roads and housing. A is incorrect because artists and photographers were employed by the Works Progress Administration (WPA). C is incorrect because jobs and electricity were provided by the Tennessee Valley Authority (TVA).

See Part 2 of the U.S. History Review.

9. The correct answer is C. Nat Turner's Rebellion was a violent slave uprising in 1831, prior to the Civil War. Sit-ins, boycotts, picket lines, and marches are all examples of nonviolent protests.

See Part 5 of the U.S. History Review.

10. The correct answer is E. During the colonial period, New England colonies were characterized by economies based on trade. Inhabitants

led stable lives focused on work and religion. Southern colonies relied on large-scale farming supported by an aristocratic plantation culture, so B and D are incorrect. Indentured servitude was prevalent primarily in the South, so C is incorrect.

See Part 1 of the U.S. History Review.

11. The correct answer is C. The Grange movement, which arose to support agrarian interests in the late 1800s, was the precursor to the Populist Party of the 1890s. The Populist Party was also known as the People's Party, so D is incorrect.

See Part 3 of the U.S. History Review.

12. The correct answer is A. Stephen A. Douglas defeated Abraham Lincoln in the Illinois Senate race in 1858. Central to his success was his role in the Lincoln-Douglas debates of 1858, which centered around the issue of slavery. D is incorrect because Douglas did run against Lincoln for president in 1861, but Lincoln won the campaign.

See Part 3 of the U.S. History Review.

13. The correct answer is D. The *Roe v. Wade* decision was significant for women's rights. In this 1973 decision, the U.S. Supreme Court struck down various state laws restricting abortion. The Court argued that the right to privacy granted by a provision of the Fourteenth Amendment includes a woman's right to decide to have an abortion. A is incorrect because the primacy of federal power was established in *McCulloch v. Maryland* (1819). B is incorrect because *Brown v. Board of Education* (1954) established that separate educational facilities for blacks were inherently unequal. C is incorrect because the doctrine of "separate but equal" was established by *Plessy v. Ferguson*.

See Part 5 of the U.S. History Review.

14. The correct answer is C. Two prominent factors contributed to the lengthening of the Civil War. First, neither the Union nor the Confederate armies had a well-designed strategy going into the war. As a result, the war dragged on as each side repeatedly altered its course. In addition,

this war was the first to employ trench warfare, which made the war last longer and increased casualties on both sides. Soldiers in trenches were able to have sufficient protection from enemy fire while at the same time having the ability to hit oncoming soldiers in an advance. So trench warfare made large-scale infantry advances ineffective.

See Part 3 of the U.S. History Review.

15. The correct answer is E. In 1773, colonists rebelled to protest against the Townshend Acts of 1767 that levied taxes on multiple luxury goods, including sugar, glass, paint, and tea. Passage of the tea tax prompted an uprising known as the Boston Tea Party, during which rebels dumped shiploads of tea into Boston Harbor. B is incorrect because, while passage of the Townshend Acts led to the Boston Massacre, the Boston Massacre itself did not prompt the Boston Tea Party.

See Part 1 of the U.S. History Review.

16. The correct answer is B. The Twenty-First Amendment was significant because it repealed Prohibition. From 1920 to 1933, the Eighteenth Amendment to the Constitution prohibited the manufacture and sale of alcoholic beverages in the United States. This period, known as Prohibition, reduced the total amount of liquor consumed in the country, but it also fueled illegal liquor sales through underground clubs known as speakeasies and gave rise to organized crime. Prohibition ended in 1933, when the Twenty-First Amendment repealed the Eighteenth Amendment.

See Part 3 of the U.S. History Review.

17. The correct answer is A. Government ownership of all property is a tenet of Communism. In Soviet Communism, for instance, the Communist Party maintained ownership of all property and business. The book *Wealth of Nations*, published in 1776 by British economist Adam Smith, supported the concepts of the economic philosophy of capitalism. A capitalist economy operates according to the law of supply and demand, so B and C are incorrect. In *Wealth of Nations*, Smith argues

that the "invisible hand" of market forces can have a profound impact on economic progress, so E is incorrect. Economists after Smith used the French term *laissez-faire* to refer to the hands-off capitalist policy of allowing market forces to encourage economic efficiency, so D is also incorrect.

See Parts 1 and 5 of the U.S. History Review.

18. The correct answer is E. James Garfield was one of four U.S. presidents to be assassinated. The other three presidents are Abraham Lincoln, William McKinley, and John F. Kennedy. D is incorrect because Reconstruction ended before Garfield's term, which was in 1881. B and C are incorrect because Prohibition and the League of Nations occurred after Garfield's term.

See Leadership section, Big Ideas in U.S. History.

19. The correct answer is B. The Scopes trial of 1925 reflected the increasing controversy in the country between creationism, or the theory that humans were created by God, and evolutionism—Charles Darwin's philosophy that humans evolved over time. William Jennings Bryan, an influential politician and attorney, pressed for schools to make it unlawful to teach evolution. When the state of Tennessee passed such a law, the American Civil Liberties Union (ACLU) issued a pledge to support any teacher who would challenge the legislation with a legal case. A teacher named John Scopes went to trial.

See Part 4 of the U.S. History Review.

20. The correct answer is C. George Washington's administration was characterized by adherence to Federalist Party policies as proposed by Alexander Hamilton. These included a strong central government, emphasis on a loose constructionist interpretation of the Constitution, and the implementation of protective tariffs to bolster manufacturing. So A, B, and E are incorrect.

See Part 2 of the U.S. History Review.

21. The correct answer is D. The time period to which the author refers in the passage was the Great Depression, the most widespread, serious,

and longest-lasting economic crisis of the twentieth century. This passage is excerpted from John Steinbeck's Depression-era novel *The Grapes of Wrath*, published in 1939. A, B, and C are incorrect because these occurred during a more uplifting period in U.S. history (the 1920s) that preceded the Depression.

See Part 4 of the U.S. History Review.

22. The correct answer is A. The cartoon represents the League of Nations as a rabbit staring intently at a snake that represents the international community. This depiction portrays the League of Nations as doomed from the start; the rabbit does not stand a chance against the snake.

See Part 4 of the U.S. History Review.

23. The correct answer is E. Large conglomerates such as U.S. Steel were developed during the Gilded Age, in the late 1800s. Big businesses flourished during this period because of the great deal of wealth accumulated, often through unscrupulous means.

See Part 3 of the U.S. History Review.

24. The correct answer is A. This passage from *The Jungle* was written by muckraker Upton Sinclair and published in 1904. It describes the evils of big business, which Sinclair refers to as "organized and predatory Greed." B and D are incorrect because these time periods predated the era of big business. C and E are incorrect because these time periods came after the era described in the passage.

See Part 3 of the U.S. History Review.

25. The correct answer is E. Anne Hutchinson was banished from the Massachusetts Bay Colony in 1638 because she challenged certain aspects of Puritan religious ideology. In particular, her views were perceived to threaten the leadership of colony founder John Winthrop. Hutchinson was tried for heresy and banished from the colony. She eventually settled in Rhode Island with her followers.

See Part 1 of the U.S. History Review.

26. The correct answer is B. The *Liberator* newspaper was published by William Lloyd Garrison before the Civil War to spread his abolitionist message. Garrison called for the immediate emancipation of all slaves. A, D, and E are incorrect because Garrison's work occurred before the Civil War, prior to the implementation of poll taxes, segregation by race, and Jim Crow laws.

See Part 3 of the U.S. History Review.

27. The correct answer is D. The statement was excerpted from a speech given by George H. W. Bush to a joint session of Congress in September 1990. Bush was responsible for leading the nation through the Persian Gulf War in 1991.

See Part 5 of the U.S. History Review.

28. The correct answer is D. The passage was excerpted from the slave narrative of Frederick Douglass, published in 1845. As a former slave, Douglass was likely to have supported the Emancipation Proclamation, which freed certain slaves during the Civil War; passage of the Thirteenth Amendment abolishing all slavery; and passage of the Fourteenth Amendment granting citizenship to blacks. He was not likely to have supported the cause of the proslavery Confederacy, which seceded from the Union.

See Part 3 of the U.S. History Review.

29. The correct answer is C. Jane Addams is best known for her work in founding Hull House. Well-known members of the transcendentalist movement include authors Nathaniel Hawthorne, Ralph Waldo Emerson, and Henry David Thoreau.

See Part 2 of the U.S. History Review.

30. The correct answer is A. The election of Andrew Jackson (1829–1837) marked the beginning of what was known as the Second Party System. In this system, two new political parties arose: the Democratic Party, headed by Jackson, and the Whig Party, led by Henry Clay. The

Democratic Party arose from Thomas Jefferson's Democratic-Republican Party—of which Jackson had been a member—so B and C are incorrect.

See Part 2 of the U.S. History Review.

31. The correct answer is E. Bill Clinton went through impeachment proceedings for his role in a scandal involving White House intern Monica Lewinsky. Clinton was ultimately acquitted. A is incorrect; Richard Nixon resigned before being impeached. B, C, and D are incorrect. Gerald Ford, George H. W. Bush, and Barack Obama were not impeached.

See Part 5 of the U.S. History Review.

32. The correct answer is B. The energy crisis of 1973 occurred when Arab nations cut off oil supplies to nations that had supported Israel during the Arab-Israeli War. This war, which occurred in October 1973, prompted oil-rich Arab nations to retaliate by curtailing oil supplies to the United States and other pro-Israel countries. By 1972 the United States had increased its dependence on foreign oil, and the oil shortage created an energy crisis. During the energy crisis, many Arab nations controlled oil supplies rather than running short of them, so A is incorrect. C is incorrect as well, since the energy crisis was caused by a shortage of oil, not coal.

See Part 5 of the U.S. History Review.

33. The correct answer is C. The battle of Yorktown in 1781 was significant because it was the last major battle of the American Revolution. It resulted in a decisive victory for American and French troops over British general Charles Cornwallis. B and D are incorrect because the French joined the war in support of the American forces after the battle of Saratoga (1777), and Spain joined as France's ally at that time.

See Part 1 of the U.S. History Review.

34. The correct answer is C. The statement was made by President Richard M. Nixon as he announced his resignation from office in 1974. Nixon resigned to avoid impeachment for his role in the Watergate scandal. A is incorrect because, although Bill Clinton was impeached for his role

in a scandal involving White House intern Monica Lewinsky, Clinton did not resign from office and was eventually acquitted.

See Part 5 of the U.S. History Review.

35. The correct answer is D. Lincoln's plan for Reconstruction was characterized by leniency for the South compared to Congress' plan. Congress wanted a stricter program than that proposed by Lincoln, so progress was deadlocked.

See Part 3 of the U.S. History Review.

36. The correct answer is A. Blacks were granted the right to vote by the Fifteenth Amendment, passed in 1870 during Reconstruction. The Thirteenth Amendment (1865) abolished slavery, so D is incorrect. The Fourteenth Amendment, passed in 1866, declared that blacks were citizens and guaranteed due process and equal protection under the law, so B is incorrect. C and E are incorrect because the Seventeenth and Nineteenth Amendments were passed after Reconstruction.

See Part 3 of the U.S. History Review.

37. The correct answer is B. George Washington and John Adams held the office of president during the Federalist period. Both Washington and Adams were members of the Federalist Party, as was Alexander Hamilton, who did not hold presidential office. Thomas Jefferson represented the Democratic-Republican Party, as did James Madison (1809–1817), James Monroe (1817–1825), and John Quincy Adams (1825–1829).

See Part 2 of the U.S. History Review.

38. The correct answer is D. Former slave Sojourner Truth was best known for her "Ain't I a Woman?" speech, given at the Ohio Women's Rights Convention in 1854. A and C are incorrect; although Harriet Jacobs and Harriet Tubman were both former slaves, they did not give the speech. Harriet Jacobs was best known for her slave narrative, and Harriet Tubman assisted runaway slaves on the underground railroad.

See Part 2 of the U.S. History Review.

39. The correct answer is E. Nat Turner's revolt in 1831 was one incident that led to the Civil War. This slave rebellion occurred in Virginia and was led by a slave, Nat Turner. Approximately sixty white persons were killed in the rebellion, causing great tension in the South. Many innocent slaves were injured or killed as part of the public reaction, and fifty-six accused participants were formally executed by the state. A is incorrect because it was during the Boston Massacre (1770) that British guards fired into a crowd, hitting eleven men. B is incorrect because indentured servitude fell out of favor with plantation owners after Bacon's Rebellion of 1676.

See Part 3 of the U.S. History Review.

40. The correct answer is C. In the late 1800s, many believed in the notion of a moral responsibility to spread civilization to other parts of the world. *Our Country*, an ideological work by minister Josiah Strong, helped to promote the idea of an ethical imperative for colonization.

See Part 3 of the U.S. History Review.

41. The correct answer is B. The Articles of the Confederation established a provisional government for the United States during the American Revolution. The powers of the government were significantly limited, however, so D is incorrect. A, C, and E are incorrect because the Articles of Confederation gave Congress no ability to regulate foreign trade, levy taxes, or regulate interstate commerce.

See Part 2 of the U.S. History Review.

42. The correct answer is E. John Winthrop was the founder of the Massachusetts Bay Colony, established in 1630. He saw the settlement as a "city on a hill" that would abide by righteous precepts and serve as a model for others. D is incorrect because Winthrop's vision concerned Massachusetts Bay Colony, not Plymouth Colony. B is incorrect because Winthrop was a Puritan leader whose religious philosophy called for improvement or "purification" of the Protestant Church, not separation from it.

See Part 1 of the U.S. History Review.

43. The correct answer is A. Publication of Alfred T. Mahan's book *The Influence of Sea Power upon History* was significant because it advocated a strong navy and motivated U.S. imperialism. At the turn of the twentieth century, imperialism was expanded in part because Americans believed there was a need for a strong navy to maintain its economic prowess and protect its shipping lanes. Mahan's book was very influential in spreading this notion.

See Part 3 of the U.S. History Review.

44. The correct answer is C. The quotation most clearly expresses the views of Tecumseh, a Shawnee tribal leader. Together with his brother, known as The Prophet, Tecumseh attempted to unite Native American tribes. Fearful that Tecumseh was planning to collaborate with the British against the United States in the War of 1812, U.S. troops attacked the Shawnees in the battle of Tippecanoe in 1811. Tecumseh did later collaborate with the British in the War of 1812.

See Part 3 of the U.S. History Review.

45. The correct answer is E. Advocates of Prohibition argued that alcohol consumption should be banned entirely. Unlike members of the Temperance movement, Prohibition supporters did not urge a reduction in alcohol consumption, but rather the prohibition of it. Prohibition was legalized from 1920 to 1933, when the Eighteenth Amendment to the Constitution prohibited the manufacture and sale of alcoholic beverages in the United States.

See Part 3 of the U.S. History Review.

46. The correct answer is D. The graphs show that immigration from southeastern Europe surged compared to immigration from southeastern Europe over the previous twenty-year period. The light gray portions of the graphs represent immigration from southeastern Europe, while the darker gray portions of the graphs represent immigration from northwestern Europe. In the years between 1881 and 1890, the light gray portion of the graph is much smaller than the dark gray portion. In

the years between 1901 and 1910, by contrast, the light gray portion of the graph is much larger than the dark gray portion. C is incorrect because it represents the opposite of what is shown in the graphs.

See Part 3 of the U.S. History Review.

47. The correct answer is C. During the Federalist period, Thomas Jefferson was opposed to the imposition of protective tariffs. A, B, and D are therefore incorrect. E is incorrect because Jefferson disagreed with Hamilton's position regarding the role of the tariffs. Jefferson also opposed other elements of Federalist policies put forth by Hamilton, including a strong central government and the creation of a national bank.

See Part 2 of the U.S. History Review.

48. The correct answer is A. Unlike Jefferson's Democratic-Republican Party, which was pro-aristocracy, Jackson's Democratic Party supported universal suffrage for white men—the belief that all white men should have voting rights, not just landowners. Individual rights in general and protection from self-incrimination in particular were embodied in the Bill of Rights and the Fifth Amendment respectively, both of which were implemented when the Constitution was established.

See Part 2 of the U.S. History Review.

49. The correct answer is E. The chart shows the growth of religious denominations from 1780 to 1860. In particular, the growth of religions is strong from 1820 to 1860. This growth was influenced by the Second Great Awakening, a religious revival that occurred during the mid-1800s. This revival sparked renewed interest in salvation, and many religions increased in membership. A is incorrect because, although the transcendentalist movement was popular in the mid-1800s, it did not influence the growth of religions.

See Part 2 of the U.S. History Review.

50. The correct answer is B. The passage is excerpted from Martin Luther King Jr.'s "Letter from a Birmingham Jail," written in 1963. King

was a minister and activist whose efforts profoundly influenced the civil rights gains of the 1950s and 60s.

See Part 5 of the U.S. History Review.

51. The correct answer is D. The quoted passage is taken from the Declaration of Independence.

See Part 1 of the U.S. History Review.

52. The correct answer is C. The dot-com boom of the 1990s involved technology investments, particularly Internet companies. It was called the dot-com boom because the companies involved were typically named with the Internet extension "dot-com," such as "CompanyX.com."

See Part 5 of the U.S. History Review.

53. The correct answer is A. The Treaty of Paris brought an end to the Spanish-American War. Guam, Puerto Rico, and the Philippines came under U.S. control as a result of the treaty. The United States also annexed **Hawaii** at this time. B is incorrect because the Treaty of Versailles ended World War I. The War of 1812 was concluded by the Treaty of Ghent in 1814, so E is incorrect. The Cold War did not end with a formal treaty, so C is incorrect.

See Part 3 of the U.S. History Review.

54. The correct answer is E. Roger Williams was a minister who was banished from the Massachusetts Bay Colony because he advocated the separation of church and state. He founded the Rhode Island Colony based on religious tolerance. C is incorrect because John Winthrop was the leader of Massachusetts Bay Colony at the time and was part of the government that banished Williams.

See Part 1 of the U.S. History Review.

55. The correct answer is B. The construction of the Panama Canal from 1904 to 1914 established a connection between the Atlantic and Pacific waterways. C is incorrect because this response describes the transcontinental railroad.

See Part 3 of the U.S. History Review.

56. The correct answer is D. The concept of asceticism refers to the philosophy of a rigid way of life devoid of worldly pleasures. This way of life was practiced by the Puritans, who believed that those who labored diligently, amassed riches, and lived very frugally were serving the glory of God.

See Part 1 of the U.S. History Review.

57. The correct answer is E. The statement was made by President Ronald Reagan in 1987 and is known as the "Speech at the Brandenburg Gate," just before the end of the Cold War. Reagan was addressing Soviet leader Mikhail Gorbachev, who was ultimately responsible for leading the Soviet Union to end the Cold War in 1989. A, B, C, and D are incorrect because these individuals served before the term of Gorbachev.

See Part 5 of the U.S. History Review.

58. The correct answer is A. The diplomatic efforts of George Kennan were significant because they helped establish the U.S. policy of containment during the Cold War. Kennan was stationed in Moscow as a diplomat at the onset of the Cold War in 1946. He shared his perspective on Soviet intentions in a dispatch called the Long Telegram. Kennan argued that the Soviets were inherently expansionist and would always be at war with capitalism. Kennan's views encouraged the United States to develop a foreign policy designed to "contain" the spread of Communism. C is incorrect because Kennan's efforts assisted the United States, not the Soviet Union.

See Part 5 of the U.S. History Review.

59. The correct answer is D. The Civil War was inspired in part by the creation of the Confederate States of America. As tensions over slavery mounted, the Southern states seceded from the Union in 1860 and 1861. They declared themselves the Confederate States of America, and a temporary government was set up under the leadership of Jefferson Davis. The first military attack of the war was made by the Confederate army at Fort Sumter in April 1861. C and E are incorrect because these events were associated with the American Revolutionary War.

See Part 3 of the U.S. History Review.

60. The correct answer is A. The quotation is from the book *The Feminine Mystique*, by feminist researcher and activist Betty Friedan. B is incorrect because Lucretia Mott was a suffragist and was particularly active in the Civil War period. D and E are incorrect because both Geraldine Ferraro and Hillary Rodham Clinton were active in politics and ran for office. Ferraro was the first female candidate for vice president, and Clinton was the first female presidential candidate. Both Ferraro and Clinton were unsuccessful in their vice presidential and presidential campaigns, respectively. However, Clinton held the positions of Senator, representing New York, and secretary of state.

See Part 5 of the U.S. History Review.

61. The correct answer is B. The table shows that the number of bales of cotton produced in the Confederate States decreased significantly from 1860 to 1864. This is the only topic for which comparison data are provided in 1860 and in 1864, so A, C, D, and E are not supported by the data in the table.

For more on the Civil War period, see Part 3 of the U.S. History Review.

62. The correct answer is C. The War on Poverty was a series of domestic programs launched by President Lyndon B. Johnson. Among the programs were Head Start, Vista, the Job Corps, Medicare, and Medicaid. A and B are incorrect because the SSA and WPA were passed during the New Deal period in response to the Great Depression. E is incorrect because the Iraq War was part of the War on Terror launched by the Bush administration in 2003.

See Part 5 of the U.S. History Review.

63. The correct answer is E. Ponce de León was the explorer who discovered Florida in 1513. Ferdinand Magellan was the first to circumnavigate the globe in 1519, so A is incorrect. Hernando de Soto discovered the Mississippi River in 1539, so B is incorrect. Amerigo Vespucci explored South America under Spanish sponsorship in 1499, so C is

incorrect. Finally, Vasco Balboa discovered the Pacific Ocean in 1513, so D is incorrect as well.

See Part 1 of the U.S. History Review.

64. The correct answer is C. Monopolies are companies that grow so large that they dominate a market and hedge out their competitors. Because the U.S. economy is based on the capitalist principle of free market competition, monopolies present a threat to business efficiency and can hurt consumers as well. Since monopolies are the only companies selling a particular good or service, they have the freedom to set prices as they choose; prices are often high under monopolies.

See Part 3 of the U.S. History Review.

65. The correct answer is B. In the antebellum period, a Georgia plantation owner would most likely have been dependent on the slave trade for economic survival. A is incorrect because Northern economies did not rely on the slave trade. E is incorrect because although the mid-Atlantic states relied on a mix of industry and agriculture, plantations in the South were typically run using slave labor.

See Parts 2 and 3 of the U.S. History Review.

66. The correct answer is A. The Iran-Contra affair was a scandal during the Reagan administration. The cover-up concealed the use of funds for military aid that had not been authorized by Congress. The United States sold arms to the Iranians and used some proceeds from the sale to fund military operations of anti-Communist Contra forces in Central America. In exchange for the arms sale, the Iranians used their influence with Lebanon to secure the release of several U.S. hostages. Iran was under an arms embargo at the time, and the news of secret operations conducted without congressional approval met with a great uproar and controversy. The ensuing investigation did not find conclusive evidence regarding Reagan's knowledge of the operation.

See Part 5 of the U.S. History Review.

67. The correct answer is A. Henry Kissinger was secretary of state under

Richard Nixon and played a crucial role in establishing détente with the Soviet Union during the Cold War. Détente was a period during the 1970s in which U.S. relations with the Soviet Union improved. Kissinger was instrumental in carrying out this policy under Nixon's leadership. B is incorrect because Ronald Reagan was president at the end of the Cold War in the 1980s, not during détente. D is incorrect because Joseph Stalin was the Soviet leader at the onset of the Cold War. E is incorrect because Senator Joseph McCarthy was decidedly anti-Communist and was involved in domestic attacks against alleged Communist sympathizers, not foreign policy.

See Part 5 of the U.S. History Review.

68. The correct answer is E. The passage of the Fifteenth Amendment granted blacks the right to vote. In practice, however, black citizens were prevented from voting due to certain obstacles, such as poll taxes. Poll taxes required voters to pay a fee; individuals who did not pay the tax were not permitted to vote, thus blocking African Americans from voting despite the amendment. D is incorrect because segregation laws dealt with keeping whites and African Americans separate in public facilities. Segregation laws were also known as Jim Crow laws, so C is incorrect. *Plessy v. Ferguson* declared segregation laws constitutional; school segregation ended due to the decision in *Brown v. Board of Education*.

See Part 3 of the U.S. History Review.

69. The correct answer is B. The Puritans migrated to North America primarily because they wished to escape religious persecution in England. The Puritans migrated from England, so D is incorrect. Escape from religious persecution was a primary motive for Puritan migration, so E is correct.

See Part 1 of the U.S. History Review.

70. The correct answer is D. Roger Williams was closely associated with the concept of religious tolerance. Originally a member of the Massachusetts

Bay Colony, Williams was a minister who advocated the separation of church and state. He was banished and later founded the Rhode Island Colony based on religious tolerance.

See Part 1 of the U.S. History Review.

71. The correct answer is C. The cartoon depicts the head of scientist Charles Darwin on the body of a monkey. Darwin's theory supported the notion of scientific evolution and was hotly debated in the late 1800s.

See Part 3 of the U.S. History Review.

72. The correct answer is A. The Indian Removal Act of 1830 was prompted by the discovery of gold on Cherokee land in Georgia. It led to the large-scale resettlement of Native Americans in Oklahoma. B is incorrect because the battle of Tippecanoe resulted from the suspicion that Shawnee troops were colluding with the British. This battle occurred years before the Indian Removal Act, just prior to the War of 1812.

See Part 2 of the U.S. History Review.

73. The correct answer is E. During the George Washington's presidency, the United States remained neutral in foreign affairs. Washington believed that neutrality was the most prudent course of action for the new nation. In 1793, he issued a Proclamation of Neutrality in response to the question of whether the United States should assist France in its conflict with Britain during the time of the French Revolutionary Wars.

See Part 2 of the U.S. History Review.

74. The correct answer is B. In the War of 1812, the battle of New Orleans was significant because it gave the false impression that the United States had won the war. In actuality, the war ended in a stalemate. The battle of New Orleans was fought after the treaty had officially ended the war, though U.S. and British forces did not realize this at the time. When the Treaty of Ghent was signed in 1814, its intent was to maintain the status quo with Britain. Before news of the treaty signing had reached the United States, however, the battle of New Orleans was won unexpectedly by troops commanded by Andrew Jackson. This served to

boost morale for the United States and inspired a surge of nationalism, so A is incorrect. D is incorrect because the battle of New Orleans was won by American troops. E is incorrect because the Treaty of Ghent had been signed before the battle of New Orleans ended.

See Part 2 of the U.S. History Review.

75. The correct answer is C. Former slave Harriet Tubman was best known for her work with the underground railroad during the antebellum era. Through the underground railroad, Tubman helped runaway slaves escape from the South and obtain their freedom. A is incorrect; *Uncle Tom's Cabin* was published by abolitionist Harriet Beecher Stowe. B is incorrect because the *Liberator* newspaper was published by abolitionist William Lloyd Garrison.

See Part 3 of the U.S. History Review.

76. The correct answer is D. The quotation is excerpted from the book *Walden*, published in 1854 by Henry David Thoreau. In the book, Thoreau details his two-year commitment to simple living in a remote location known as Walden Pond.

See Part 2 of the U.S. History Review.

77. The correct answer is B. Stanton was a prominent advocate for women's suffrage. Her historical efforts contributed most to passage of the Nineteenth Amendment to the Constitution, which gave women the right to vote. C is incorrect because the Equal Rights Amendment to the Constitution was never ratified.

See Part 2 of the U.S. History Review.

78. The correct answer is E. During the colonial period, tobacco was instrumental to Jamestown Colony, which flourished economically due to tobacco sales. Tobacco was introduced to Jamestown by a settler named John Rolfe; before the introduction of the crop, Jamestown suffered economically due to harsh conditions and the inexperience of the settlers.

See Part 1 of the U.S. History Review.

79. The correct answer is A. After World War I, Wilson pushed to form the League of Nations in the hope of preventing such large-scale devastation in the future. A precursor to the United Nations, the League of Nations was the first international organization formed for the purpose of maintaining world peace. It was established in 1920 after the end of the war. At its height, from September 1934 to February 1935, it had fifty-eight members, but the United States was not among them. Although Wilson received the 1919 Nobel Peace Prize for his efforts to establish the League of Nations, he was unable to convince the U.S. Senate to ratify its covenants. This failure of ratification was primarily due to Republican opposition in the U.S. Senate.

See Part 4 of the U.S. History Review.

80. The correct answer is D. Shays's Rebellion of 1786 and the Whiskey Rebellion of 1794 differed in that only one involved suppression by U.S. government forces. Both incidents involved the use of military force to quell the uprising, so C is incorrect. However, U.S. government forces were only used to suppress the Whiskey Rebellion, not Shays's Rebellion. Shays's Rebellion occurred under the government of the Articles of Confederation, which was ineffective in responding to the incident; this uprising was quelled by an army paid for by Boston merchants.

See Part 2 of the U.S. History Review.

81. The correct answer is A. During the late 1800s, the name robber barons was given to American businessmen and financiers who amassed wealth by unethical practices. Well-known robber barons included Andrew Carnegie, John D. Rockefeller, Cornelius Vanderbilt, and J. P. Morgan. Many robber barons exploited workers and engaged in questionable stock-market tactics. A is incorrect because Alexander Hamilton's participation in government occurred during the late 1700s, when the government was first established. George Kennan was a diplomat during the Cold War, and Herbert Hoover was president of the United States during the Depression. Theodore Roosevelt was president from 1901 to 1909.

See Part 3 of the U.S. History Review.

82. The correct answer is D. Jacob Riis was a well-known muckraker who wrote the book *How the Other Half Lives*. His work, like that of other muckrakers, was significant because it exposed crime and corruption in American during the Gilded Age. A, B, and C are incorrect because Riis was a writer, not an inventor.

See Part 3 of the U.S. History Review.

83. The correct answer is C. The passage is excerpted from a 1925 book called *The Great Gatsby*, published by F. Scott Fitzgerald. The description of the music from the period sounds most like the Jazz Age, so C is correct.

See Part 4 of the U.S. History Review.

84. The correct answer is E. Though farmers did press for reform in the late 1800s, this was not one of the main factors motivating U.S. imperialism at the turn of the century. Imperialism in the early 1900s was motivated by the election of pro-imperialist presidents such as McKinley, the perceived need for a strong navy, the sense of moral responsibility to spread civilization, and the need to expand overseas to obtain raw materials and new markets for U.S. exports.

See Part 3 of the U.S. History Review.

85. The correct answer is B. The "house divided" speech was an address by Abraham Lincoln on June 16, 1858, in Springfield, Illinois, upon accepting the Illinois Republican Party's nomination as that state's U.S. senator. E is incorrect because secession from the Union occurred prior to the Emancipation Proclamation.

See Part 3 of the U.S. History Review.

86. The correct answer is A. Jim Crow laws were passed in the 1880s to impose segregation for blacks and whites or to prevent blacks from having access to certain public facilities. B is incorrect because slavery was abolished by the Thirteenth Amendment to the Constitution. C and D are incorrect because Jim Crow encouraged discrimination.

See Part 3 of the U.S. History Review.

87. The correct answer is E. The Treaty of Versailles imposed a harsh peace for Germany that required war reparations. France demanded war reparations from Germany and refused to support a more lenient treaty. Wilson's Fourteen Points were essentially abandoned in the final treaty, which created difficult economic conditions for Germany that ultimately led to the emergence of the Nazi regime. A is incorrect because Wilson's Fourteen Points were not included in the treaty. B is incorrect because the bombing of Pearl Harbor occurred in World War II. C is incorrect because the Yalta Conference was held at the end of World War II.

See Part 4 of the U.S. History Review.

88. The correct answer is D. The Harlem Renaissance was a cultural movement centered in New York City's Harlem neighborhood and spanning the 1920s and 1930s. The movement was characterized by a surge in literature, art, and music created by African Americans, as well as a new sense of racial pride. The Harlem Renaissance also influenced a group of black writers who lived in Paris but were originally from French-speaking African and Caribbean colonies. Notable figures of the Harlem Renaissance included authors Langston Hughes, James Weldon Johnson, Zora Neale Hurston (Their *Eyes Were Watching God*), and Claude McKay.

See Part 4 of the U.S. History Review.

89. The correct answer is B. The cartoon illustrates popular reaction to concept of popular sovereignty, which allowed the question of slavery to be determined by popular vote.

See Part 3 of the U.S. History Review.

90. The correct answer is E. The Gulf of Tonkin Resolution, passed under Lyndon B. Johnson in 1964, authorized the Vietnam War. This resolution was controversial because it allowed the president to commit troops without a formal declaration of war.

See Part 5 of the U.S. History Review.

91. The correct answer is D. At the turn of the twentieth century, muckrakers exposed crime and corruption in American industry and politics. Muckrakers used a writing style known as sensationalism, designed to arouse people's emotions. Famous muckrakers of the period include Ida Wells, Upton Sinclair, and Jacob Riis.

See Part 3 of the U.S. History Review.

92. The correct answer is C. Economic policies during the Reagan administration were characterized by lower taxes, less government spending, fewer governmental regulations (deregulation), and low inflation achieved through federal control of the money supply.

See Part 5 of the U.S. History Review.

93. The correct answer is B. The Platt Amendment was a provision written into the Cuban constitution granting the American government the right to intervene in Cuba. C is incorrect because the Open-Door Policy (1899) concerned trade relations in China. D is incorrect because the Roosevelt Corollary to the Monroe Doctrine (1904) occurred after the establishment of the Cuban constitution. It concerned U.S. intervention in Latin America as a whole.

See Part 3 of the U.S. History Review.

94. The correct answer is A. La Follette was a staunch supporter of anti-monopoly legislation. He also founded the Progressive Party and ran for president as the Progressive Party candidate in 1924, so C is incorrect. He supported women's rights and fought against corruption in big business and government, so D and E are incorrect.

See Part 3 of the U.S. History Review.

This book contains two practice tests. Visit mymaxscore.com to download your free third practice test with answers and explanations.

Practice Test 2

<u>Directions:</u> Choose the answer choice that best answers the question or incomplete statement below.

1. Newfoundland was first discovered by

    A. Portuguese explorer Vasco da Gama in 1498
    B. Norse explorer Leif Ericsson around 1000
    C. Spanish explorer Christopher Columbus in 1492
    D. English explorer John Cabot in 1497
    E. Portuguese explorer Ferdinand Magellan in 1519

2. The Marshall Plan allowed for the recovery of

    A. the United States after World War I
    B. Germany after World War I
    C. the United States after World War II
    D. Europe after World War II
    E. the Soviet Union after the Cold War

3. Which of the following helped to established naval superiority as a motivation behind U.S. imperialist expansion?

    A.   Robert M. La Follette
    B.   Adam Smith
    C.   Alfred T. Mahan
    D.   Charles Darwin
    E.   Josiah Strong

4. Each of the following was a robber baron of the Gilded Age EXCEPT

    A.   Andrew Carnegie
    B.   J. P. Morgan
    C.   Cornelius Vanderbilt
    D.   John D. Rockefeller
    E.   H. L. Mencken

5. What was the name given to individuals who gained passage to North America by agreeing to work on Southern plantations in exchange for their freedom at the end of the defined work period?

    A.   Indentured servants
    B.   Pilgrims
    C.   Puritans
    D.   Slaves
    E.   *Mayflower* passengers

6. The Montgomery bus boycott of 1956 led to which of the following?

    A.   The arrest and trial of Montgomery seamstress Rosa Parks
    B.   National attention for civil rights activist Dr. Martin Luther King Jr.
    C.   Overturning of the Supreme Court decision in *Brown v. Board of Education*

D. The Supreme Court declaration that forced integration was unconstitutional

E. Overturning of the Supreme Court decision in *Marbury v. Madison*

7. The Mexican War was triggered by which of the following?

A. A U.S. alliance with France

B. U.S. annexation of Texas

C. U.S. annexation of Hawaii

D. U.S. support of Cuba

E. U.S. intervention in Puerto Rico

8. During the American Revolutionary War, the battle of Saratoga was significant because it

A. was the last major conflict of the war

B. was the conflict in which the first shots were fired in the war

C. represented a sound victory for the British

D. prompted the French to join the war in support of the United States

E. prompted the surrender of British General Cornwallis

9. President Franklin D. Roosevelt's New Deal programs were significant because

A. they helped the United States recover from the Great Depression

B. they provided economic repair for Europe after World War II

C. they provided for the creation of an international justice tribunal

D. they continued economic policies initiated under Herbert Hoover

E. they provided the rationale for ratification of the League of Nations

10. Harry Truman was responsible for which of the following?

   A.   Declaring war against Japan after the bombing of Pearl Harbor
   B.   Passage of the Gulf of Tonkin Resolution regarding Vietnam
   C.   Authorizing use of atomic bombs to end World War II
   D.   Entering World War II to support the allies against Germany
   E.   Ordering an invasion of mainland Japan in 1945

11. The War of 1812 resulted in a permanent loss of political power for

   A.   the Democratic-Republican Party
   B.   Henry Clay
   C.   Andrew Jackson
   D.   the Democratic Party
   E.   the Federalist Party

12. The Neutrality Act of 1794 was issued in response to the question of whether the United States should assist

   A.   Latin America in preventing colonization by the Spanish
   B.   France against Britain during the time of the French Revolutionary Wars
   C.   China in establishing free trade with European nations
   D.   Cuba in its attempts to free itself from Spanish imperialist rule
   E.   Russia against Japan during the Russo-Japanese War

13. During Reconstruction in the 1860s, many former slaves continued to live at a subsistence level through

   A.   carpetbagger arrangements
   B.   copperhead agreements
   C.   indentured servitude
   D.   sharecropping
   E.   scalawag alliances

14. Which of the following is an accurate statement about the Equal Rights Amendment?

    A.   It was never ratified by Congress.

    B.   It was introduced in 1972.

    C.   It prohibited discrimination based on race.

    D.   It was passed as the Twenty-Eighth Amendment.

    E.   It passed only one chamber of Congress.

15. Which of the following issues was a hallmark of John F. Kennedy's presidency?

    A.   Worsening economic inflation and recession

    B.   Cessation of the U.S. space program

    C.   Easing of tensions with the Soviet Union

    D.   Normalization of relations with Cuba

    E.   Advances in civil rights

16. The Fugitive Slave Law, passed as part of the Compromise of 1850, became significant for which of the following reasons?

    A.   It led to the emancipation of many Southern slaves.

    B.   It was overturned by the Kansas-Nebraska Act of 1854.

    C.   It increased North-South tensions leading up to the Civil War.

    D.   It outlawed the possibility of capture for runaway slaves.

    E.   It prompted South Carolina to secede from the Union.

17. The Treaty of Paris established

    A.   an end to the Nazi dictatorship

    B.   war reparations for Germany after World War I

    C.   a provisional government for the United States

    D.   the United States of America as an independent nation

    E.   a truce between Britain and the United States in the War of 1812

18. Booker T. Washington advocated

    A.   accommodating the Jim Crow segregation laws

    B.   organization of the March on Washington in 1963

    C.   nonviolent civil disobedience in the Montgomery bus boycott

    D.   staunchly opposing the Jim Crow segregation laws

    E.   resistance to oppression "by any means necessary"

19. Each of the following was established at the time of the signing of the Treaty of Paris in 1898 EXCEPT

    A.   U.S. control of Guam and Puerto Rico

    B.   U.S. control of the Philippines

    C.   U.S. annexation of Hawaii

    D.   an end to the Spanish-American War

    E.   overturning of the Platt Amendment

20. The Protestant work ethic reflected the belief that

    A.   hard work was required only for some occupations

    B.   laziness and time wasting were sinful

    C.   only members of the church could accumulate wealth

    D.   church leaders had the ability to communicate with God

    E.   church members were not required to work as hard as non-Protestants

21. The motto "Speak softly and carry a big stick" signified

    A.   the U.S. quest for naval superiority

    B.   the ideology of U.S. neutrality

    C.   the Monroe Doctrine

    D.   the doctrine of Manifest Destiny

    E.   the Roosevelt Corollary to the Monroe Doctrine

22. The *Federalist Papers* put forth the argument that

    A.   the colonies should be independent from British rule

    B.   the Constitution gave the government too much power

    C.   ratification of the U.S. Constitution should be postponed

    D.   a strong central government was beneficial for the United States

    E.   the colonists were declaring themselves citizens of the United States

23. The Progressive Party was founded by

    A.   Robert M. La Follette

    B.   Henry Clay

    C.   Andrew Jackson

    D.   Daniel Webster

    E.   Stephen A. Douglas

24. "It is a curious subject of observation and inquiry, whether hatred and love be not the same thing at bottom. Each, in its utmost development, supposes a high degree of intimacy and heart-knowledge; each renders one individual dependent for the food of his affections and spiritual life upon another; each leaves the passionate lover, or the no less passionate hater, forlorn and desolate by the withdrawal of his object."

The passage above is most likely excerpted from

    A.   Zora Neale Hurston's *Their Eyes Were Watching God*

    B.   Arthur Miller's *The Crucible*

    C.   Nathaniel Hawthorne's *The Scarlet Letter*

    D.   Jane Addams's *Twenty Years at Hull House*

    E.   Upton Sinclair's *The Jungle*

25. The French and Indian War and the American Revolution are similar in that

    A. both ended with a treaty entitled the Treaty of Paris
    B. both ended with heavy war reparations for the Americans
    C. both ended with heavy war reparations for the Native Americans
    D. both resulted in a stalemate with the British
    E. both resulted in large territorial gains for the British

26. Each of the following is an example of checks and balances in the U.S. government EXCEPT

    A. Congress must ratify treaties proposed by the president
    B. the judicial branch interprets the laws passed by Congress
    C. the president has veto power over legislation passed by Congress
    D. Congress can remove Supreme Court judges from office
    E. legal cases can be appealed at higher levels of the judicial system

27. "We owe it, therefore, to candor and to the amicable relations existing between the United States and those powers to declare that we should consider any attempt on their part to extend their system to any portion of this hemisphere as dangerous to our peace and safety."

The quotation above most clearly expresses the views of

    A. Woodrow Wilson
    B. James Monroe
    C. Ulysses S. Grant
    D. Douglas MacArthur
    E. John Adams

28. *Brown v. Board of Education* was significant because it

    A. protected convicts from cruel and unusual punishment

B.   determined that students could not be forced to salute the American flag

C.   established the concept of suspects' rights, including the right to remain silent

D.   established that school segregation was unconstitutional

E.   upheld students' rights to freedom of speech

29. The Townshend Act of 1767 was imposed to

A.   tax the sale of domestic goods by American merchants

B.   tax exports of goods from the American colonies

C.   tax imports of goods into the American colonies

D.   create trade barriers against French trade with the colonies

E.   tax goods sold by merchants in Britain

30. South Carolina was led in nullifying the Tariff of 1832 by

A.   William Lloyd Garrison

B.   Stephen A. Douglas

C.   Andrew Johnson

D.   Robert M. La Follette

E.   John C. Calhoun

31. Barack Obama appointed which of the following as Secretary of State in 2009?

A.   Hillary Rodham Clinton

B.   Madeleine Albright

C.   Henry Kissinger

D.   George Kennan

E.   Condoleezza Rice

32. Colonies that were granted to individuals by the British government were known as

    A. appointed colonies
    B. self-governing colonies
    C. royal colonies
    D. joint-stock colonies
    E. proprietary colonies

33. In the first half of the nineteenth century, before the Civil War, the economies of the western states were dependent on

    A. cash crops
    B. fur trade
    C. tobacco
    D. industry
    E. cotton

RECENT ADDITIONS TO THE U.S. PUBLIC DEBT

FISCAL YEAR (BEGINS 10/01 OF PREV. YEAR)	ANNUAL DEFICIT	% OF GDP	TOTAL DEBT	% OF GDP
1994	$281.0 billion	4.0%	$4.70 trillion	67.3%
1995	$281.5 billion	3.8%	$4.95 trillion	67.8%
1996	$251.0 billion	3.2%	$5.20 trillion	67.7%
1997	$188.5 billion	2.3%	$5.40 trillion	65.9%
1998	$113.0 billion	1.3%	$5.55 trillion	63.8%
1999	$130.0 billion	1.4%	$5.65 trillion	61.4%
2000	$18.0 billion	0.2%	$5.65 trillion	57.8%
2001	$133.5 billion	1.3%	$5.80 trillion	56.8%
2002	$421.0 billion	4.0%	$6.25 trillion	59.1%
2003	$555.0 billion	5.1%	$6.80 trillion	61.8%
2004	$596.0 billion	5.1%	$7.40 trillion	63.1%
2005	$553.5 billion	4.4%	$7.95 trillion	63.7%

FISCAL YEAR (BEGINS 10/01 OF PREV. YEAR)	ANNUAL DEFICIT	% OF GDP	TOTAL DEBT	% OF GDP
2006	$536.5 billion	4.1%	$8.50 trillion	64.3%
2007	$500.5 billion	3.6%	$9.00 trillion	64.8%
2008	$1,017 billion	7.1%	$10.0 trillion	69.6%
2009	$1,885 billion	13.4%	$11.9 trillion	84.5%
2010	$1,652 billion	11.4%	$13.6 trillion	93.5%
2011 (1st Quarter)	$463.5 billion		$14.0 trillion	~96.5%

SOURCE: *Bureau of Economic Analysis: Gross Domestic Product; December 2010*

34. The chart above shows the progression of U.S. public debt from 1994 to 2011. Which of the following statements is supported by the chart?

   A. George W. Bush's balanced budget legislation significantly reduced the national debt.
   B. Bill Clinton's administration oversaw the largest increase of the national debt in the country's history.
   C. Under the administration of George W. Bush, the national debt nearly doubled.
   D. Deficit spending over the last decade has led to economic recession.
   E. Tax increases enacted during the Gulf War helped bolster the economy.

35. Which of the following resulted in the relocation of Indian tribes along the route known as the Trail of Tears?

   A. The Indian Relocation Act of 1956
   B. The Indian Citizenship Act of 1924
   C. The Mexican War
   D. The Indian Removal Act of 1830
   E. The 1811 battle of Tippecanoe

36. During the Federalist period under the presidency of George Washington, which of the following was proposed by Alexander Hamilton?

   A.   Strict constructionist interpretation of the Constitution
   B.   The establishment of a national bank
   C.   A weakening of the central government
   D.   A ban on protective tariffs
   E.   State responsibility for paying off state debts

37. In colonial America, the proliferation of tobacco plantations in the Southern colonies had which of the following consequences?

   A.   Decreased trade imbalance with Great Britain
   B.   Decline of agriculture and rise of industrialism
   C.   Falling cost of exports to France and Spain
   D.   New social agendas leading to Prohibition
   E.   Increased demand for slave labor

38. In the 1950s, forced integration occurred after racial segregation was declared to be a violation of which of the following?

   A.   The equal protection clause of the Fourteenth Amendment
   B.   The Fifth Amendment
   C.   The Seventeenth Amendment
   D.   The Thirteenth Amendment
   E.   The due process clause of the Fourteenth Amendment

39. The War Hawks advocated for war against Britain in 1812 for each of the following reasons EXCEPT

   A.   they believed the war would help reduce hostilities by the Native Americans
   B.   they believed war might help the United States regain its honor with respect to Britain

C. they had their sights on the acquisition of Canada

D. they wanted to win the territory of Louisiana

E. the British were forcing captured Americans to serve in the British navy

40. President Herbert Hoover's response to the Great Depression included which of the following?

A. The Smoot-Hawley Tariff

B. The Works Progress Administration

C. The Agricultural Adjustment Act

D. The Tennessee Valley Authority

E. The Social Security Act

41. When settlers first arrived in the colonies in the early 1600s, Native American tribes were characterized by

A. united resistance against the settlers

B. refusal to participate in armed conflict

C. scattered tribes and unique languages

D. peaceful coexistence between the tribes

E. use of a single tribal dialect

42. Which of the following was true of slave ownership in the antebellum United States?

A. About half of all Southerners owned slaves.

B. Most slave owners had five slaves or fewer.

C. Slaves were owned by most white households.

D. Slaveholders were typically wealthy merchants.

E. Most slave owners had twenty slaves or more.

43. The Cuban Missile Crisis of 1962 was a standoff between

    A. the United States under Ronald Reagan and the Soviet Union under Mikhail Gorbachev

    B. the Soviet Union under Mikhail Gorbachev and Cuba under Fidel Castro

    C. the United States under Dwight D. Eisenhower and France under Charles de Gaulle

    D. the United States under John F. Kennedy and the Soviet Union under Nikita Khrushchev

    E. the United States under Dwight D. Eisenhower and the Soviet Union under Joseph Stalin

44. Each of the following was an important muckraker during the early 1900s EXCEPT

    A. Ida Tarbell

    B. Upton Sinclair

    C. Ida Wells

    D. Jacob Riis

    E. Langston Hughes

45. "Men who had made five thousand, year before last, and ten thousand last year, were urging on nerve-yelping bodies and parched brains so that they might make twenty thousand this year; and the men who had broken down immediately after making their twenty thousand dollars were hustling to catch trains, to hustle through the vacations which the hustling doctors had ordered."

The passage above is most likely excerpted from

    A. Sinclair Lewis's *Babbitt*

    B. Kurt Vonnegut's *Breakfast of Champions*

    C. Nathaniel Hawthorne's *The Scarlet Letter*

D.   Louisa May Alcott's *Little Women*

E.   Richard Wright's *Native Son*

46. The Pilgrims and the Puritans who settled New England in the 1600s differed in that

A.   only the Puritans wished to separate from the Church of England

B.   the Puritans were Protestant, and the Pilgrims were not

C.   the Pilgrims were Protestant, and the Puritans were not

D.   only the Pilgrims wished to separate from the Church of England

E.   only the Puritans viewed the Church of England as corrupt

47. During the presidency of Bill Clinton, the U.S. economy was characterized by

A.   recession

B.   depression

C.   economic growth

D.   stagflation

E.   deregulation

48. Black codes were enforced in the United States during which period?

A.   Reconstruction

B.   The colonial era

C.   The Civil War

D.   The antebellum period

E.   The Critical Years

49. In the 1600s and 1700s, European imperialism was fueled by

    A. joint-stock companies
    B. conquistadors
    C. socialism
    D. Communism
    E. mercantilism

50. Charles Lindbergh became significant for which of the following in 1927?

    A. Circumnavigating the globe
    B. Completing a transatlantic flight
    C. Inventing the light bulb
    D. Inventing the steam turbine
    E. Making a phonograph recording

51. The outbreak of World War I was triggered by

    A. the establishment of the League of Nations
    B. the signing of the Treaty of Versailles
    C. the assassination of Austria-Hungary's archduke Franz Ferdinand
    D. the sinking of the British liner *Lusitania*
    E. the publication of the Zimmerman Note

52. The Watergate incident in 1972 resulted in

    A. the resignation of Richard Nixon to avoid impeachment
    B. the impeachment and conviction of Richard Nixon
    C. the imposition of the Oil Embargo of 1973
    D. the dissolution of the Democratic National Committee
    E. the impeachment and acquittal of Richard Nixon

53. Each of the following was a member of the Whig Party that arose in the Second Party System EXCEPT

   A. Zachary Taylor
   B. Abraham Lincoln
   C. Daniel Webster
   D. Henry Clay
   E. Andrew Jackson

54. In the years before the Revolutionary War, the British enforced laws in the colonies through a policy known as

   A. the Coercive Acts
   B. encomiendas
   C. the invisible hand
   D. salutary neglect
   E. taxation without representation

55. The Reconstruction period under Republican control was characterized by

   A. military rule and corruption
   B. leniency for the Southern governments
   C. equality for black citizens
   D. the decline of black codes
   E. the lifting of poll taxes

56. In the late 1800s and early 1900s, immigration was generally viewed with which of the following perspectives?

   A. Creationist theory
   B. Darwinism theory
   C. Melting pot theory
   D. Romanticist theory
   E. Salad bowl theory

57. A 1920s drawing of a flapper would most likely depict a woman representing which of the following points of view?

    A. Concern with economic hardships during the Great Depression
    B. Disdain for social conventions following World War I
    C. Disagreement with government policy during the Vietnam War
    D. Acceptance of women's traditional roles following World War II
    E. Fear of Soviet domination during the Cold War

58. Which of the following is true regarding the Salem witch trials of 1692?

    A. Many of the accused individuals were killed for refusing to stand trial.
    B. The Salem trials were the first witch trials to occur in the colonies.
    C. A great number of people were accused in the trials, but all were acquitted.
    D. Most of the individuals accused of witchcraft were slaves.
    E. Many of the accused were from upstanding Salem families.

59. The Mayflower Compact was significant because

    A. it established Plymouth Colony as a theocratic government
    B. it established protection of religious freedom for the Pilgrims
    C. it established the first form of independent government in the colonies
    D. it established the governmental principle of separation of church and state
    E. it established the governing structure for the Jamestown Colony

AN AVAILABLE CANDIDATE.

Library of Congress

60. The cartoon above, created during the 1848 presidential election, refers to which political party?

A.   The Whig Party
B.   The Republican Party
C.   The Progressive Party
D.   The Democratic Party
E.   The Democratic-Republican Party

61. "BUT I AM NOT tragically colored. There is no great sorrow dammed up in my soul, nor lurking behind my eyes. I do not mind at all.... Even in the helter skelter skirmish that is my life, I have seen that the world is to the strong regardless of a little pigmentation more of less. No, I do not weep at the world. I am too busy sharpening my oyster knife."

The passage above was most likely published during

    A.   the American Revolution

    B.   the colonial era

    C.   the Gilded Age

    D.   World War I

    E.   the Harlem Renaissance

62. Proponents of social Darwinism in the late 1800s argued that

    A.   social policies should provide strong welfare for the poor

    B.   social policies should not support those unable to support themselves

    C.   individuals from different religious backgrounds should not marry

    D.   domestic economics should discourage competition

    E.   social policies should be designed to protect individuals from economic discrimination

63. Each of the following presidents was a member of the Democratic-Republican Party EXCEPT

    A.   Thomas Jefferson

    B.   John Quincy Adams

    C.   James Monroe

    D.   John Adams

    E.   James Madison

64. "I am acutely aware that you have not elected me as your President by your ballots, and so I ask you to confirm me as your President with your prayers.... My fellow Americans, our long national nightmare is over.... Our Constitution works; our great Republic is a government of laws and not of men. Here the people rule."

The statement above was made by

A. Gerald Ford, taking the oath of office following Richard Nixon's resignation

B. Ronald Reagan, accepting the Republican presidential nomination

C. Bill Clinton, accepting the Democratic nomination for president

D. John F. Kennedy, addressing the General Assembly of the United Nations

E. Franklin D. Roosevelt, addressing Congress after the attack on Pearl Harbor

65. The Civil Rights Act of 1964 established which of the following?

A. The unconstitutionality of "separate but equal" facilities

B. The jurisdiction of the U.S. Department of Agriculture

C. The unlawfulness of discrimination against blacks and women

D. The unlawfulness of discrimination based on disability

E. The primacy of states' rights over federal rights

66. In 1892 Elizabeth Cady Stanton stated: "The strongest reason why we ask for woman a voice in the government under which she lives; in the religion she is asked to believe; equality in social life, where she is the chief factor; a place in the trades and professions, where she may earn her bread, is because of her birthright to self-sovereignty; because, as an individual, she must rely on herself."

Which of the following movements do Stanton's comments address?

    A.   Nationalism
    B.   Women's suffrage
    C.   Postmodernism
    D.   Reproductive rights
    E.   Ecofeminism

67. Aggressive expansion under Manifest Destiny was promoted by

    A.   Dwight D. Eisenhower
    B.   John Quincy Adams
    C.   James Monroe
    D.   James K. Polk
    E.   Herbert Hoover

68. Which of the following caused a reduction in the use of indentured servants in the American colonies?

    A.   Shays's Rebellion
    B.   The Whiskey Rebellion
    C.   Bacon's Rebellion
    D.   Nat Turner's Rebellion
    E.   The Boston Tea Party

69. Authors Nathaniel Hawthorne, Ralph Waldo Emerson, and Henry David Thoreau were all proponents of

   A. transcendentalism
   B. the temperance movement
   C. Prohibition
   D. education reform
   E. prison reform

70. Which of the following white supremacist organizations arose during the Reconstruction era?

   A. The Aryan Nation
   B. The Ku Klux Klan
   C. The Nazi Party
   D. The Minutemen
   E. The White Patriot Party

71. "It is, then, the strife of all honorable men and women of the twentieth century to see that in the future competition of the races the survival of the fittest shall mean the triumph of the good, the beautiful, and the true; that we may be able to preserve for future civilization all that is really fine and noble and strong, and not continue to put a premium on greed and imprudence and cruelty."

The passage above is most likely excerpted from

   A. John Steinbeck's *The Grapes of Wrath*
   B. Ernest Hemingway's *The Sun Also Rises*
   C. Ralph Ellison's *Invisible Man*
   D. Willa Cather's *My Antonia*
   E. W. E. B. Du Bois's *The Souls of Black Folk*

72. President Jimmy Carter helped to ease tensions between Israel and Egypt through which of the following?

    A. Rapprochement policy
    B. Détente policy
    C. Camp David Peace Accords
    D. SALT I talks
    E. GATT

73. Which of the following overturned the Supreme Court decision established in *Plessy v. Ferguson*?

    A. *Roe v. Wade*
    B. *McCulloch v. Maryland*
    C. *Brown v. Board of Education*
    D. *Miranda v. Arizona*
    E. *Dred Scott v. Sandford*

74. The Second Great Awakening arose in the United States in reaction to which of the following?

    A. Rationalism
    B. Religious fundamentalism
    C. Evangelicalism
    D. Protestantism
    E. Social reforms

75. The term "Bleeding Kansas" refers to conflict in Kansas between

    A. big businesses and anti-monopoly groups
    B. union organizers and corporation owners
    C. agrarian reformists and railroad companies
    D. proslavery and antislavery factions
    E. women suffragists and abolitionists

76. Samuel Gompers championed which of the following causes?

    A. Repeal of Prohibition

    B. Worker's rights

    C. Women's suffrage

    D. Black suffrage

    E. Medicare reform

DISTRIBUTION OF SLAVES IN THE UNITED STATES, 1790–1870

CENSUS YEAR	# OF SLAVES	# OF FREE BLACKS	TOTAL BLACKS	% FREE BLACKS	TOTAL U.S. POPULA-TION	% BLACKS OF TOTAL
1790	697,681	59,527	757,208	7.9%	3,929,214	19%
1800	893,602	108,435	1,002,037	10.8%	5,308,483	19%
1810	1,191,362	186,446	1,377,808	13.5%	7,239,881	19%
1820	1,538,022	233,634	1,771,656	13.2%	9,638,453	18%
1830	2,009,043	319,599	2,328,642	13.7%	12,860,702	18%
1840	2,487,355	386,293	2,873,648	13.4%	17,063,353	17%
1850	3,204,313	434,495	3,638,808	11.9%	23,191,876	16%
1860	3,953,760	488,070	4,441,830	11.0%	31,443,321	14%
1870	0	4,880,009	4,880,009	100%	38,558,371	13%

SOURCE: U.S. Census Bureau

77. The chart above shows the distribution of slaves in the United States between 1790 and 1870. Which of the following statements is best supported by the chart?

    A. Slavery was most prominent on large plantations with high-value cash crops.

    B. The percentage of free blacks increased steadily between 1790 and 1860.

    C. Slavery was a principal issue leading to the American Civil War.

    D. The majority of slaves lived in the Southern coastal regions.

    E. Slavery declined following the passage of the Thirteenth Amendment.

78. The concept of the iron curtain referred to a division between

 A. mercantilism and capitalism during the imperialist era
 B. socialism and fascism during World War II
 C. Communism and democracy during the Cold War
 D. big business and government during the Progressive era
 E. moderates and teetotalers during Prohibition

79. President Lyndon B. Johnson is credited with which of the following?

 A. The War on Poverty
 B. The Afghanistan War
 C. The War on Terror
 D. The Persian Gulf War
 E. The 9/11 attacks

80. Which of the following took a leadership role in ensuring the survival of the Jamestown settlers, particularly by organizing food supplies?

 A. John Winthrop
 B. Pocahontas
 C. John Rolfe
 D. John Smith
 E. Daniel Shays

81. The concept of "rugged individualism" was put forth by which of the following?

 A. Harry Truman at the end of World War II
 B. Herbert Hoover in a 1928 campaign speech
 C. William McKinley at the end of the Spanish-American War
 D. Warren G. Harding in an address to Congress
 E. Woodrow Wilson in his Fourteen Points speech

82. Journalist H. L. Mencken was known for his coverage of which of the following in 1925?

    A. The Rosenberg trial
    B. The Sacco and Vanzetti trial
    C. The Red Scare
    D. The XYZ Affair
    E. The Scopes trial

83. A graph depicting high stock market closing values from 1994 to 2002 would most likely reflect which of the following?

    A. Post-Keynesian economics
    B. Comparative advantage
    C. The dot-com boom
    D. Non-equilibrium economics
    E. Cost-push inflation

84. Thoreau's 1854 publication *Walden* centered around which of the following?

    A. Simple living
    B. Prohibition
    C. Abolition
    D. Women's suffrage
    E. Education reform

85. Which of the following was true of the Sherman Anti-Trust Act of 1890?

    A. It was passed to support monopolies.
    B. It was very loosely enforced.
    C. It prevented big business from influencing politics.
    D. It was passed during the term of Grover Cleveland.
    E. It was supported by big business interests.

86. "There is not a liberal America and a conservative America—there is the United States of America. There is not a Black America and a White America and Latino America and Asian America—there's the United States of America."

The statement above was most likely made by which of the following?

    A.   George W. Bush regarding lack of public support for social programs

    B.   Ronald Reagan regarding the War on Poverty

    C.   Bill Clinton regarding liberalization of foreign trade

    D.   Barack Obama regarding American racial and political divisiveness

    E.   John F. Kennedy regarding changes to American immigration policy

87. Which of the following is the subject of the cartoon above?

    A.   Theodore Roosevelt's Progressive Party platform

    B.   Herbert Hoover's policies of economic modernization

C. Harry Truman's briefings on the Manhattan Project

D. Dwight D. Eisenhower's establishment of the Eisenhower Doctrine

E. Woodrow Wilson's League of Nations negotiations

88. The doctrine of Manifest Destiny was inspired by

A. the Monroe Doctrine

B. the Roosevelt Corollary to the Monroe Doctrine

C. the California Gold Rush of 1848

D. the Stimson Doctrine

E. the Gulf of Tonkin Resolution

89. In the abolitionist movement, those who called for a gradual end to the institution of slavery were known as

A. carpetbaggers

B. scalawags

C. immediatists

D. free-soilers

E. moderates

90. Which of the following triggers of the stock market crash of 1929 refers to the approach of purchasing stocks with borrowed funds?

A. Bull market speculation

B. Futures manipulation

C. Options trading

D. Buying on margin

E. Counter purchasing

91. Which of the following best reflects the U.S. role in the Spanish-American War?

   A. The United States provided support for Cuba in its rebellion against Spain.
   B. The United States fought with Spain over access to Asian trading ports.
   C. The United States served to mediate a civil war in Hawaii.
   D. The United States provided support for Spain in maintaining control over Guam.
   E. Americans fought the Spanish to gain territory in the western United States.

UNEMPLOYMENT % OF LABOR FORCE, 1930s AND 1940s

YEAR	SOURCE #1	SOURCE #2
1933	24.9	20.6
1934	21.7	16.0
1935	20.1	14.2
1936	16.9	9.9
1937	14.3	9.1
1938	19.0	12.5
1939	17.2	11.3
1940	14.6	9.5
1941	9.9	8.0
1942	4.7	4.7
1943	1.9	1.9
1944	1.2	1.2
1945	1.9	1.9

SOURCE: *Historical Statistics US (1976)*

92. The chart above shows U.S. rates of unemployment between 1933 and 1945. Which of the following statements is best supported by the chart?

A. As a result of World War II, unemployment in the United States continued to escalate.

B. Following the implementation of Roosevelt's New Deal programs, unemployment rates improved in the mid-1930s.

C. Unemployment in the United States peaked during the Spanish-American War.

D. By limiting cartels and monopolies, the Sherman Anti-Trust Act had a devastating effect on the nation's unemployment rate during the 1930s.

E. During the Great Depression, unemployment rates fell below 10 percent.

Practice Test 2: Answer Key

1. B		17. D
2. D		18. A
3. C		19. E
4. E		20. B
5. A		21. E
6. B		22. D
7. B		23. A
8. D		24. C
9. A		25. A
10. C		26. E
11. E		27. B
12. B		28. D
13. D		29. C
14. A		30. E
15. E		31. A
16. C		32. E

33. B	59. C
34. C	60. A
35. D	61. E
36. B	62. B
37. E	63. D
38. A	64. A
39. D	65. C
40. A	66. B
41. C	67. D
42. B	68. C
43. D	69. A
44. E	70. B
45. A	71. E
46. D	72. C
47. C	73. C
48. A	74. A
49. E	75. D
50. B	76. B
51. C	77. E
52. A	78. C
53. E	79. A
54. D	80. D
55. A	81. B
56. C	82. E
57. B	83. C
58. E	84. A

85. B   89. E

86. D   90. D

87. A   91. A

88. C   92. B

Practice Test 2: Explanations

1. The correct answer is B. Newfoundland was first discovered by Norse explorer Leif Ericsson around 1000. D is incorrect; although English explorer John Cabot did sail to Newfoundland, the Norse led by Leif Ericsson were the first to discover the territory. E is incorrect because Portuguese explorer Ferdinand Magellan was the first to circumnavigate the globe in 1519.

See Part 1 of the U.S. History Review.

2. The correct answer is D. The Marshall Plan was enacted in 1948 to provide recovery support for post–World War II Europe. Through the Marshall Plan, the United States allocated funds to rebuild Europe after its devastation from the war. The plan was named for its champion, Gen. George C. Marshall, who was secretary of state at the time. C is incorrect because the United States provided funds for the Marshall Plan; it did not receive funds for U.S. recovery. A and B are incorrect because the Marshall Plan was instituted after World War II, not World War I.

See Part 5 of the U.S. History Review.

3. The correct answer is C. Capt. Alfred T. Mahan helped to established naval superiority as a motivation behind U.S. imperialist expansion. Mahan's book, *The Influence of Sea Power upon History*, was very influential in spreading the notion that there was a need for a strong navy to maintain U.S. economic prowess and protect its shipping lanes

at the turn of the twentieth century. E is incorrect because Josiah Strong helped to promote the idea of an ethical imperative for colonization, not a naval imperative.

See Part 3 of the U.S. History Review.

4.   The correct answer is E. H. L. Mencken was a well-known journalist who reported on the Scopes trial in 1925. Carnegie, Morgan, Vanderbilt, and Rockefeller were all considered robber barons of the Gilded Age.

For a discussion of the Gilded Age, see Part 3 of the U.S. History Review. For information about the Scopes trial, see Part 4 of the U.S. History Review.

5.   The correct answer is A. During the colonial era, settlers often gained passage to the New World by committing themselves to indentured servitude. Indentured servants made agreements to work on Southern plantations in exchange for their freedom and in some cases a portion of land.

See Part 1 of the U.S. History Review.

6.   The correct answer is B. The Montgomery bus boycott of 1956 led to national attention for civil rights activist Martin Luther King Jr. The arrest and trial of Montgomery seamstress Rosa Parks prompted the boycott, so A is incorrect.

See Part 5 of the U.S. History Review.

7.   The correct answer is B. The Mexican War was sparked when the United States annexed Texas, a territory in dispute with Mexico. This angered the Mexican leadership, who promptly declared war. U.S. annexation of Hawaii occurred at the end of the 1898 Spanish-American War. This was after the Mexican War, which occurred in 1846.

See Part 2 of the U.S. History Review.

8.   The correct answer is D. During the American Revolutionary War, the battle of Saratoga was significant because it prompted the French to join the war in support of the American forces. The battle of Yorktown was the last major conflict of the war, prompting Cornwallis to surrender,

and the first shots of the war were fired at Lexington, Massachusetts. So A, B, and E can be eliminated.

See Part 1 of the U.S. History Review.

9. The correct answer is A. The New Deal programs implemented by Franklin D. Roosevelt were significant because they helped the United States recover from the Great Depression. These programs did not primarily continue economic policies initiated under Herbert Hoover, so D is incorrect. Hoover's policies were on the whole ineffective for addressing the Depression; Roosevelt was elected on the promise that he could help the country pull through the period, which he did.

See Part 4 of the U.S. History Review.

10. The correct answer is C. Harry Truman was responsible for authorizing use of atomic bombs to end World War II. Truman took office before the war's end. A and D are incorrect because Truman was president at the end of World War II, not at the beginning. E is incorrect because the United States did not invade mainland Japan to end the war. The decision to drop the bombs was based in part on the belief that an invasion of Japan would have cost hundreds of thousands of American lives.

See Part 5 of the U.S. History Review.

11. The correct answer is E. The War of 1812 resulted in a permanent loss of political power for the Federalist Party. Before the war's end, a group of Federalist Party members had met at the Hartford Convention and developed several proposed amendments to the Constitution, including a requirement for a two-thirds majority in Congress for a declaration of war. The Federalists brought the amendments to Washington just as news of Jackson's victory at New Orleans was breaking. With American morale soaring, the Federalists were seen as traitors and secessionists. They lost power permanently as a result. C and D are incorrect because Jackson and the Democratic Party came into power as a result of the war.

See Part 2 of the U.S. History Review.

12. The correct answer is B. During his term in office, Washington established the foreign policy of the country as neutral vis-à-vis other nations. Washington believed that neutrality was the most prudent course of action for the new nation. In 1793 Washington issued a Proclamation of Neutrality in response to the question of whether the United States should assist France in its conflict with Britain during the time of the French Revolutionary Wars. The proclamation was followed by the Neutrality Act of 1794, which declared that the United States would remain neutral.

See Part 2 of the U.S. History Review.

13. The correct answer is D. In the 1860s, blacks continued to live at a subsistence level with sharecropping arrangements that required them to give large parts of their harvests to their landlords in exchange for the right to use the land. A and E are incorrect because the alliances formed with carpetbaggers and scalawags concerned political control and not economic subsistence.

See Part 3 of the U.S. History Review.

14. The correct answer is A. The Equal Rights Amendment was a proposed amendment to the U.S. Constitution prohibiting discrimination based on gender, so C is incorrect. It was introduced in Congress in 1923, so B is incorrect. The amendment eventually passed both chambers of Congress in 1972, so E is incorrect. It failed, however, to be ratified by the required number of states, which eliminates choice D. A is correct.

See Part 5 of the U.S. History Review.

15. The correct answer is E. John F. Kennedy was the thirty-fifth president of the United States from 1961 until his assassination in 1963. During the 1960s, state-sanctioned racial discrimination and segregation of public institutions were halted. School desegregation was finally implemented following the 1954 Supreme Court decision that racial segregation in public schools was unconstitutional. Kennedy supported racial

integration and civil rights and was a supporter of Dr. Martin Luther King Jr.

See Part 5 of the U.S. History Review.

16. The correct answer is C. The Fugitive Slave Law became significant because it increased North-South tensions leading up to the Civil War. The law required citizens to help capture runaway slaves, so A and D are incorrect. As part of the overall Compromise of 1850, it helped temporarily to avoid civil war by preventing the Southern states from seceding from the Union at the time, so E is incorrect.

See Part 3 of the U.S. History Review.

17. The correct answer is D. The Treaty of Paris (1783) brought an end to the American Revolution. It established the United States of America as an independent nation recognized by Britain. B is incorrect because World War I ended with the Treaty of Versailles. E is incorrect because the War of 1812 ended with the Treaty of Ghent.

See Part 1 of the U.S. History Review.

18. The correct answer is A. Booker T. Washington advocated accommodating the Jim Crow segregation laws during Reconstruction. Washington was an activist in the late 1800s, not in the 1950s and 60s, so B and C are incorrect. Dr. Martin Luther King helped organize the March on Washington and was a leader in the Montgomery bus boycott.

See Part 3 of the U.S. History Review.

19. The correct answer is E. Signed in 1898, the Treaty of Paris brought an end to the Spanish-American War, so D is incorrect. It also gave the United States control of Guam, Puerto Rico, and the Philippines, so A and B can be eliminated. The United States annexed Hawaii at this time, which rules out C; in addition, the United States gained the right to intervene in Cuban affairs through passage of the Platt Amendment to the Cuban constitution, so E is correct.

See Part 3 of the U.S. History Review.

20. The correct answer is B. The Protestant work ethic reflected the belief that laziness and time wasting were sinful. Those who followed this ideology believed that hard work was necessary to serve God, and members of the church were expected to devote themselves to industry. A and E are incorrect because hard work was seen as a virtue overall, and church members were expected to labor diligently.

See Part 1 of the U.S. History Review.

21. The correct answer is E. The motto "Speak softly and carry a big stick" was coined by Theodore Roosevelt and signified the Roosevelt Corollary to the Monroe Doctrine.

See Part 3 of the U.S. History Review.

22. The correct answer is D. *The Federalist Papers* put forth the argument that a strong central government was beneficial for the United States. They supported ratification of the Constitution, so B and C are incorrect. Choice A describes the argument of the pamphlet *Common Sense* by Thomas Paine, and E describes the Declaration of Independence.

See Part 1 of the U.S. History Review.

23. The correct answer is A. La Follette founded the Progressive Party and ran for president as the Progressive Party candidate in 1924. Henry Clay and Daniel Webster were active members of the Whig Party in the mid-1800s, which opposed Andrew Jackson.

See Part 3 of the U.S. History Review for a discussion of the Progressive Party. For a discussion of the Whig Party, see Part 2 of the U.S. History Review.

24. The correct answer is C. The text is excerpted from Nathaniel Hawthorne's *The Scarlet Letter*, a novel about a Puritan woman and a minister who commit adultery in the mid-1600s. B is incorrect because *The Crucible* concerns the Salem witch trials.

See Part 2 of the U.S. History Review.

25. The correct answer is A. Both the American Revolution and the

French and Indian War ended with a treaty entitled the Treaty of Paris. The Treaty of Paris ending the French and Indian War was signed in 1763. The Treaty of Paris that ended the American Revolution was signed in 1783.

See Part 1 of the U.S. History Review.

26. The correct answer is E. The appeals system is not an example of checks and balances in the U.S. government. Checks and balances are specifically built in to ensure that no one branch of government has a preponderance of power. A, B, C, and D are examples of checks and balances.

See Part 2 of the U.S. History Review.

27. The correct answer is B. This quotation most clearly expresses the views of James Monroe announcing the Monroe Doctrine. This doctrine, established in 1823, declared that the United States would intervene militarily to thwart any attempts at colonization by European powers within the Americas, because these attempts would be seen as acts of aggression.

See Part 2 of the U.S. History Review.

28. The correct answer is D. *Brown v. the Board of Education* established an important precedent in 1954 that segregation of children in public schools on the basis of race, even if the facilities were similar, led to an inherently unequal education. C is incorrect because *Miranda v. Arizona* upheld the right of an individual to be protected against self-incrimination. B is incorrect because *West Virginia State School Board v. Barnette* established that students could not be forced to demonstrate their allegiance to the American flag.

See Part 5 of the U.S. History Review.

29. The correct answer is C. The Townshend Act was imposed on the American colonies in 1767 as a way to raise revenue for the British treasury. These duties taxed goods imported into the American colonies, including tea, glass, paper, lead, and paint. The Townshend Act was

named after British chancellor Charles Townshend, who proposed the duties as part of the Revenue Act of 1767. The duties were hotly protested in the colonies, leading ultimately to the Boston Massacre. A is incorrect because the tax focused on imported goods rather than domestic goods. B is incorrect because imports were taxed, not exports. E is incorrect; although the tax was imposed by Britain, it was paid by the American colonists, not by those who bought goods sold in Britain.

See Part 1 of the U.S. History Review.

30. The correct answer is E. South Carolina nullified the Tariff of 1832 under the leadership of Senator John C. Calhoun. This tariff reduced tariffs imposed by the act of 1828, but it was rejected by the Southern states.

See Part 3 of the U.S. History Review.

31. The correct answer is A. Hillary Rodham Clinton was appointed secretary of state by Obama in 2008. Madeleine Albright served as secretary of state under Bill Clinton, and Condoleezza Rice served as secretary of state under George W. Bush.

See Part 5 of the U.S. History Review.

32. The correct answer is E. In colonial America, proprietary colonies were granted to individuals by the British government; the owners would then appoint a governor for the colony. Royal colonies were owned by the British Crown, so C is incorrect. Self-governing colonies were developed when the king granted a charter to a joint-stock company.

See Part 1 of the U.S. History Review.

33. The correct answer is B. In the antebellum United States, the economies of the western states were dependent on fur trade and commercial farming. Southern economies were dependent on agriculture and cash crops, including tobacco and cotton. So A, C, and E are incorrect. Northern states were dependent on industry and manufacturing. So D is incorrect.

See Part 2 of the U.S. History Review.

34. The correct answer is C. Although Bill Clinton's administration oversaw budget surpluses in the late 1990s, the national debt grew to the largest in U.S. history during the George W. Bush administration (2001–2009). From September 30, 2002, through September 30, 2004, the deficit increased nearly 50 percent, and the national debt increased from $5.7 trillion in January 2001 to $10.7 trillion by December 2008.

For more on presidential economic policies in the 1990s and 2000s, see Part 5 of the U.S. History Review.

35. The correct answer is D. The Indian Removal Act of 1830 resulted in the relocation of Indian tribes along the route known as the Trail of Tears. The Trail of Tears was traveled in 1838, so A is incorrect.

See Part 2 of the U.S. History Review.

36. The correct answer is B. Alexander Hamilton, as a leader of the Federalist Party, proposed establishment of a national bank. The bank was established during George Washington's term. Hamilton maintained a "loose constructionist" approach to interpreting the Constitution, while Thomas Jefferson and the Democratic-Republicans were "strict constructionists." Hamilton also supported a strong central government, protective tariffs, and raising taxes to pay off state debt. So C, D, and E are incorrect.

See Part 2 of the U.S. History Review.

37. The correct answer is E. The first commercial tobacco crop was planted in the United States during the 1600s. Increased demand for tobacco in the American colonies and in Europe created a need for large plantations with inexpensive labor. Since tobacco sold for only pennies per pound at this time, the solution to growing profitable tobacco crops in the colonies was to use an increased number of slaves to greatly expand tobacco production.

See Part 1 of the U.S. History Review.

38. The correct answer is A. Forced integration occurred after racial segregation was declared to be a violation of the equal protection clause of the Fourteenth Amendment. The due process clause of the Fourteenth

Amendment protects individual rights to fairness in criminal proceedings. So E is incorrect.

See Part 5 of the U.S. History Review.

39. The correct answer is D. The Louisiana Purchase was made by Jefferson in 1803, so this territory was not at stake in the War of 1812.

See Part 2 of the U.S. History Review.

40. The correct answer is A. President Herbert Hoover's response to the Great Depression included the Smoot-Hawley Tariff. B, C, D, and E are incorrect because these were all programs passed by Franklin D. Roosevelt, who served after Hoover.

See Part 4 of the U.S. History Review.

41. The correct answer is C. When the American settlers first arrived, Native American tribes were scattered, independent groups that spoke unique languages. E is therefore incorrect. A is a common misconception regarding the early Indian tribes; in fact, there was no united resistance by the tribes when the settlers first arrived. Some tribes were at war with other tribes, and the introduction of metal tools increased this intertribal friction, which eliminates choices B and D.

See Part 1 of the U.S. History Review.

42. The correct answer is B. Most slave owners in the antebellum United States had five slaves or fewer. Only about 25 percent of American Southerners owned slaves, so A is incorrect. The majority of slaveholders were aristocratic plantation owners, not merchants, so D is incorrect.

See Part 3 of the U.S. History Review.

43. The correct answer is D. In 1962, the Cuban missile crisis occurred as a conflict between the United States and the Soviet Union. Nikita Khrushchev was the Soviet leader at the time; John F. Kennedy was president of the United States. The crisis involved a military standoff that narrowly averted nuclear war. The Soviet government was supplying missiles to Cuba at the time and refused to concede when the U.S. government

discovered the missiles and asked that they be removed. Eventually, tensions eased when Khrushchev agreed to remove the missiles. Choice A is incorrect because Reagan and Gorbachev were leaders at a later time, at the end of the Cold War. E is incorrect because Eisenhower and Stalin were leaders of the United States and Soviet Union before the Cuban missile crisis. B and C are incorrect because the conflict was between the United States and the USSR.

See Part 5 of the U.S. History Review.

44. The correct answer is E. Langston Hughes was a celebrated figure of the Harlem Renaissance in the 1920s. A, B, C, and D are incorrect because these individuals were all muckrakers during the early 1900s.

See Part 3 of the U.S. History Review.

45. The correct answer is A. The passage is excerpted from *Babbitt*, an American novel published by Sinclair Lewis in 1922. *Babbitt* offered a critique of big business during the Roaring Twenties and Americans' relentless and conformist pursuit of wealth during the early part of the twentieth century. In his characterizations of George Babbitt's work and preoccupation with material possessions, Lewis explores the negative implications of capitalism in an increasingly materialistic society.

For an overview of the Roaring Twenties, see Part 4 of the U.S. History Review.

46. The correct answer is D. Both the Pilgrims and the Puritans were Protestants, so B and C are incorrect. As Protestants, both groups broke with the latent Catholicism of the Anglican Church, or the Church of England; both groups saw the church as highly corrupt, so E is incorrect. The Pilgrims themselves were Puritans, but they wished to separate completely from the Anglican Church. The Puritans wished to "purify" the church and not to separate from it—which rules out A.

See Part 1 of the U.S. History Review.

47. The correct answer is C. The United States experienced significant economic growth during the Clinton presidency. Stagflation

characterized the economy during the presidency of Jimmy Carter; deregulation was the prominent economic policy during the Reagan years.

See Part 5 of the U.S. History Review.

48. The correct answer is A. Black codes were enforced in the United States during Reconstruction, in the late 1800s, after the Civil War.

See Part 3 of the U.S. History Review.

49. The correct answer is E. European imperialism in the 1600s and 1700s was fueled by mercantilism. Conquistadors were Spanish explorers who conquered the peoples they discovered. Joint-stock companies funded colonization efforts in North America, but they were not a factor fueling imperialism.

See Part 1 of the U.S. History Review.

50. The correct answer is B. Charles Lindbergh became significant for completing the first transatlantic flight in 1927. The globe was first circumnavigated by Portuguese explorer Ferdinand Magellan in 1519, so A is incorrect. The light bulb (Thomas Edison) and steam turbine (Charles Parson) were invented in the late 1800s, prior to Lindbergh's flight, so C and D are incorrect.

For a list of significant inventions, see Part 3 of the U.S. History Review.

51. The correct answer is C. The outbreak of World War I was precipitated by the assassination of Austria-Hungary archduke Franz Ferdinand. The archduke was assassinated by Serbian nationals dissatisfied with Austro-Hungarian rule. After the assassination, Austria-Hungary declared war on Serbia, and Russia came to Serbia's aid. Germany declared war on France, Russia's ally, and Great Britain declared war on Germany to support France. Choices D and E are incorrect because these events happened after the war started. B is incorrect because the Treaty of Versailles ended the war instead of triggering it. The League of Nations was established after the end of the war.

See Part 4 of the U.S. History Review.

52. The correct answer is A. After his attempted cover-up of the Watergate break-ins became public knowledge, President Nixon resigned to avoid near-certain impeachment. B and D are incorrect because Nixon resigned before being impeached. The Oil Embargo of 1973 occurred after the Watergate incident, but the direct result of Watergate was Nixon's resignation.

See Part 5 of the U.S. History Review.

53. The correct answer is E. In the Second Party System of the 1830s, the Whig Party arose to oppose Andrew Jackson's Democratic Party. Abraham Lincoln was the Illinois leader of the Whig Party before the party disbanded.

See Part 2 of the U.S. History Review.

54. The correct answer is D. In the pre-Revolutionary period, the British policy of enforcing colonial law was known as salutary neglect. This policy involved the failure to enforce laws, or a purposefully relaxed approach to enforcement. A is incorrect because the Coercive Acts were passed by the British in response to the Boston Tea Party. The phrase "taxation without representation" was used by Americans in response to Britain's imposition of taxes in the years prior to the war, so E is incorrect.

See Part 1 of the U.S. History Review.

55. The correct answer is A. The Reconstruction period under Republican control was characterized by military rule and corruption. B is therefore incorrect. C, D, and E can be eliminated because they represent the opposite of what occurred during Reconstruction under the Republicans.

See Part 3 of the U.S. History Review.

56. The correct answer is C. In the late 1800s and early 1900s, immigration was generally viewed through the lens of the melting pot theory. In this view, the United States was likened to a melting pot, where peoples from all backgrounds came together and merged to create a unique culture. E is incorrect; the salad bowl theory did not arise until the 1970s.

See Part 3 of the U.S. History Review.

57. The correct answer is B. The term *flapper* was used to describe young women in the 1920s who embraced transatlantic culture and rejected post–World War I behavioral conventions. Flappers were known for wearing heavy makeup, driving automobiles, and listening to jazz music.

See Part 4 of the U.S. History Review.

58. The correct answer is E. Many of those accused in the Salem witch trials were from upstanding Salem families. A is incorrect; of the people killed in the trials, most were tried and found guilty; only one refused to stand trial. B is incorrect because other witch trials had occurred in the colonies prior to this one. C is incorrect because nineteen accused persons were found guilty.

See Part 1 of the U.S. History Review.

59. The correct answer is C. The Mayflower Compact was significant because it established the first form of independent government in the colonies. The agreement was signed aboard the *Mayflower* before the Pilgrims landed. E is incorrect because the Mayflower Compact was signed by the Pilgrims who founded Plymouth Colony.

See Part 1 of the U.S. History Review.

60. The correct answer is A. The Whig Party was formed following the Mexican War (1846–1848). This political cartoon presents a scathing attack of either Gen. Zachary Taylor or Winfield Scott. Both Taylor and Scott were decorated war heroes and subsequently became contenders for the Whig Party nomination. Operating from the 1830s to the 1850s, the Whig Party was formed in opposition to the policies of Andrew Jackson and the Democratic Party and supported increased congressional power and economic protectionism.

See Part 2 of the U.S. History Review.

61. The correct answer is E. The passage is excerpted from "How It Feels to Be a Colored Me," by Zora Neale Hurston. It was published during the Harlem Renaissance, a movement characterized by a surge

in literature, art, and music created by African Americans, as well as a new sense of racial pride.

See Part 4 of the U.S. History Review.

62. The correct answer is B. Social Darwinism was a political and economic philosophy that gained popularity in the United States before the turn of the twentieth century. It was based on ideas developed by Charles Darwin, an English scientist who believed in the theory of natural selection. In Darwin's view, the strong members of each species survived the competition inherent in the process of evolution. Applied to societies, Darwin's ideas led social Darwinists to conclude that competition was healthy for the development of a strong economy. Proponents of this view argued that social policies should not support those who were unable to support themselves.

See Part 3 of the U.S. History Review.

63. The correct answer is D. John Adams was not a member of the Democratic-Republican Party. He was a member of the Federalist Party and served as second president of the United States from 1797 to 1801. John Adams was the father of the sixth president of the United States, John Quincy Adams (1825–1829). Jefferson, Madison, Monroe, and John Quincy Adams were all Democratic-Republican presidents.

See Part 2 of the U.S. History Review.

64. The correct answer is A. The quoted text is excerpted from Gerald Ford's first presidential address in 1974. Following the Watergate scandal and Richard Nixon's subsequent resignation, Ford became the first U.S. president to serve without being elected as either president or vice president. Ford's speech addresses the uniqueness of his position in American presidential history.

See Part 5 of the U.S. History Review.

65. The correct answer is C. The Civil Rights Act of 1964 established the unlawfulness of discrimination against blacks and women.

See Part 5 of the U.S. History Review.

66. The correct answer is B. Elizabeth Cady Stanton was an advocate for all women's right to vote, a right that was granted in 1920 by the passage of the Nineteenth Amendment. Reproductive rights pertain to legislation involving reproduction and reproductive health, so D is incorrect. Eco-feminism is a recent social and political movement that links environmentalism and feminism in terms of power relationships, so E is incorrect.

See Part 2 of the U.S. History Review.

67. The correct answer is D. President James K. Polk supported aggressive expansion under Manifest Destiny during his term.

See Part 2 of the U.S. History Review.

68. The correct answer is C. Indentured servitude fell out of favor with plantation owners after Bacon's Rebellion of 1676. In this uprising, an immigrant named Nathaniel Bacon led a group of former indentured servants in a series of violent attacks on neighboring Native American tribes and then on the Jamestown capital. The colonies moved more toward the use of slave labor after the incident. A is incorrect because Shays's Rebellion occurred in 1786 when the poor—especially poor farmers—revolted over their high debt and taxes. D is incorrect because Nat Turner's rebellion was a slave rebellion in 1831. It did not involve indentured servants.

For more on Bacon's Rebellion and the Boston Tea Party, see Part 1 of the U.S. History Review. For more on Shays's Rebellion and the Whiskey Rebellion, see Part 2 of the U.S. History Review. Nat Turner's rebellion is discussed in Part 3 of the U.S. History Review.

69. The correct answer is A. Nathaniel Hawthorne, Ralph Waldo Emerson, and Henry David Thoreau were all proponents of transcendentalism. Horace Mann and John Dewey were known for their role in education reform, and Dorothea Dix was active in prison reform.

See Part 2 of the U.S. History Review.

70. The correct answer is B. The Ku Klux Klan (KKK) white supremacists organized during Reconstruction to resist black rights through

violent scare tactics. The KKK saw a resurgence of activity in the United States in the 1920s.

See Part 3 of the U.S. History Review.

71. The correct answer is E. The passage is excerpted from *The Souls of Black Folk*, written by W. E. B. Du Bois. Published in 1903, Du Bois's collection of essays chronicles the continuing struggle of African Americans with discrimination decades after the Civil War. *The Souls of Black Folk* is known not only as a classic of American literature but also as an early seminal work in the field of sociology, exploring group struggles related to race. Du Bois cofounded the National Association for the Advancement of Colored People (NAACP) in 1909.

See Part 3 of the U.S. History Review.

72. The correct answer is C. During his term, Carter organized the Camp David Peace Accords to help ease tensions between Israel and Egypt.

See Part 5 of the U.S. History Review.

73. The correct answer is C. *Plessy v. Ferguson* was overturned by the *Brown* decision. The *Plessy* case established the doctrine of "separate but equal," which was declared unconstitutional by the *Brown* decision.

See Part 5 of the U.S. History Review.

74. The correct answer is A. The Second Great Awakening arose in the United States as a backlash against rationalism. It helped to motivate social reforms, so E is incorrect.

See Part 2 of the U.S. History Review.

75. The correct answer is D. The term "Bleeding Kansas" refers to a series of conflicts that concerned whether Kansas should be a free state or a slave state. The Kansas-Nebraska Act had allowed states to determine the issue by popular vote, and violence broke out between proslavery and antislavery factions in Kansas from 1854 to 1858. Kansas was admitted as a free state in 1861.

See Part 3 of the U.S. History Review.

76. The correct answer is B. Samuel Gompers was a labor organizer who promoted cooperation among craft unions, favored collective bargaining over strikes, and encouraged union members to take an active role in political elections.

See Part 3 of the U.S. History Review.

77. The correct answer is E. Slavery was a form of unpaid labor prominent in the southern United States for nearly three hundred years, until the passage of the Thirteenth Amendment in 1865, during Reconstruction. The Thirteenth Amendment abolished slavery and involuntary servitude, so E is correct. A, B, and C are not supported by the chart because they are outside the scope of what the chart addresses. D is incorrect because it is the opposite of what the chart indicates. The percentage of free blacks did not increase steadily during the time period indicated; instead, it increased from 1790 to 1810, then decreased and increased slightly until a final decrease to 11 percent in 1860.

See Part 3 of the U.S. History Review.

78. The correct answer is C. The iron curtain referred to a division between Communism and democracy during the Cold War. The term was coined by Winston Churchill, a former British prime minister, who declared that an iron curtain separated the countries of Eastern and Western Europe. Soviet Communism was a political system that involved the control of resources by the central government. In contrast to Western democracy, which involved a mix of federal and state government, the Communist central government maintained total control.

See Part 5 of the U.S. History Review.

79. The correct answer is A. President Lyndon B. Johnson is credited with carrying out the War on Poverty, a series of domestic programs designed to combat poverty in the 1960s and improve living standards among the nation's poor. B, C, D, and E all took place after Johnson's term.

See Part 5 of the U.S. History Review.

80. The correct answer is D. John Smith, Pocahontas, and John Rolfe were all important figures in the Jamestown settlement, but it was John Smith who took over command and helped the settlers organize their food supplies. Pocahontas negotiated with Native Americans to spare Smith's life and decrease hostilities against the settlers. She married John Rolfe, who introduced tobacco to Virginia, thereby enabling the colony to thrive.

See Part 1 of the U.S. History Review.

81. The correct answer is B. The concept of "rugged individualism" was put forth by Herbert Hoover in a 1928 campaign speech. At the end of World War I, Hoover contended, the American people were "challenged with a…choice between the American system of rugged individualism and a European philosophy of diametrically opposed doctrines of paternalism and state socialism." Hoover argued that the acceptance of the European philosophy would have threatened "the individual initiative and enterprise through which our people have grown to unparalleled greatness."

See Part 4 of the U.S. History Review.

82. The correct answer is E. Mencken was known for his coverage of the Scopes trial in 1925, also known as the Scopes monkey trial.

See Part 4 of the U.S. History Review.

83. The correct answer is C. The "dot-com bubble" occurred between 1995 and 2000 and reflected rising equity in the Internet and technology sectors for stock markets in industrialized countries. Spawned by the Internet's commercial growth, the period was noted by both the spectacular successes and sweeping failures of start-up technology companies known as "dot-coms." In March 2000, the stock market's NASDAQ Composite index peaked at 5132.52, reflecting the pinnacle of the dot-com boom.

See Part 5 of the U.S. History Review.

84. The correct answer is A. Thoreau's book *Walden* detailed his

two-year commitment to simple living in a remote location known as Walden Pond.

See Part 2 of the U.S. History Review.

85. The correct answer is B. The Sherman Anti-Trust Act of 1890 was passed to outlaw monopolies, so A is incorrect. In effect, it was very loosely enforced. Even after passage of the act, big businesses continued to influence politics and many aspects of the economy.

See Part 3 of the U.S. History Review.

86. The correct answer is D. The quoted text is excerpted from Barack Obama's keynote address at the 2004 Democratic National Convention in Boston, Massachusetts, which drew national attention and catapulted Obama's status within the Democratic Party. Obama was elected president in 2008 and is the first African American to hold the office.

See Part 5 of the U.S. History Review.

87. The correct answer is A. In 1912, Theodore Roosevelt, who had already served two terms in office, sought a third term as president and formed his own political party, the Progressive Party, in order to run against Republican President Howard Taft. The Progressive Party had a sweeping social and political agenda, calling for the establishment of a national health service, social insurance for the needy, farm relief, workers' compensation, federal income tax, election reform, and women's suffrage.

For more on the Progressive Era, see Part 3 of the U.S. History Review.

88. The correct answer is C. The doctrine of Manifest Destiny significantly affected U.S. growth during the 1800s. It was based on the belief that Americans had the God-given right to expand throughout the content of North America from coast to coast. The doctrine was inspired in part by the 1848 California gold rush, which motivated many prospectors to move west.

A, B, D, and E are incorrect because these elements concerned U.S. foreign policy, not expansion within the nation.

See Part 2 of the U.S. History Review.

89. The correct answer is E. Moderate abolitionists wished to bring a gradual end to the institution of slavery. Immediatists called for the immediate emancipation of all slaves, so C is incorrect.

See Part 3 of the U.S. History Review.

90. The correct answer is D. The stock market crash occurred because too many investors purchased through a method called "buying on margin." This method involves purchasing stocks with borrowed funds.

See Part 4 of the U.S. History Review.

91. The correct answer is A. Cuba was an imperial colony of Spain in 1898, and it rebelled against Spain in a war for independence. The United States entered the war to protect its investments in Cuba.

See Part 3 of the U.S. History Review.

92. The correct answer is B. Unemployment decreased rapidly from 1933 to 1937 following Franklin D. Roosevelt's enactment of the New Deal, a complex set of programs designed to produce higher employment, economic recovery, and reform. The economy went into a deep recession in 1938 but improved dramatically during the economic stimulus provided by World War II. The Spanish-American War was a conflict in 1898 between Spain and the United States, and the Sherman Anti-Trust Act was passed in 1890 to limit monopolies, so answers C and D are incorrect.

See Part 5 of the U.S. History Review.

About the Author

Cara Cantarella is a test preparation author with thirteen years of professional experience in the field. She has created test preparation courses, practice materials, and study guides for the ACT, SAT, GRE, GMAT, LSAT, MCAT, TOEFL, PSAT, GED, DSST, and AP exams.

Cara gained her start in the field of test prep as an instructor for Kaplan Education Centers, where she provided lecture-style classroom instruction, individualized tutoring, and advising to students.

She holds a bachelor's degree cum laude in government from Harvard University. She completed her master's degree in international relations and PhD studies in political science at the University of Chicago.

Also Available

My Max Score SAT Math 1 & 2 Subject Test
by Chris Monahan • 978-1-4022-5601-1

My Max Score SAT Literature Subject Test
by Steven Fox • 978-1-4022-5613-4

$14.99 U.S./£9.99 UK

Also Available

My Max Score AP English Literature and Composition
by Tony Armstrong • 978-1-4022-4311-0

My Max Score AP English Language and Composition
by Jocelyn Sisson • 978-1-4022-4312-7

My Max Score AP Calculus AB/BC
by Carolyn Wheater • 978-1-4022-4313-4

My Max Score AP U.S. Government & Politics
by Del Franz • 978-1-4022-4314-1

My Max Score AP U.S. History
by Michael Romano • 978-1-4022-4310-3

$14.99 U.S./$17.99 CAN/£9.99 UK

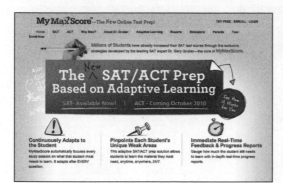

Essentials from
Dr. Gary Gruber
and the creators of My Max Score

"Gruber can ring the bell on any number
of standardized exams."
—*Chicago Tribune*

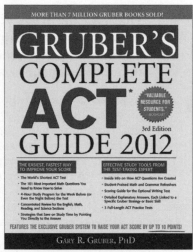

$19.99 U.S./£14.99 UK
978-1-4022-6058-2

$19.99 U.S./£14.99 UK
978-1-4022-5331-7

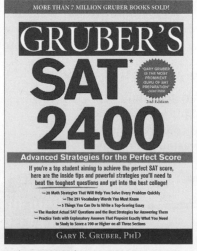

$16.99 U.S./$19.99 CAN/£11.99 UK
978-1-4022-4308-0

$13.99 U.S./£9.99 UK
978-1-4022-5334-8

"Gruber's methods make the questions
seem amazingly simple to solve."
—*Library Journal*

"Gary Gruber is the leading expert on the SAT."
—*Houston Chronicle*

$14.99 U.S./£9.99 UK
978-1-4022-5337-9

$14.99 U.S./£9.99 UK
978-1-4022-5340-9

$14.99 U.S./£9.99 UK
978-1-4022-5343-0

$12.99 U.S./£8.99 UK
978-1-4022-6072-8

Notes

Notes

Notes